# DEMOCRACY WITHIN PARTIES

# COMPARATIVE POLITICS

Comparative Politics is a series for students, teachers, and researchers of political science that deals with contemporary government and politics. Global in scope, books in the series are characterised by a stress on comparative analysis and strong methodological rigour. The series is published in association with the European Consortium for Political Research. For more information visit www.essex.ac.uk/ecpr

The Comparative Politics series is edited by Professor David M. Farrell, School of Politics and International Relations, University College Dublin, Kenneth Carty, Professor of Political Science, University of British Columbia, and Professor Dirk Berg-Schlosser, Institute of Political Science, Phillipps University, Marburg.

## OTHER TITLES IN THIS SERIES

# Democracy within Parties

*Candidate Selection Methods
and Their Political Consequences*

REUVEN Y. HAZAN AND GIDEON RAHAT

OXFORD

UNIVERSITY PRESS

# OXFORD
### UNIVERSITY PRESS

Great Clarendon Street, Oxford OX2 6DP

Oxford University Press is a department of the University of Oxford.
It furthers the University's objective of excellence in research, scholarship,
and education by publishing worldwide in

Oxford  New York

Auckland  Cape Town  Dar es Salaam  Hong Kong  Karachi
Kuala Lumpur  Madrid  Melbourne  Mexico City  Nairobi
New Delhi  Shanghai  Taipei  Toronto

With offices in

Argentina  Austria  Brazil  Chile  Czech Republic  France  Greece
Guatemala  Hungary  Italy  Japan  Poland  Portugal  Singapore
South Korea  Switzerland  Thailand  Turkey  Ukraine  Vietnam

Oxford is a registered trade mark of Oxford University Press
in the UK and in certain other countries

Published in the United States
by Oxford University Press Inc., New York

British Library Cataloguing in Publication Data
Data available

Library of Congress Cataloging in Publication Data
Data available

Typeset by SPI Publisher Services, Pondicherry, India
Printed in Great Britain
on acid-free paper by
MPG Books Group, Bodmin and King's Lynn

ISBN 978–0–19–957254–0

1 3 5 7 9 10 8 6 4 2

*For*
*Sara and Albert Hazan*
*Ana and the late Menachem Rahat*

# Acknowledgments

We are very grateful to those who made our research possible. We are indebted to our colleagues, both in Israel and across many countries, for providing an encouraging environment and insightful comments that helped us improve our work as we painstakingly gathered data and presented our developing framework at conferences from the mid-1990s onwards. We hope that they will find true value in our endeavor, and that this book will draw more scholars to the subject of candidate selection. We have surely made some mistakes, and trust that future studies will check our research and improve on it.

We want to thank Shlomit Barnea, Yael Hadar, Reut Itzkovitch-Malka, Naomi Mandel, Ayelet Banai, Hila Shtayer, Nir Atmor, and David Korn for their research assistance. Francine Hazan's editing was of crucial assistance to us; without her incessant efforts our thoughts could not have been expressed properly in writing. We are especially appreciative for the backing we received from David Farrell, our Comparative Politics series editor, and from Dominic Byatt, our publisher at Oxford University Press.

This research was supported by The Israel Science Foundation (Grant No. 390/05).

# Contents

# What is Candidate Selection and Why is it Important for Understanding Politics?

We begin with a story, one that has strong links to events that really took place. Deborah is a party stalwart and yearns to be a member of parliament. After years of party affiliation and activity, she decided it was time to give it her best shot. For the past three years she had participated in every meeting of the party's central committee. This forum, composed of approximately 1,000 delegates, decides who the party candidates will be prior to the general election. Deborah also took part in every political activity organized by any member of the central committee, wrote position papers on the major issues which were distributed to all the committee members, sent gifts to each member on every birthday and anniversary, and attended every wedding or family festivity to which she was invited. In short, she spent a large amount of time, effort, and funds in order to curry favor with those who could make her one of the party's candidates. As the general election approached, the party leadership decided to shift the decision of who would be the party's list of candidates from its central committee to its rank-and-file membership – internal democracy, the leadership proclaimed, would attract more voters and members to the party. Deborah quickly realized that the painstaking activities which had brought her to the attention of 1,000 central committee members did nothing to advance her candidacy among over 100,000 party members. She did not give up, however, because she believed in her party and its cause. The party members eventually made their decision, but Deborah was near the bottom of their list when the votes were tallied.

Michael is the head of a workers' union at one of the largest companies in the country. He is not a supporter of any particular party, and dislikes what it takes to make a successful foray into politics. As the general election approached, Michael geared up his union members for their traditional rally in favor of the pro-labor candidates. As he prepared to inform over 10,000 workers at his company of the date and place of the rally, he learned that the party leadership had decided to allow all party members to partake in the process of selecting its candidates. Michael quickly realized that since his union's members were also party members, they could now take part in the selection process. He promptly mounted a campaign asking each union member to enlist his or her family and friends as party members. His goal was to expand his union's voting bloc and to get himself elected to parliament, where he could serve his union in a much better way than he had done until that time. Michael's union quickly doubled its party membership numbers, and mobilized behind his candidacy. When the party members' votes were counted, Michael was near the middle of the party list – a "safe" position – and knew that even if his party faired poorly in the general election, he would soon be a member of parliament.

The party leadership was proud of its decision to allow all party members to participate in selecting its candidates for public office. The media covered the party in a more favorable light, making endless comparisons between the internal democracy of this party, and the party hacks and their internal deals found among the other parties. The party also saw an increase in its membership, which added not only prospective voters but also finances to its coffers, while making the party look new, energetic, forward-thinking, and headed toward victory. What the leadership did not prepare for was that after the members made their choice, the candidates seemed to lose interest in the general election, which was only weeks away. Those in safe positions, like Michael, participated in few election activities, while those who knew that they had little chance to be elected, like Deborah, stayed at home. Moreover, after the election victory, the leadership realized that there were numerous party representatives who refused to follow their directives. Michael, for one, told the party whip that he was selected as a party candidate due to his abilities to mobilize a personal support base, which he could mobilize again next time, and not due to the influence of the party leadership. His legislative activities would first and foremost be guided by what was good for his union, and only after that by what was best for his party. The party leaders had no credible way to bring him back into line, even after he voted against the party line on several important issues. This was true for several other members of parliament as well, who quickly became known as the party "rebels." As party cohesion ceased to be the standard operating procedure and became a goal that had to be constantly maintained, talk of a possible change in the candidate selection method once again surfaced.

The party leader, and sitting prime minister, realized that the rebels in his party made it impossible to govern efficiently, and that their number was enough not only to make him lose important policy votes in the legislature, but also to be no longer able to count on a cohesive majority in parliament. As the situation deteriorated, the party leader took the initiative – he decided to split from his party and dissolve the parliament, thus heralding a snap election. The charismatic and assertive party leader was very popular at the time, and his newly declared party was well received in the public opinion polls. The remaining party representatives realized that they had gone too far, and their leadership also decided it was time to reassert control.

As the election neared, the old and the new party each adopted a different candidate selection method in order to reign in the internal chaos. The prime minister, along with a small circle of his close confidants, formed a selection committee to choose a list of candidates. Those who had been loyal to the party leader were retained, while other political associates and personal acquaintances were recruited to augment the new party list. The old party, trailing in the polls and left with less than one-half of its elected representatives, decided to return the candidate selection process to its central committee. Practically overnight, Michael and the other rebellious party representatives fell into line and followed the guidelines issued by their leadership. Internal democracy thus did not survive for long in the party – its unexpected consequences not only brought about a quick return to more exclusive candidate selection methods, they also decapitated the ruling party and drastically diminished its representation in the legislature.

Those who believe that Deborah, Michael, and the party leadership are examples of strange, even deviant, behavior are not aware of the significance of the internal dynamics associated with how parties decide who their candidates will be. This arena, which normally functions far from the attention of the general public and largely remains uncovered by the media, has consequences not only for the candidates and their parties, but also for their parent legislature and its performance. The realm of candidate selection, which in most countries is within the purview of each party to do with as it sees fit, influences the balance of power within the party, determines the personal composition of parliaments, and impacts on the behavior of legislators. In short, it is central to politics in any representative democracy. A party leadership that implements a reform in its candidate selection method may encounter unexpected consequences concerning key democratic parameters such as participation, representation, competition, and responsiveness. For example, does an increase in quantity influence the quality of participation? Do women fare better or worse in more open selection arenas? Are incumbents more likely to be reselected in more inclusive bodies? Does the opening up of parties create more responsive legislators, and to whom are they more responsive? These core characteristics of a polity are but the tip of the iceberg when it comes to assessing the political consequences of different candidate selection methods.

## DEFINING CANDIDATE SELECTION

Leon Epstein (1967: 201) argued over a generation ago that "the selection of party candidates is basically a private affair, even if there are legal regulations." Austin Ranney (1981: 75, emphasis in original) built on this in his definition of candidate selection as "the predominantly *extralegal* process by which a political party decides which of the persons legally eligible to hold an elective public office will be designated on the ballot and in election communications as its recommended and supported candidate or list of candidates." Candidate selection is, therefore, an intraparty issue; it takes place almost entirely inside a particular party arena and is largely unregulated.[1] There are very few veteran established democracies – for example, Finland, Germany, New Zealand, and Norway (until 2002) – where the legal system specifies criteria for candidate selection, and only in the United States does the legal system extensively regulate the process of candidate selection. In most countries, the parties themselves are allowed to determine the rules of the game for their selection of candidates.

The recent phenomenon of increased judicial involvement in politics is likely to lead to an increase in the adjudication of internal party affairs, including candidate selection.[2] However, such involvement is still largely limited to the question of whether parties have adhered to the rules and regulations they have decided for themselves (Gauja 2006). Constitutional amendments, alongside legislation that concerns both women and minority representation, have also been on the increase since the 1990s (Htun 2004). Yet, they do not dictate the methods for selecting candidates, but rather instruct parties as to the required consequences of their chosen candidate selection methods.

Candidate selection methods are thus the nonstandardized and predominantly unregimented particular party mechanisms by which political parties choose their candidates for general elections. The result of this process is the designation of a candidate, or list of candidates, as *the* candidate(s) of the party. The party then becomes effectively committed to the candidate(s), and to mobilizing its strength behind the chosen candidate(s).

In the study of candidate selection, therefore, the unit of analysis is the *single* party, in a particular country, at a specific time. Only in cases where several parties in a particular country use similar candidate selection methods, or in the rare case where legal requirements force parties to use analogous methods, can we make uicler generalizations.

---

[1] Our focus is on candidate selection to national legislatures, although, when it is helpful, we also refer to analyses of selection methods that were used to select candidates to regional, local, and supranational councils and parliaments. We refrain from analyzing leadership selection and selection of candidates to national, regional, and local executive positions. While the study of both candidate and leadership selection may be mutually beneficial, they require separate treatment since there are substantial differences between the two in terms of the methods that are in use and also in their political consequences (Kenig 2009*a*, 2009*b*).

[2] Rush (1988) already pointed to the developing trend in the UK of appealing to the courts as a result of conflicts regarding candidate selection back in the 1980s. A prominent case was the judicial decision that did not allow Labour to continue using all-women short lists, and led to the legislation of the Sex Discrimination (Election Candidates) Act of 2002, which allowed it (McHarg 2006).

## CANDIDATE SELECTION VERSUS POLITICAL RECRUITMENT

The term political recruitment belongs to the behavioral tradition. It is a central concept in the functionalist approach suggested by Almond (1960), and together with socialization it is one of the four input functions that are found in any political system. According to Czudnowski (1975: 155), political recruitment is "...the process through which individuals or groups of individuals are inducted into active political roles." Scholars in the behavioral tradition have invested much effort in mapping the demographic differences between the elite and the masses. The well-known bias in favor of white, middle-class, educated men in politics was substantiated repeatedly in studies of political elites throughout the democratic world. Within this school, candidate selection was seen, at best, as one aspect of a complex and comprehensive process (Wright 1971). While Czudnowski (1975) recognized the institutional element as a part of the recruitment phenomenon, his approach concerning candidate selection methods is clearly behavioral, emphasizing societal variables and perceiving institutions as their mere reflection, and hence of little relevance:

> One should add, however, that considering selection systems as independent variables leads to descriptive analyses of little theoretical relevance. Selection systems serve political purposes; they are adopted for political purposes and can be changed for political purposes. The rigidity of selection systems is itself a politically relevant cultural variable, which should focus attention on recruitment systems as indicators of rewards—or of access to the distribution of rewards—in the context of those values which are the object of collective action in any given system. (Czudnowski 1975: 228)

In more recent years, when the institutional approach re-emerged in its new version – neo-institutionalism – scholars began to look at candidate selection methods not only as reflecting politics, but also as affecting it. A central work pioneering this path of inquiry was Gallagher and Marsh (1988). Norris (1997*a*, 2006; see also Best and Cotta 2000*a*) successfully bridged between the behavioral tradition and the neo-institutional approach when she described candidate selection as one element within a more comprehensive process of legislative recruitment, which includes additional institutional aspects (e.g. the electoral system) alongside "softer" structural elements such as "supply and demand" and "opportunity structures." Comprehensive overviews of studies of legislative recruitment also treat candidate selection as part of this field of study (Matthews 1985; Patzelt 1999).

The increase in the importance of the institutional element within recruitment analysis reflects the rise and consolidation of the neo-institutional approach. Yet, other real-world developments also contribute to this phenomenon. A major developing field of study is that of the representation of women. Recent increases in the representation of women in legislatures seem to result, at least partially, from the adoption of an institutional mechanism – quotas – at the national and/or the party levels (Caul 2001; Dahlerup 2006; Krook 2009). In other words, the study of recruitment, which in the past concentrated on the impact of societal values, especially culture, has begun to pay attention to institutional elements. If in the past counting the number of women in parliament was a classic behavioral research strategy, it is now also recognized as a result of institutional mechanisms, such as the use of quotas and certain elements of the electoral system. In short, institutions in general, and candidate selection methods in particular, can stand now on their own as independent variables (Kunovich and Paxton 2005).

This study adopts the institutional approach, and analyzes the various aspects of candidate selection methods as the independent variables. Yet, in order to avoid repeating past mistakes, we do not presuppose that institutions can explain everything, but rather that institutions matter. We also admit that institutions, and particularly the relatively less stable arena of candidate selection methods, can be studied as dependent variables – as reflecting rather than affecting both society and politics. We chose the institutional path because we believe that by examining candidate selection methods as independent variables, we can gain a valuable anchor which allows us to better assess and explain the wide and somewhat vague phenomenon of legislative recruitment.

## THE IMPORTANCE OF CANDIDATE SELECTION

Selecting candidates is one of the first things that political parties must do prior to an election. Candidate selection is also one of the defining functions of a political party in a pluralist democracy and maybe *the* function that separates parties from other organizations. According to Sartori's (1976: 64) definition, "A party is any political group that presents at elections, and is capable of placing through elections, candidates for public office." Those who are elected to office will be the successful candidates previously selected, and they are the ones who will determine much of how the party looks and what it does. Moreover, a party's candidates will help define its characteristics – demographically, geographically, and ideologically – more than its organization or even its manifesto. The outcome of the candidate selection process, like the results of the general elections, will affect the legislators, the party, and the legislature for a long time after the (s)election itself is over.

Both the essence and the relevance of candidate selection were indicated long ago. It is no less than astounding that so little has been written – until lately – to expand and expound upon this. Most political science scholars, and even those who focus on political parties and electoral systems, have viewed candidate selection as one of the more obscure functions performed by political parties.

It seemed to be of interest only to those directly involved or influenced by it, and it apparently had little significance outside of these circles. This dearth of scholarly literature raised a formidable obstacle in the path of researchers who wished to undertake cross-national analyses of the subject. A few pioneering ventures did take place, with initial attempts to produce a theory or a framework for analysis, but they remain few and far between. What Ranney (1965: viii–ix) noted long ago is regrettably still largely true today. "Thus the literature of political science provides few empirical descriptions of candidate selection outside the United States, and even fewer efforts to build a general comparative theory from such descriptions. This constitutes a major lacuna in our knowledge of the institutions and problems of modern democracies."

A quick search of the term "electoral systems" in the Worldwide Political Science Abstracts produced 2,783 references to published works, whereas a similar search for "candidate selection methods" comes up with only 34 items. A more general search for "elections" reveals almost 28,534 publications, whereas the equivalent term "candidate selection" results in merely 251 works (World-wide Political Science Abstracts). This lack of attention is also partially due to the objective difficulties and obstacles one encounters in any attempt to conduct research on candidate selection – namely, the lack of, and inaccessibility to, empirical data. A researcher who wants to compare electoral systems and analyze the election results of several democracies can gather most of this data from the internet. A researcher who wishes to compare the candidate selection methods within his or her own country will need months of fieldwork and access to data that is either not public or perhaps even unavailable. In the early 1950s, Duverger (1954: 354) described candidate selection as a "private act which takes place within the party. Often it is even secret, as parties do not like the odours of the electoral kitchen to spread to the outside world." A decade later, Anthony Howard (quoted in Ranney 1965: 3) described the selection of parliamentary candidates as "the secret garden" of British politics. In 1988, the first cross-national study of candidate selection (Gallagher and Marsh 1988) used this phrase in its title. More than twenty years later, it is still appropriate to describe candidate selection as one of the less discussed mysteries that make up the system of democratic government.

However, the more recent research into this subfield, particularly in the last decade, eschews many of the earlier assumptions, penetrates new grounds of empirical research, and shows that candidate selection has wide-ranging and significant implications for political parties, party members, leaders, and demo-cratic governance (Hazan and Pennings 2001; Narud, Pedersen, and Valen 2002c; Ohman 2004; Siavelis and Morgenstern 2008).

The fact that research on candidate selection is underdeveloped does not testify to its insignificance. On the contrary, the relevance of this topic for the study of politics was made clear long ago. Ostrogorski (1964[1902]: 210) noted the importance of candidate selection, arguing:

> It confers on the candidate an incontestable superiority over all his competitors of the same party; he becomes in truth the anointed of the party. He is "the adopted candidate." . . . Even the sitting member would not stand again if the Caucus were to start another candidate in opposition to him. His position with regard to his party would somewhat resemble that of an excommunicated sovereign in the Middle Ages, whose subjects, so devoted to him the day before, are released from their loyalty to him.

Almost a century ago, Michels (1915: 183–4) recognized the importance of candidate selection, stressing its relevance for the power struggles within parties between the leaders themselves. Schattschneider's (1942: 64) argument concerning this issue is almost seventy years old, and is still worth citing at length:

> The bid for power through elections has another consequence: it makes the nomination the most important activity of the party. In an election the *united front* of the party is expressed in terms of a nomination. For this reason nominations have become the distinguishing mark of modern political parties; if a party cannot make nominations it ceases to be a party. . . . The nomination may be made by a congressional caucus, a delegate convention, a mass meeting, a cabal, an individual, or a party election. The test is, does it bind? Not, how was it done? Unless the party makes authoritative and effective nominations, it cannot stay in business, for dual or multiple party candidacies mean certain defeat. As far as elections are concerned, the united front of the party, the party concentration of numbers, can be brought about only by a binding nomination. The nominating process thus has become the crucial process of the party. The nature of the nominating process determines the nature of the party; he who can make the nominations is the owner of the party. This is therefore one of the best points at which to observe the distribution of power within the party.

Ranney (1981: 103) endorses this statement, "It is therefore not surprising that the most vital and hotly contested factional disputes in any party are the struggles that take place over the choice of its candidates; for what is at stake in such a struggle, as the opposing sides well know, is nothing less than control of the core of what the party stands for and does." Gallagher (1988*a*: 3) takes it a step further, stating ". . . the contest over candidate selection is generally even more intense than the struggle over the party manifesto." Indeed, after an election, what largely remains as the functioning core of almost any party is its officeholders – its successful candidates.

Moreover, in parliamentary systems it is usually the case that one cannot become a member of the executive branch nor a party leader without first having served in parliament, and in order to serve in parliament one must first be selected as a candidate. The successful candidates thus also form the recruitment pool from which party leaders and executive officeholders will be drawn. In addition, in the case of closed and semi-closed list systems, the higher the position that a candidate wins in the candidate selection competition, the better the chances to get a senior parliamentary or ministerial position (Kenig and Barnea 2009).

Candidate selection is more than just a high-stakes power struggle within the party, it is more than just a battle over the party's image and policy, and it is more than a narrowing of the roster from which leaders and officeholders will be drawn. Candidate selection can determine the extent of the party's ability to remain united in the legislature. Gallagher (1988a: 15) argued, "Where nominations are controlled centrally, we might expect to find that deputies follow the party line faithfully in parliament, as disloyalty will mean deselection. . . . If they do not depend on any organ of the party for reselection, one might expect to find low levels of party discipline in parliament. . . . Party cohesion may be threatened unless control of selection procedures is maintained." The ability of prospective politicians to appeal directly to the party membership – in those parties where candidate selection is more inclusive – and not just to the party organization thus changes the locus of responsibility of the party representatives. If the party does not function as a filtering mechanism, then the key actors in the process may become the candidates themselves, who will mobilize supporters directly. The whole selection process could then be driven by the candidates and not by the parties. The result could be a weakening of partisan discipline and cohesiveness, leading to a decline in the ability of the parties to function as a stable basis for the political process and to operate effectively in the parliamentary arena. In the end, such partisan disarray may even lead the party to suffer an electoral setback.

An alternative approach to the consequences of democratizing candidate selection is based on the model of the cartel party (Katz and Mair 1995). According to this approach, parties require a considerable degree of elite autonomy in order to participate effectively in the cross-party cartel. The cartel model suggests that one possible strategy used by party leaders in order to achieve this is to empower the ordinary party members, thereby diluting the influence of the ideologically motivated and organizationally entrenched activists, because they are the ones who might be able to coordinate an effective challenge to the autonomy of the party leaders. The rationale behind this option is that the less intensely involved rank-and-file party members are more likely to be swayed by such factors as name recognition, and hence are more likely to take cues from the highly visible party leadership. In other words, an increase in the nominal power of the base of the party will come at the expense of the power of the middle-level ideological activists. Moreover, this strategy will maintain, or even increase, the power of the party leaders, rather than diminish it, and may help to sustain party unity.

Whether the democratization of candidate selection is real, leading to a decline in party unity, or whether it is used as an instrument of the party elite in an attempt to simultaneously empower and control the base, both approaches point to a connection between candidate selection and party cohesion. In short, both perspectives see candidate selection as a key variable in the process of eroding or sustaining party unity.

Reform of a party's candidate selection method can be a result of developments at three levels: the political system level, the party system (or interparty) level, and the intraparty level. At the political system level, democratization – empowering individual party members by letting them decide who their representatives will be – may be the strategy that parties adopt to cope with the decline of ideology and increased individualism. In the interparty arena, competition may lead parties – especially after they suffer electoral defeat – to look for innovations that can help rehabilitate their image. Opening up the candidate selection method can create a more popular democratic image. If a party that democratizes its selection method enjoys electoral success, other parties are likely to follow suit. At the intraparty level, internal power struggles can also lead to reform of a party's candidate selection method. Forces from within the parties may push for democratization in order to change the existing power balance between different forces: personal factions, ideological groups, different generations, or any other grouping that is relevant to a specific party at a certain point in time (Barnea and Rahat 2007).

The autonomy of parties in the arena of candidate selection means that there are many possible reasons for change, be it toward more inclusion or away from it. But regardless of the motivating factor, parties change their candidate selection methods more often than nations reform their electoral systems. On the one hand, since candidate selection methods are unregulated intraparty processes, they are less stable mechanisms than state institutional mechanisms (such as electoral systems), and are relatively more prone to change. As such, they should be seen as reflecting politics. On the other hand, these changes are not frequent enough to justify an inclusive treatment of them as only a mirror. Thus, candidate selection methods should be treated as institutional mechanisms that both *reflect* the nature of the parties and *affect* party politics. The study of candidate selection can therefore help us understand the dynamics of party organization. For example, the evolution of parties from elite to mass to catch-all influenced how the party organized its selection of candidates; and in the less ideological era of the catch-all party, Kirchheimer (1966: 198) concluded that "the nomination of candidates for popular legitimation as office holders thus emerges as the most important function of the present-day catch-all party." This claim seems to be even stronger when related to the cartel party.

Candidate selection determines not only the choices before voters – while influencing how these choices are perceived and made – but also the composition of the parties in the legislature and, through them, the government and the opposition. It thus influences the interests most likely to be addressed and the resulting policy decisions that will be enacted. In short, candidate selection affects the fundamental nature of modern democratic politics and governance.

The importance of candidate selection methods for understanding politics stems from a combination of the three elements elaborated above:

- First, candidate selection reflects and defines the character of a party and its internal power struggle.
- Second, it is relatively easy for parties to alter their candidate selection methods, and they do so much more often than nations change their electoral systems.
- Third, a change in candidate selection methods will affect both what goes into politics – from the quality of intraparty participation to the kind of candidates chosen – and also what emerges from politics – from the extent of competition and turnover to the behavior of legislatures and their locus of responsiveness.

In other words, candidate selection is a key institutional crossroad, a crucial political arrangement that can be relatively easily altered and can cause a transformation of behavioral patterns by parliamentarians, parties, and parliaments in both expected and unexpected ways. Three additional elements, elaborated below, complete the picture concerning the relevance of candidate selection:

- Fourth, country-specific variables can increase the importance of candidate selection beyond its inherent value.
- Fifth, the chain of democratic delegation starts with candidate selection.
- Sixth, the rise of individual-based politics enhances the significance of candidate selection.

The consequences of candidate selection can be more or less significant as a result of other characteristics of a particular nation's politics. For example, in countries with single-member districts, if the number of safe seats is either large or growing, then the selection process of the winning party could be more decisive than the election itself. In both the United States and Great Britain, more than one-half of the constituencies are safe for one party or the other, with majorities of greater than 10%, which means that the effective choice of who will become a legislator is made not by the voters in the general election but by the candidate selection process. As Rush (1969: 4) stated about safe seats in Britain, "*selection* is *tantamount* to election." Norris and Lovenduski (1995: 2) concluded, "In choosing candidates the selectorate therefore determines the overall composition of parliament, and ultimately the pool of those eligible for government."

Moreover, even in marginal seats, the correct choice of a candidate by a party could make the decisive difference between winning the seat and losing it. In countries using proportional systems, the selection of candidates at the top of a party list can virtually guarantee election, particularly in the major parties, practically regardless of the results of the general election. In short, in the majority of democratic nations, in a majority of the parties, selection is equal to election. As Gallagher (1988*a*: 2) posited, "It is clear that the values of the selectorate, often a small number of activists, frequently have more impact than those of the voters. This applies especially under electoral systems which do not permit any degree of choice between candidates of the same party; picking candidates often amounts to picking deputies."

Studying the consequences of candidate selection could therefore be as important as studying electoral systems, the subject of an entire industry of scholarly writing over the past decades. Ranney (1987: 73) is correct when he argues, "Candidate selection is as essential to realizing the ideal of free elections as free elections are to realizing the ideal of government by the consent of the governed." The rationale for this claim becomes apparent when the chain of democratic delegation is understood as beginning with candidate selection. Before the executive delegates power to the bureaucracy, before the legislature delegates power to the government (in parliamentary regimes), before the voters delegate power to their representatives, the first stage in the chain of delegation is the selection of candidates for public office by the parties. The institutional determinants of the candidate selection process inaugurate the chain of delegation and shape both the tactical decisions of the candidates, alongside the prospective ones, and the strategic choices of the parties (Mitchell 2000).

Last, but not least, democratic politics are becoming more candidate-centered, more personalized, and more "presidentialized" (Poguntke and Webb 2005). Even in those countries with pure parliamentary systems, proportional elections, and fixed party lists, the focus on the individual is increasing at the expense of the collective, the ideological, and the organizational – in other words, the party. The result is that the political character of a polity is now being shaped more by candidate selection than ever before. The personal and personnel implications of candidate selection are critical; candidate selection is becoming the locus of political activity, at times overshadowing the dominance of the parties in the legislative elections.

If candidate selection expresses the internal make-up of the party and impacts on how factions struggle for power; if it is a central aspect of the recruitment process influencing the type of legislators elected and their behavior in office, and thus the performance of legislatures; if it is the preliminary stage in the democratic chain of delegation, which is becoming increasingly candidate focused even in party-centered contexts; and if candidate selection is not only one of the basic functional definitions of political parties but also mostly what still remains under the purview of parties in an era of "party decline," then it is incumbent upon those who seek to understand the key elements of the democratic process to shed the traditional myopic perspective which has kept candidate selection on the backbenches of political science and to move it to the forefront of the research agenda.


## CHALLENGES FOR CANDIDATE SELECTION RESEARCH

The major challenge for the study of candidate selection methods is to bring it closer to the state that the study of electoral systems was approximately forty years ago, when Rae's (1967) seminal work, *The Political Consequences of Electoral Laws*, was published. That is, we need cross-party and cross-national empirical studies of the political consequences of candidate selection methods.

Achieving this is by no means easy. Indeed, existing theoretical frameworks, particularly those concerning party politics, provide substantial propositions for the study of candidate selection. The problem with a cross-national empirical study is that it requires familiarity with local politics and accessibility (in terms of language, as well as in other, more basic terms) to intraparty data. The lack of cross-national empirical studies is, thus, the Achilles' heel of any attempt to make further progress.

Candidate selection methods not only affect party politics, they also reflect it. There is, therefore, a need to analyze candidate selection methods both as a dependent and as an independent variable. Prominent examples of treating candidate selection as a dependent variable, in the rather exceptional case of the United States, range from Key (1949) to Ware (2002). When it comes to the origins and the politics of reform of candidate selection methods, here too there is a dire need for cross-national empirical data if we are to reach any conclusive findings. We require a more integrative look at the phenomenon of candidate selection, one that would account not only for trends but also for the differences among parties and among nations that may result from interactions at the inter- and intraparty levels.

Sailing the uncharted waters of candidate selection could help us better understand the nature of party membership, the kind of candidates selected, the dynamics exhibited within the party, the power and performance of the party in parliament, and could enhance our overall ability to evaluate politics in general and party politics in particular. Behind closed party doors, this "secret garden" of politics is still largely unexplored. This book aims at opening the gate, at penetrating the restrictive party "gatekeepers", at shedding light on this hitherto largely uncharted ground.

## DEFINING "REALISTIC" POSITIONS AND CONSTITUENCIES

Our book concentrates not only on how candidates are selected, but also, and primarily, on the political consequences of candidate selection. We thus focus on the selection of candidates with real chances to be subsequently elected in the general elections. We are not interested in the way that parties determine candidacies for the positions at the bottom of the list that have no possibility of being elected, nor in candidacies in those single-member districts in which rather than selecting candidates, the parties simply try to convince someone to stand in their name, with no chance of even giving a good fight.

The concept of *safe* positions on the candidate list, or safe seats when dealing with majoritarian systems, is used quite freely in the research literature. We use the concept of realistic candidacies – realistic positions or realistic districts. These include all those positions/districts that are seen at least as winnable before the elections. Our study, as stated above, is therefore about realistic candidacies.[3]

Thus, for example, if a party won five seats under a closed list electoral system (or even a semi-closed one), we are interested in the selection of the candidates for the first five positions – possibly even the next few positions just in case the party does surprisingly well in the elections – but we are not concerned with positions quite far down the list. For example, a party with forty seats might have serious competition between candidates for the first fifty positions prior to the next election. The same party could produce a list of one hundred candidates, with the lower half simply allocated, possibly to those who lost in the selection contest or to well-known public figures with no political aspirations in order to attract positive media attention. While these "symbolic" candidacies are not of no value, and may have some political significance, they are largely irrelevant for our purposes.[4] If we analyze all of the candidacies, both realistic and unrealistic, we would be misguided about the most basic aspects of candidate selection, such as assessing which are the relevant selectorates. The same is true for the noncompetitive districts. In the case of single-member districts, we are interested in those districts where there is a reasonable chance of winning, and not in those districts where the candidates are doing their party a "favor" by agreeing to stand in its name.

## THE ORGANIZATION OF THE BOOK

This book is divided into two main parts. Part I is an attempt to delineate candidate selection methods. The classification suggested is based on four major dimensions:

---

[3] It should be noted that when the concept of "realistic" candidacies is operationalized, there is a need for a clear-cut and fixed delineation of the "realistic" from the "unrealistic." In that case, we use the existing number of seats/constituencies that the party has as our fixed criterion. Moreover, although the size of the party's legislative representation is not known in advance – intraparty selection is made before general elections – both the parties and the politicians tend to relate to their party's *actual* representation as the one that distinguishes the realistic candidacies from the unrealistic ones. When it comes to new parties, we cannot relate to their existing size, so we are forced to estimate according to their *projected* size through the use of public opinion polls, which makes the criterion of projected size more fluid, especially in regard to marginal seats/positions.

[4] For example, in a single-member district electoral system, "third" parties might make an effort to put forth candidates in as large a number of districts as possible in order to send a message of being serious contenders. In list systems, the final positions may be allotted to well-known public figures, or to former senior politicians held in high esteem, as a sign of support for the party in the campaign. In both types of electoral systems, candidates may agree to, and even aspire for, such positions in order to signify the start of a political career.

candidacy, the selectorate, decentralization, and voting versus appointment systems. Each dimension is described and analyzed in a separate chapter. Part II of the book analyzes the political consequences of candidate selection on the basis of the above classification. The consequences of using different candidate selection methods are assessed according to four important aspects of democracy: participation, representation, competition, and responsiveness. Each aspect is explained and analyzed in a distinct chapter. The book concludes with an overall appraisal of candidate selection methods and democratic politics.

# Part I

---

## Candidate Selection Methods:
## A Framework for Analysis

Part I presents a fourfold classification of candidate selection methods. Each chapter is dedicated to one of the four dimensions that delineate candidate selection methods. Each of the four dimensions answers a major question: Candidacy – Who can be selected as the party's candidate? The selectorate – Who selects the candidates? Decentralization – Where does selection takes place? Appointment and voting – How are the candidates selected? We hope that by dedicating the first part of our book to conceptualization and classification we will contribute to the creation of a common, shared language for the study of candidate selection methods.

Differentiating between candidate selection methods is a precondition for conducting any meaningful studies regarding the origin, preservation, and reform of candidate selection methods – not to mention their political consequences. We present what we believe is the relevant menu for scholars to choose from. In some studies it might suffice to address only the (arguably) two main dimensions: the selectorate and decentralization. Yet, in most studies – especially those that focus on the internal life of parties in general, and their democratization in particular – the other two dimensions will prove to be significant as well.

We collected data about both new and old democracies around the world, in order to demonstrate how our classification can be used, as well as its applicability. In some cases the data were readily accessible, especially regarding the selectorate and decentralization. When it came to candidacy, the data were sketchy. Much to our regret, empirical information on appointment and voting systems is quite rare. Hopefully, shedding light on the analytical potential and the significance of these four dimensions will lead scholars to invest more time and effort in studying them. The systematic accumulation of cross-national data is a necessary precondition in order to make further progress in the study of candidate selection methods.

# 2

# Candidacy

In any attempt to assess candidate selection methods, the first dimension that should be addressed is the question of candidacy: Who can be selected? This is, on the one hand, the simplest of the four dimensions that describe candidate selection methods; but on the other hand, it is the most brutal of dimensions because it has the potential to eliminate an overwhelming majority of the population from the pool of candidates.

Candidacy tells us who can present himself or herself in the candidate selection process of a single party at a particular point in time. Are there any restrictions on presenting candidacy in a given party? If so – how strict are these limitations? How much do they affect the size and nature of the potential candidate pool? The restrictions applied to potential candidates are the defining elements that will allow us to classify candidacy on a continuum according to the level of inclusiveness or exclusiveness, as elaborated later in Figure 2.1.

At one end, the inclusive pole, every voter can stand as a party candidate. Most states in the United States are close to this pole. This phenomenon can be attributed to the fact that state laws, rather than party rules, regulate the candidate selection process.[1] Under such candidacy requirements, or lack thereof, the party has little to no influence as a gatekeeper for potential candidates. In other words, aspirants for office practically impose themselves on the party, which must accept their candidacy, reluctantly or otherwise. Politics in the United States have been described as candidate-centered (Wattenberg 1991), and in the arena of candidacy, possibly the strangest example was the cross-filing system in the state of California where, between 1913 and 1959, a candidate did not need to be a member of any party and could compete in the primaries of more than one party at the same time (Key 1967).

At the exclusive pole, we encounter a series of restrictive conditions. One example is Obler's (1974: 180) account of the requirements that applied to potential candidates in the Belgian Socialist Party. Here the party's role as gatekeeper, already at the candidacy stage, was both strong and influential.

---

[1] This fact led Epstein (1986) to liken the American parties to "public utilities," such as water or electric companies.

While the exact requirements vary from one constituency to another, they generally stipulate that to be placed on the primary ballot aspirants must (1) have been a member of the Socialist party, trade union, co-operative and insurance association for at least five years prior to the primary; (2) have made annual minimum purchases from the Socialist co-op; (3) have been a regular subscriber to the party's newspaper; (4) have sent his children to state rather than Catholic schools; and (5) have his wife and children enrolled in the appropriate women's and youth organizations. These conditions, in effect, require that a candidate serve as a member of an activist subculture before he becomes eligible to run for Parliament. They involve a form of enforced socialization during which it is assumed (or hoped) that the aspirant will absorb the appropriate values and attitudes as well as a keen commitment to the party.

The more common requirements set by parties for candidacy are less demanding, such as a minimal length of membership prior to the presentation of candidacy and pledges of loyalty to the party. The multitude of real-world examples result in a candidacy continuum, as presented in Figure 2.1, based on the extent of inclusiveness or exclusiveness imposed by the party – in most cases – or the state on eligibility.

Why would a party adopt more inclusive, or more exclusive, candidacy requirements? Inclusivity might be the result of legal regulations, as is the case in the United States. But it may also be a trait of a party whose main interest is electoral success, and is therefore open to any candidate who could help increase the party's share of the vote. Where little to no membership requirements exist, such as even a minimal membership period, the resulting candidates could be newcomers to the party. For example, in Canada, among the nonincumbent candidates elected to parliament in 1988, 14 percent joined their parties during the year prior to the elections (Erickson and Carty 1991).

Exclusivity, on the other hand, may be due to an attempt by the party to control the supply side of potential candidates, so that those who fulfill the enhanced eligibility requirements, and are subsequently both selected and elected, will behave according to party dictates. In other words, additional requirements can not only remove those candidates with potential personal problems, but also assure certain behavioral patterns once in office. A party with strict candidacy requirements can arrive in office as a cohesive unit, manifesting a patent party culture, thereby removing the need to utilize disciplinary measures in order to keep their

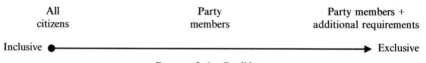

FIGURE 2.1. Candidacy

*Source*: Updated from Rahat and Hazan (2001).

elected representatives in line (Hazan 2003). Moreover, the party leadership can use the more exclusive candidacy requirements to reward loyalists and long-time activists, thereby creating a structure of selective incentives for potential candidates.

Overall, the more electorally oriented and catch-all parties might decide to pursue inclusive candidacy requirements, while the more ideological parties may adopt exclusive restrictions that ensure a candidate's "socialization" into the party culture. The adoption of particular candidacy requirements can thus be a trade-off between different electoral and programmatic goals. Gallagher (1988c: 247) argued that variations among parties in their candidacy requirements cut along ideological lines. Left-wing parties instituted more formal candidacy requirements for selection than right-wing parties; that is, left-wing parties are more exclusive. Thiébault (1988: 82) also found that in France the parties of the right, more so than those on the left, selected candidates who were not even party members before-hand. Obler (1970) showed that the very stringent candidacy requirements of the Belgian Socialist Party, described above, were quite different from those of the Belgian Christian Social Party, where the relatively inclusive candidacy requirements were limited to one year of party membership and (in some districts) a maximum age of sixty-five.

At times, parties will ignore their own candidacy regulations, largely due to electoral considerations. For example, even the rather exclusive Italian Commu-nist Party included nonmembers as candidates. These "prestigious independents not previously identified with the party" were "a central feature of the party's electoral (and image-building) strategy" (Wertman 1988: 154). The Irish Labour Party required candidates to be party members for at least one year prior to the elections, but when it came to those unaffiliated potential candidates who the party thought were attractive, this requirement was overlooked (Galligan 2003). The Czech Christian and Democratic Union – Czechoslovak People's Party placed nonparty members on its candidate list for the European Parliament although the selection rules did not allow this (Linek and Outly 2006).

Before outlining some of the more common candidacy requirements cross-nationally, it is important to distinguish between party-level requirements and state-level candidacy restrictions. This chapter is concerned with the former, which is independently decided by each individual party. In other words, there is likely to be variation across parties because each can choose the criteria it wants to focus on. One party can decide to concentrate on general rules such as district residency, age, and a monetary deposit, while another might focus on ideological loyalty and a history of party activities. Moreover, each party can set the standard for the particular requirements it chooses – residency, age, and a monetary deposit might be similar criteria across several parties, but the degree of each could vary significantly.

State-level candidacy restrictions are a different, yet related world. They are different because they are typically delineated in a formal document, such as the constitution, the election law, laws governing the legislature, etc. Some restrictions are "hidden" because they are implicit. For example, if the election law states that in order to be a candidate one must have the right to vote, then all the limitations placed on voting eligibility – from age to residency to serving time in prison, etc. – are automatically imposed on candidacy as well.

The most common national-level qualifications on who has the right to be a candidate are age, citizenship, residence (country and/or district), monetary deposit, and incompatibility with other offices. Additional common eligibility restrictions include the establishment of certain standards for prospective politicians – candidates are frequently disqualified on the grounds of insanity, criminal convictions, undischarged bankruptcy, and in some underdeveloped countries educational and literacy disqualifications (Inter-Parliamentary Union 1986).[2]

State-imposed candidacy restrictions are related to party candidacy requirements because they set the lowest common denominator to which all parties must adhere. For example, if the state decides that all candidates for legislative office must be citizens by birth (Bolivia, Brazil, Ecuador, the Philippines, and Venezuela), or by naturalization (most countries), or that they need not be citizens (Jamaica and St. Vincent) (Massicotte, Blais, and Yoshinaka 2004: 55), then either it is ludicrous for a party to adopt a lesser limit, or parties do not have to address this issue because the state has already taken care of it. State-level restrictions, whether describing ineligibility criteria – such as incompatibility with other public offices – or eligibility requirements – such as citizenship, number of signatures required on a nomination paper, etc. – create a uniform base which is standard for all parties. No variation across parties in either the criteria or their extent is to be found.[3]

Since our interest lies in how parties select their candidates, we are less concerned with the restrictions imposed by the state, as they do not allow us to distinguish differences between parties nor, as a result, to assess the political consequences of these variations within the state. State-level candidacy restrictions versus party-level requirements are akin to the national electoral law versus the candidate selection method of each party. This book focuses on the latter; we are interested in differences between parties rather than between states. When candidate selection is regulated by law, studying it tells us more about the legal regulations of the political process than about the political parties themselves. However, we do not ignore the restrictions on candidacy emanating from the state

---

[2] A comprehensive cross-national sample of state-level candidacy requirements is presented by Massicotte, Blais, and Yoshinaka (2004: 42–9).

[3] A curious case is Finland, where the Election Act regulates parties, but the parties are allowed to deviate from many of the stipulations. Most of the provisions of the act apply unless a party enacts rules on candidate selection (Ministry of Justice, Finland). Sundberg (1997) and Kuitunen (2002) point out that the parties have chosen to follow the legal text almost verbatim, but there are still some differences between parties, as well as deviations from the Election Act.

because they define the playing field on which the parties must compete, and thus they are important, yet preliminary, to our discussion.

Common party-level candidacy requirements include criteria that are similar to the state-level restrictions, such as age, but many are quite different. For example, a minimal period of party membership is extremely common, as are pledges of loyalty, usually to the party platform, and a collection of signatures in support of candidacy. Data on party-level candidacy restrictions are quite hard to find. The criteria are delineated either in party statutes, available usually in the local language only and rarely translated or disseminated in a more general manner – that is, the internet – or they are to be found in party documents that are inaccessible to most. The scholarly literature rarely covers this aspect of candidate selection, if at all. An expansive reading of the academic literature, along with years of searching for these data, allows us to present a preliminary delineation of party-level candidacy requirements along with cross-national examples. Prior to analyzing candidacy requirements at the party level, though, we must delineate the unit of analysis.

Our unit of analysis is the single party, in a particular country, at a specific point in time. Only in cases where several parties in a country impose similar candidacy restrictions (usually due to legal requirements), where a single party implements similar candidate requirements more than once, or when both similarities occur, can we make generalizations over time and across parties.

The tools offered in this chapter, and the ones that follow, can be easily used when analyzing a simple, one-stage, uniform candidate selection method. Such a simple method is one in which all potential candidates face similar restrictions. Empirically, however, we face complex candidate selection methods. Since these largely come into play when we discuss the selectorate – our second dimension – they will be delineated and analyzed in Chapter 3. When it comes to analyzing candidacy requirements we must be careful, because even in one specific party, different candidacy restrictions might be imposed in different constituencies or regions.

## AGE RESTRICTIONS

Age limit is a common requirement placed on potential candidates. For example, the Austrian Socialist Party did not have any age restrictions in 1945, but by 1959, it imposed a detailed restriction: all candidates had to be under the age of sixty-five and those who had never been candidates before, or were nonincumbents, had to be less than sixty years old (the Austrian People's Party copied this ten years later). Circumventing this candidacy restriction was possible, but only with a two-thirds majority in the full party executive (Müller 1992). Most of the Belgian parties imposed an age limit of sixty-five for candidates (De Winter 1988). In the Australian Labour Party of New South Wales, as well as in the Labour Party of New Zealand, a candidate's age could not surpass seventy at the end of the prospective term in office the candidate wished to fill (Norris et al. 1990; Sheppard 1998).

The fact that many parties impose an age limit on candidates raises important questions. For example, what leads parties to impose such limits? Are parties disinterested in representing the elderly and in mobilizing their supporters? Are long-term incumbents, many of whom are nearing the age limit, not experienced legislators that the party could use? Age restrictions, it seems, are a reaction to multiple-term incumbents who have become professional politicians with no desire to be replaced. The "young Turks" of the party feel frustrated by these perennial legislators, and conclude that their entrance into politics is stymied by the "old-timers." Moreover, some of the older incumbents can tarnish the party's image, especially if they are perceived to possess health or mental problems that may impair their ability to function. Imposing an age limit thus both creates vacancies and relieves the party from having to deal with problematic personal cases.

It will be interesting to see whether age restrictions will be changed or challenged as life expectancy increases and people are able to be productive well beyond their sixties, as the electorate grows older and pensioners become increasingly successful in their attempts to establish political organizations. An attack on age restrictions could also be a matter of principle in the name of antidiscrimination laws, as the experience of the United States testifies, since these limitations are clearly targeted at a specific segment of the population and are indeed prejudiced.

## PARTY MEMBERSHIP REQUIREMENTS

A minimal membership period in the party is one of the most common political candidacy requirements. There are, however, many parties that do not impose a party membership period as a candidacy requirement. Among these are the Swedish Liberals, who even invited people not associated with the party to run as candidates in the 2004 European elections (Aylott 2005); the Left Party in Sweden (Pierre and Widfeldt 1992); the Japanese Liberal Democratic Party (Shiratori 1988); the Social Democrats in Iceland (Kristjánsson 2002); and the three main parties in Ireland – Fianna Fail, Fine Gael, and the Progressive Democrats (Gallagher 1988b). A study of political parties in Bangladesh, India, Nepal, Pakistan, and Sri Lanka noticed a willingness by parties across south Asia to run candidates who were not party members, but who had a good chance of winning (Suri 2007).

Our research has shown that membership requirements can be quite minimal. In Finland, where parties are somewhat regulated by the state, the law did not require a candidate to be a party member, although the parties expected this to be the case (Kuitunen 2002). In New Zealand's National Party, a candidate simply had to be a paid member at the time of selection (Jackson 1980). In the Finnish Social Democrats, candidates needed to be members for only four months before the primary (Kuitunen 2002), and in the Irish Greens the minimal membership period for candidacy stood at six months (Galligan 2003).

Variation across parties in a single country is common. For example, in Ireland while the three main parties (Fianna Fail, Fine Gael, and the Progressive Democrats) did not prescribe any minimum period of party membership, the Labour Party had a minimal period of six months, Sinn Fein had a one-year eligibility minimum, and the Workers' Party restricted candidates to those who had been members for at least two years (Gallagher 1988*b*).

Many parties set membership requirements of at least one year, and often two years, before a member could be selected as their candidate. The extreme cases were some of the Belgian and Italian parties, which required their candidates to be members of the party for at least five years – which effectively meant that they had to be party members for at least two elections and could only attempt to become candidates in the second election. It seems that significant candidacy restrictions are more characteristic of the ideological era of the mass party. Catch-all and cartel parties tend to ease and bypass these requirements, largely due to electoral considerations.

## ADDITIONAL REQUIREMENTS

Most parties do not mention criteria such as citizenship and residency in their candidacy requirements, mainly because they are already stipulated in national election law.[4] There are, however, a series of requirements that parties impose in addition to those that the state requires of all candidates across parties.

A monetary deposit, which some countries impose at the state level, can also be found within parties. The Canadian Conservatives required a $1,000 deposit (Conservative Party of Canada 2009). The Christian Democratic Union – Czechoslovak People's Party required payment of a nomination fee of CZK 10,000 (about $500) from their candidate to the European Parliament (Linek and Outly 2006). These sums are not returned to the candidate unless they

---

[4] The Christian Democrats in Germany can be seen as a counterexample, when it stipulated that only German natives were eligible for candidacy to parliament (Poguntke and Boll 1992).

obtain a certain percentage of the vote. In Kenya, the National Rainbow Coalition required parliamentary aspirants to pay a nomination fee of approximately \$380 (Ohman 2004).

As cited above, the candidacy requirements of the Belgian Socialist Party in the 1960s seem to be quite excessive. Beyond five years of party membership and membership in the Socialist trade union and health insurance fund also for at least five years, the party required membership and minimal purchases at the socialist cooperative, a subscription to the party's newspaper, and the holding of some party office. All of these pertained mainly to the potential candidate, but there were requirements placed on the candidate's family as well: his wife had to be a party member in the relevant organization, enrolled in the trade union and insurance fund, while his children had to go to state schools and be members in the party youth organization (Obler 1974; De Winter 1988). These stringent eligibility requirements are no longer strictly enforceable, due to a decline in the pillarized structure of Belgian society – for example, the disappearance of party newspapers and cooperatives – resulting from the waning of consociational politics.

Other parties impose their own particular requirements on potential candidates, but they seem to be a far cry from this extreme example. The Irish Workers' Party, beyond a two-year membership period and a record of party activities, required candidates to take an internal educational course. The party's National Executive could, however, suspend this requirement. Fine Gael and the Progressive Democrats, on the other hand, required candidates to make a pledge, before being selected by the party convention, that they would "contribute" an amount of money decided by the parliamentary party to the party's election campaign (Farrell 1992).

A common political requirement is a pledge of loyalty, usually to the party platform, as practiced by the three main Irish parties (Gallagher 1988b). These pledges could include provisions for supporting whichever candidate is eventually selected by the party, as was the case in several of the parties in New Zealand (Milne 1966), or, once elected, promising to vote in parliament based on the party's decision. While such a requirement may influence the potential pool of candidates, its significance compared to other candidacy requirements is secondary.

Some parties require written recommendations by existing party members, regardless of whether the candidate is a member or not. The Labour Party in New Zealand allowed six members to nominate a candidate, while the National Party required that ten paid members should recommend a candidate (Milne 1966). Both the Liberal and Conservative parties in Canada require twenty-five signatures (Liberal Party of Canada 2009; Conservative Party of Canada 2009). In Finland, candidates could be nominated by fifteen members of a local organization, or by thirty members of different local organizations all in the same district (Ministry of Justice, Finland). In Iceland, candidates needed between twenty and fifty endorsements by party members, depending on the size of the constituency (Kristjánsson 2002). The Mexican Party of the Democratic Revolution decided, in

1996, to require at least 100 member signatures for candidacy eligibility, but the candidate did not have to be a member of the party (Combes 2003). In this requirement, too, variations across parties in the same country are common. In the Netherlands, for example, the Socialist Party called for at least ten members to nominate a candidate, the Green Left required fifteen, while the Catholic People's Party insisted on twenty-five (Koole and van de Velde 1992).

In some parties, such as the British Labour Party, candidates need to be nominated by a party unit in the constituency – a party branch, an affiliated union, or another recognized group (Norris and Lovenduski 1995). In the United States, an interesting requirement for candidacy existed in several of the southern states. If a candidate had campaigned against the Democratic Party in the previous elections, he could not compete in the party's primary (Key 1967: 392).

The four main Czech political parties required knowledge of at least one world language from their candidates for the European Parliament, and two of these also required membership in the national parliament, or alternatively, experience in municipal or regional boards of representatives (Linek and Outly 2006). The Flemish wing of the Belgian Social Christian Party, prior to the 1968 elections, decided that its candidates were forbidden from holding office in local governments (unless they were composed of 30,000 inhabitants or less) and thus would have to resign before becoming candidates for the national parliament. Such a prohibition was quite significant and obliged candidates to decide which position they preferred to continue holding, as many candidates had backgrounds in local government (Obler 1970).

## INCUMBENCY

Incumbents are a special category of potential candidates. In several countries, such as Australia, Great Britain, New Zealand, and The Netherlands, incumbents in one or more parties enjoyed either automatic readoption or almost automatic readoption. In the Irish Fianna Fail, it was common at conventions to pass proposals declaring all incumbents reselected (Gallagher 1988*b*). The Japanese Liberal Democrats, almost without fail, renominated incumbent members (Shiratori 1988). Even minor parties, such as the Volksunie in Belgium, reassigned the same place on the list to incumbents who wanted to run again, unless their constituency congress voted otherwise by a two-thirds majority (De Winter 1988). Many times, those incumbents with guaranteed candidacy did not even face any of the requirements that nonincumbent candidates had to. In other words, once an aspiring candidate successfully met the candidacy requirements and was both chosen to be the candidate and elected to office, from then on there were no candidacy requirements imposed on that particular person.

Why would a party offer its incumbents automatic candidacy for an upcoming election, or at least ease their requirements? The simple answer is that parties want to win elections, and incumbents have already proven themselves in this regard. Incumbents are, therefore, likely to have a strong base of support in their constituency, making reselection especially relevant for parties who function in plurality single-member district electoral systems, and also in electoral systems that employ districts of small magnitude. Incumbents are also strong actors within the party; they know how to take care of their interests and have been working toward the goal of reselection ever since they were first chosen. Incumbent reselection can be seen as a reward given in exchange for loyalty to the party. Parties also want to minimize internal conflict on the eve of the more important general election, and the reselection of incumbents means that they do not have to fight off potential challengers before each election.

Why, then, should a party impose more demanding candidacy requirements for incumbents? The main reason is that if all incumbents are automatically reselected, then the party will appear monotonous, which is not a good image. New faces and new blood are perceived as positive projections of an interesting and exciting party prior to the general elections. But, on the other hand, a balance is needed between incumbents and aspirants – wholesale replacement of incumbents is not good for a party, and is also not likely to happen, as explained above. In order to attract new contenders to the party, the candidacy requirements for incumbents must afford competition, allowing aspirants to enter the game and feel that they have a fair chance, but also giving incumbents the feeling that they are relatively safe and can focus their attention elsewhere. Yet, the party leaders also have their political concerns, and incumbents form the pool of potential challengers for their leadership. They may thus seek to thwart leadership competition by forcing incumbents to focus more on their efforts at being reselected, not to mention the possibility that a potential contender for leadership could be removed when incumbents (but not the leader, or leaders) face special hurdles – such as the support of special majorities.

An interesting study in Britain of thirty-five attempts by the local selecting body to deselect incumbents found that the most common source was ideological, making up one-half of the cases, with other reasons – such as a lack of attention to constituency matters, personal failures, or age – far behind (Dickson 1975).[5] Nonetheless, in spite of the conflict, the local organization usually readopts the incumbent candidate because: (*a*) it fears that alternation could lead to an election defeat, (*b*) its disappointment with the incumbent can be smoothed over, (*c*) the Burkean conception holds that the local organization should not control its candidate, and (*d*) the national party organization gets involved in support of

---

[5] Almost all of the ideological conflicts involved incumbents whose ideological leanings were toward the other main party – that is, Conservatives leaning left and Labourites leaning right – and not those incumbents who held more extreme positions.

the incumbent. In short, even when readoption is not fully automatic, the incumbency advantage works in favor of the readoption of incumbents.

More recently, some parties have indeed sought to shake up their lists of candidates, mainly to present a fresh face to the public. Automatic readoption seems to be less common than it used to be, and many times incumbents have to face performance reviews. The most well-known example is the "mandatory reselection" of members of parliament adopted by the British Labour Party in the early 1980s.[6] Yet, as Gallagher (1988c: 249) stated, "Although few parties appear to have rules specifically protecting incumbents from the full uncertainties of the selection process, the great majority survive nonetheless." Indeed, Labour's adoption of mandatory reselection left few casualties.

Several parties have made it more difficult for incumbents by adding hurdles in the path to reselection. In these cases, the incumbent has different candidacy requirements to new aspirants. For example, in India the Congress Party's Central Elections Committee decided in both 1957 and 1962 that one-third of its incumbents should be replaced (Graham 1986). Moreover, the party recommended that all incumbents who held office for ten years should voluntarily resign. Prior to the 1967 elections, the party eased its requirements but nevertheless decided that incumbents would be reselected only if they had won their district by more than 1,000 votes and the district had remained unchanged. In Italy, the Christian Democrats proposed a four-term limit, but this was not adopted; and the Communists rotated candidates after two terms, unless the party decided that it was crucial for a particular candidate to remain in office (Wertman 1977).

Since 1972, the Austrian People's Party has included a stipulation that the renomination of a deputy for a fourth consecutive term requires a two-thirds majority in a secret ballot. This rule does not apply to membership in parliament or to parliamentary terms of less than two years (Müller 1992). In Israel, both Labor and the Liberals required two-term incumbents to win at least 60 percent of the votes in the party's central committee in order to be eligible for reselection (Goldberg and Hoffman 1983). In Argentina, the Radical Civic Union required incumbents to gain two-thirds of the votes in order to be reselected (Field 2006). The German Greens instituted a rotation rule, and in order to remain in office an incumbent had to gain the support of no less than 70 percent of what in the Green Party is known as the "relevant basis" (Ware 1987). In 1986, the Green Party in Sweden decided that MPs may not be elected more than twice in succession, thereby setting a three-term limit (Pierre and Widfeldt 1992).

---

[6] Mandatory reselection as opposed to automatic readoption, is " ... a process under which, in place of more or less automatic readoption, they [MPs] would have to be reselected in competition with other contenders before each general election" (Shaw 2001: 36). While automatic readoption was indeed reduced, competition for a position held by an incumbent became open only under specific conditions, rather than in all cases, and changes through the years signified some reversal of this policy – i.e. the number of "nominations" needed in order to challenge an incumbent was increased.

## OBSTACLES TO THE CLASSIFICATION OF
## CANDIDACY REQUIREMENTS

There are three main sources for gathering comparative information on candidacy requirements at the party level. The first is a data handbook on political parties. The best-known compendium of this type is Katz and Mair (1992), but many of the country specialists providing the data paid little or no attention to candidacy requirements within the parties.

The second source is volumes devoted to candidate selection, where country experts are asked to address this specific issue. The main, and practically sole source of this nature is Gallagher and Marsh (1988). Narud, Pedersen, and Valen (2002c) focus on only four Nordic countries, while Ohman (2004) covers Africa alone and concentrates mainly on Ghana. All three volumes pay scant attention to candidacy requirements at the party level.

The third source is data compiled by democracy promotion organizations, particularly those who have democracy within parties on their agenda. The National Democratic Institute, for example, presented the best and most up-to-date information on the subject in its coverage of several parties around the world (Ashiagbor 2008). In this report one learns that the British Labour Party, for example, poses somewhat minimal candidacy requirements: continuous membership in the party for at least one year, membership in a trade union recognized by the party, and contribution to the fund of that union. The Canadian Liberal Party's national candidate selection procedures for 2007 spelled out the following specific eligibility criteria (Ashiagbor 2008: 57):

- Current membership (must also be in good standing);
- Full and truthful completion of relevant forms;
- Eligibility under the laws of Canada;
- Satisfaction of any debts to the party and its constituent elements;
- Compliance with federal and relevant provincial and territorial association rules;
- The signatures of twenty-five members in good standing;
- Willingness to undergo background checks or face sanctions;
- Approval of the provincial or territorial chair to be a qualified contestant. (This approval may be revoked by the leader in his/her sole discretion at any time.)

Seemingly – but maybe not practically – more demanding eligibility requirements for selecting candidates to legislative office can be found in the party constitution (Article 11(4)) of the New Patriotic Party in Ghana, which states that in order to seek the party's nomination an individual must (Ashiagbor 2008: 61):

- Be a known and active member for at least two years;
- Be a registered member and voter in the constituency which he or she seeks to represent;

- Be of good character;
- Be of good standing;
- Qualify under the country's electoral laws;
- Pay the fee prescribed by the party's National Executive Council;
- Sign "Undertaking of Parliamentary Candidates."

Moreover, the political parties in Ghana routinely require prospective candidates to pay nomination fees. In some cases, there are two separate fees: one for the application form; and a second for filing the application with the party. The African National Congress in South Africa includes even more exceptional requirements. Its candidates must (Ashiagbor 2008: 31):

- Be a members of good standing with a proven track record of commitment to, and involvement in, the democratic movement;
- Have the requisite experience or expertise to make a constructive contribution;
- Have no criminal record, excluding politically related crimes before April 1994;
- Have no history of ill-discipline, corruption, involvement in fostering divisions, or breaching the party code of conduct.

A comprehensive database on candidacy requirements is still unavailable. The proliferation of political party websites makes this undertaking only slightly easier, because many parties do not include the details of candidate selection in general, and candidacy in particular, on their websites, and where this does appear it is usually only in the home language of the country. Hopefully, the recent increase of interest and publications on candidate selection will make such an endeavor possible in the near future. Preliminary research on this topic is thus still extremely difficult, not to mention an analysis of the change in candidacy requirements over time or of the differences across parties.


## DEMOCRATIZING CANDIDACY REQUIREMENTS


Democratization is one of the more recent and interesting trends in candidate selection methods (Bille 2001; Hazan and Pennings 2001; Hazan 2002; Kittilson and Scarrow 2003; Scarrow, Webb, and Farrell 2000). Claims concerning the occurrence of this trend are based on data about the selectorate, but not candidacy. However, we can define democratization as a widening of participation in both the supply and the selection process – that is, when parties adopt more inclusive candidacy requirements *and* selectorates. In order to democratize candidacy requirements, parties have to reduce the restrictions on eligibility, thereby creating a much larger pool of potential candidates, but in order to democratize candidate selection the selectorate must also be more inclusive.

Thus, in order to understand the significance of democratizing candidate selection, which will be addressed in the second part of this book, it is important to assess the relationship between candidacy requirements and the party selectorate – the first two dimensions in our framework for analyzing candidate selection methods. A high level of inclusiveness on both has significant political consequences, but inclusiveness on one dimension combined with exclusiveness on the other could preclude or constrain these consequences. For example, if more inclusive candidacy requirements are adopted, yet the same limited selectorate is maintained, control over the final results has not been significantly reduced. The Italian Communists included even nonmembers as candidates, but this was done under the supervision of an exclusive selectorate (Wertman 1988). The same is true for the opposite case of the Belgian Socialist Party that we described above, in which a relatively inclusive selectorate of party members was combined with highly exclusive candidacy requirements. Having described candidacy requirements for legislative office, we now turn our attention to the second and more important dimension in candidate selection methods – the selectorate.

# 3

# The Selectorate

After candidacy requirements, the second dimension in the analysis of candidate selection methods is the selectorate: Not who can be selected, but rather *who is selecting*. These two dimensions are akin to the "supply" and "demand" sides of candidate selection. While candidacy narrows the supply of contestants who can be selected, the selectorate will further decrease their numbers to those who will eventually face the voters in the general election.

The selectorate as a factor in party politics – as far as we can tell – was first addressed in a book by Paterson (1967), appropriately titled *The Selectorate*. In it, he describes candidate selection in Britain, which he finds dissatisfying, and argues for the adoption of party primaries. However, despite the focus of the book, there is no systematic treatment or definition of the selectorate. More recently, the term has been adopted by game theorists with a focus on the interplay between domestic political institutions, foreign policy, and the survival of leaders (Bueno de Mesquita et al. 2003). This model provides a definition of the selectorate as "the set of citizens who have a prospect of becoming members of an incumbent's winning coalition" (Bueno de Mesquita et al. 2002: 273), and it is the winning coalition – a subset of the selectorate – that is required for a leader to achieve or sustain political power (Enterline and Gleditsch 2000). This definition is of little help to scholars of party politics because it equates the selectorate in a democracy to the electorate, suitably adjusted for voter turnout. However, it is interesting to note that the rational choice approach emphasizes the *size* of the selectorate as an important variable.

When speaking of political parties in general, and candidate selection in particular, the selectorate is the body that selects the party's candidates for public office. It is, as Best and Cotta (2000*a*: 11) described, "an important intermediary actor ... the party organizations, the personal cliques, the groups of dignitaries or state officials involved in the selection of candidates and in their representation to constituencies." Indeed, the selectorate can be composed of one person or several people – up to the entire electorate of a given nation. While each criterion used in the classification of candidate selection methods has a distinct influence on politics, it is the selectorate that imposes the most significant and far-reaching consequences on politicians, parties, and parliaments more than any other dimension of candidate selection.

Duverger (1954: 353) argued that representatives receive a double mandate. "Before being chosen by his electors the deputy is chosen by the party. . . . The importance of each varies according to the country and the parties; on the whole the party mandate seems to carry more weight than that of the electors." Particular constraints are placed on the candidates based on the distinctive priorities of each selectorate – different selectorate priorities produce different candidates. In their study of Labour selectors, Bochel and Denver (1983: 45) posit that, "By their choices they effectively determine the range of abilities, social characteristics and ideological viewpoints present in the House of Commons." Best and Cotta (2000*a*: 11–12) expressed this most appropriately:

> Selectorates select candidates according to the result of complex choices considering the probable value of the contender's resources for electoral success, their ideological fit with and their practical function for the selectorates themselves and their likely loyalty, that is, their expected obedience to the implicit and explicit expectations of the selectors after becoming a parliamentary actor. Since selectorates have not only a demand position on the recruitment market but must also make convincing offers to the electorate, the relative weight of factors working in the selective process is variable: for example, in a situation when a selectorate is in secure control of a significant part of the electoral support market, campaign qualities of contenders will be of less importance than their expected loyalty or their ideological fit.

Changes in the selectorate are thus expected to have significant political consequences. These changes do not usually occur before each election, because candidate selection methods, like other political institutions, enjoy a certain level of stability. Yet, significant changes in candidate selection methods indeed occur – among them changes in the selectorate – much more frequently than changes in electoral systems. This makes candidate selection methods in general, and the selectorates as the most important dimension of candidate selection methods in particular, an important source for political renovation and change.

Significant changes and reforms in candidate selection methods result from the interplay between three levels of party politics. First is the intraparty arena, in which factions, camps, and individuals compete for power. At this level, changes are initiated and promoted to improve the positions of certain individuals and factions within the party. For example, the young guard might promote the adoption of party primaries, believing that they might improve its chances to advance within the party and push out the old guard. Second is the interparty arena, in which parties compete with each other for power, mainly through elections. Here, many times, changes are initiated and promoted to improve the position of one party vis-à-vis its competitors, the other parties. For example, a party that suffered defeat in the elections may reform its candidate selection method in order to improve the party's image vis-à-vis the other parties. Finally, there is the political system level – the general environment in which the parties act. Here we would expect general social, technological, and cultural developments to direct and constrain parties when they decide to preserve or reform their candidate selection methods (Barnea and Rahat 2007). The adoption of more inclusive selectorates is explained, at this level, as a reaction to general long-term developments that led to the decline or the adaptation of the parties (Scarrow 1999*a*; Katz 2001).

This chapter focuses on a delineation of the selectorate, so that researchers across political systems will have a common language when trying to classify and analyze selectorates both of their own country and of other countries. Adopting this classification allows for comparison within countries, across parties and time, and between countries. Subsequent sections of this book will address the political consequences of a democratic reform in a party's candidate selection procedure as a result of expanding the size of its selectorate.

## SIMPLE, ASSORTED, MULTISTAGE, AND WEIGHTED CANDIDATE SELECTION METHODS

A simple selection method is one in which a single selectorate selects all of the candidates. Such methods are easy to classify according to their levels of inclusiveness. As Figure 3.1 suggests, we can distinguish five archetypical kinds of selectorates:

1. The most inclusive selectorate: voters. This selectorate includes the entire electorate that has the right to vote in general elections.[1]
2. The highly inclusive selectorate: party members. Here we include party membership in its European sense; that is, not simply registration as a party affiliate

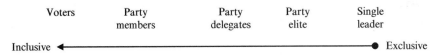

FIGURE 3.1. Party selectorates

---

[1] In some countries, the rules for this category can be even more inclusive than those for the electorate. For example, in Canada, immigrants who are not yet citizens can become party members and take part in candidate selection (Cross 2004). In Israel, an amendment to the Parties Law of 1992 (article 20A) lowered the minimum age of party members to seventeen, which allows a minor to vote in those parties that hold primaries, while the minimum age for voting in general elections is eighteen (Israel Parties Law). In Finland, the Center Party allowed its members to take part in party primaries from the age of fifteen (Kuitunen 2002).

administered by the states as in the United States – this belongs to the above category – but registration that is controlled by the party itself.[2]

3. The in-between selectorate: party delegates. This selectorate is composed of representatives selected by the party members. They can be members of party agencies (e.g. conventions, central committees, or congresses) or delegate bodies that were especially selected for this purpose alone.
4. The highly exclusive selectorate: the party elite. Here we include small party agencies and committees that were indirectly selected, or whose composition was ratified by wider party agencies, and also other less formal groupings.
5. The most exclusive selectorate: a nominating entity of a single leader.

The categories proposed above can be easily used when analyzing a simple, one-stage, and uniform candidate selection method. Such a simple method is one in which all potential candidates simultaneously face a similar selectorate. Empirically, however, we often face complex candidate selection methods – methods in which different candidates face selectorates with different levels of inclusiveness, or the same candidates face several selectorates with differing levels of inclusiveness.

We distinguish between three kinds of such complexities: the *assorted*, the *multistage*, and the *weighted* candidate selection methods. In an assorted candidate selection method, as shown in Figure 3.2, *different* candidates face selectorates that differ in their levels of inclusiveness. The Belgian parties, from the 1960s until the 1990s, serve as an example of an assorted system, one that used different selectorates for selecting candidates of the same party. Inside the main parties, some candidates were selected by party members while others were selected by delegates or members of local and central party agencies, and still others were appointed by local elites (De Winter 1988; De Winter and Brans 2003; Deschouwer 1994; Obler 1970). In Australia, candidates from the same party face substantially different selectorates across the Australian states (Norris et al. 1990).

In the multistage candidate selection method, the *same* candidates have to face more than one selectorate during the selection process. For example, in the British Conservative and Labour parties, special national party committees screened aspirants and created a list of eligible candidates. Then, a small local executive party agency (about twenty to twenty-five people) filtered candidates and compiled a "short list" from the dozens or even hundreds of aspirants, which was subsequently presented to a more inclusive party agency for selection – and in recent decades, to the even more inclusive selectorate of party members. The first selectorate (sometimes even selectorates) filters, or screens, the candidates, further minimizing the overall pool that was previously narrowed by candidacy requirements, yet the last selectorate – be it party delegates or party members – still has the last word (Norris and Lovenduski 1995).

---

[2] On the differences between US party registration and party membership, see Katz and Kolodny (1994).

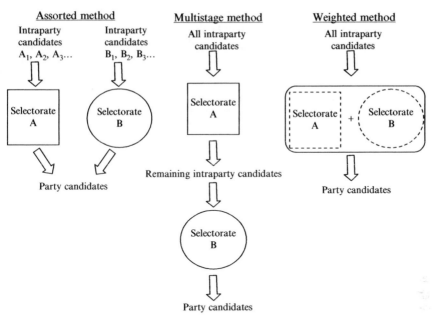

FIGURE 3.2. Complex candidate selection methods

The multistage method can also place a selected party agency after the party members. For example, candidate selection can be entrusted to the party agency after conferring with the party membership, or a party agency can exercise its veto over candidates chosen by the members. In the French Socialist Party, the executive committee at the level of the department chooses the candidates, but often after consulting the constituency party membership (Depauw 2003). The experience of British (Norris and Lovenduski 1995), Canadian (Cross 2002; Erickson 1997), New Zealand (Vowels 2002), and Irish (Gallagher 2003) parties tells us that such veto is activated only on rare occasions. The party agency still has an impact, though, because selectorates are usually sensitive enough to refrain from selecting someone who may be vetoed by the executive agency.

Weighted candidate selection methods are those in which the result is determined by weighting *together* the votes of two or more selectorates for the *same* candidate or candidates. The British Labour Party used a weighted method for selecting its candidates for the 1992 elections (Criddle 1992) in the last stage of the selection process (it was also a multistage method). The result that determined which candidate would stand as the party candidate in the constituency was based on weighting the choices of the affiliated unions (up to 40 percent) and of the party members (60 percent or more). The Labour Party of New Zealand also used a weighted method to select its candidates in the single-member districts (Mulgan 2004; Sheppard 1998). It weighted the votes of delegates nominated by the national party agency (three delegates), delegates nominated by the constituency party agency (one to two delegates), a delegate selected by party members, and the vote of the party members (as an additional, single delegate vote). In Taiwan, the Kuomintang and the Democratic Progressive Party used various weighted methods over the years. These included weighting the votes of party cadres and party members and later, in a more inclusive manner, weighting the votes of party members and the results of opinion polls (Baum and Robinson 1999; Fell 2005). Similar to the assorted and the multi-stage methods, such weighted methods spread power among several forces within the party. These may result from a compromise between forces within the party, but may also be seen as an attempt to create the optimal blend in order to produce the best possible candidates (Rahat 2009).

## Dealing with the complexities

In the case of complex candidate selection methods, classification becomes difficult. As the goal here is to offer a cross-party and cross-national analytical framework, one must integrate one-stage, uniform candidate selection methods and different complex cases, such as assorted, multistage, and weighted methods, into the same framework.

The difficulty with assorted candidate selection methods can be addressed in two steps. First, there should be a separate analysis of each distinct selectorate within the party. Second, the relative impact of each selectorate should be weighted by calculating the ratio of realistic candidacies that are filled by the particular selectorate, with the goal of "summing up" the party's candidate selection method. If one-half of the candidates are selected by party delegates and one-half by party members, then – when summing up for comparative needs – one can locate the selectorate between these zones.

The complexity of a multistage candidate selection method should be approached in a slightly different two-step method. First, there should be a separate analysis of each stage. Second, the relative importance of each stage should be estimated. If certain stages are found to be mere formalities, then they should be removed from consideration. When more than one stage has a real impact on the composition of the candidate list – in terms of the realistic candidacies – then these stages should be weighted to produce results that will enable us to locate the system along the continuum suggested.

Weighted candidate selection methods should be treated according to the relative importance that is allotted to each selectorate. When, for example, the votes of the party members and the party delegates are equally weighted, then the level of inclusiveness is between those two categories. When the vote of one selectorate carries more weight – for example, 70 percent for party members versus 30 percent for party delegates – then we are dealing with a case that is closer to party primaries in its level of inclusiveness. The following sections offer examples of the operationalization of such solutions, alongside the simpler methods, by delineating the continuum of party selectorates.

## A JOURNEY ALONG THE INCLUSIVENESS–EXCLUSIVENESS CONTINUUM

In this section we take a journey along the inclusiveness–exclusiveness continuum, starting from the most inclusive selectorate – all voters – and ending with the most exclusive one – the single leader. Our journey will pass through empirical examples from the democratic world that will refer to parties from established and new democracies. It will relate not only to the simple methods, but also to the complex ones: the assorted, multistage, and weighted selection methods.

### *Voters*

The primaries of the fifty states in the United States provide us with most of the examples at the inclusive end of the continuum. The exact location of American primaries depends on the conditions set for participation in the primaries that are defined by the different state laws (Gerber and Morton 1998; Kanthak and Morton 2001; Merriam and Overacker 1928; Ranney 1981).[3] Duverger (1954: 363) noted that in some US states there is no party affiliation beside the names of the candidates, and thus, "Really this is no longer a primary but the first ballot of an election." Indeed, at the extreme end are the American *nonpartisan* primaries, used in Louisiana from 1978 to 2006 to select candidates for Congress (Engstrom and Engstrom 2008; Maisel and Brewer 2007).[4] These primaries, where every registered voter could vote for candidates from any party, are located at the inclusive end of the continuum (Ranney 1981).

*Blanket* primaries – used in Washington (since 1938), Alaska (since 1968), and California (1998, 2000)[5] (Engstrom and Engstrom 2008) – are also at the extreme inclusiveness pole, as shown in Figure 3.3. Here voters receive a single ballot listing all the candidates from all the parties and decide, for each post separately, which party candidate to vote for. In both the nonpartisan and blanket primaries, participants do not need to declare their party affiliation in order to take part in candidate selection.

*Open* primaries, slightly less inclusive than the two previous kinds, are used in several states in the United States.[6] As in nonpartisan and blanket primaries, the

---

[3] Endorsements in preselection delegate conventions can also affect the location of the specific method, turning it into a more exclusive two-stage process. We ignore this element because it seems to have only a marginal effect on the selection process (Galderisi and Ezra 2001).

[4] Nonpartisan primaries are much more common in the lower levels of government in the United States, especially the local level.

[5] On the abolition of blanket primaries in California, as a result of a Supreme Court decision, see Persily (2001).

[6] The Democratic and Republican parties of the following states used open primaries (in parentheses are the time periods for which we have reliable data): Michigan and Montana (1960–90), Minnesota,

voters are allowed to decide in which primaries they want to take part without the need to announce their partisan preference. Yet, unlike these types, voters can take part in the primaries of only one party.

*Semi-closed* primaries are used in the United States by the Republican and Democratic parties of several states.[7] These primaries require participants to declare their party affiliation only on the selection day, and/or allow independents to take part in candidate selection of the party they announce their wish to vote in.[8] Here we are slightly away from the inclusive end of the selectorate continuum because voters need publicly to affiliate with a political party. We also have examples from Iceland, Taiwan, Mexico, and Spain.[9] According to Kristjánsson (2002), from 1971 on, parties in Iceland (Social Democrats, Progressives, and Independence Party) adopted primaries in some, and sometimes all, electoral districts, where every citizen in a particular electoral district could participate. In Taiwan, the National Party adopted primaries in which all voters could participate in 1998 (Fell 2005), and so did the Mexican Party of the Democratic Revolution in 2003 (Wuhs 2006). The Catalan Socialist Party in Spain opened its candidate selection to "registered 'sympathizers'" – non-members who could register as party supporters without paying any membership fee (Hopkin 2001).

American *closed* primaries, which demand that voters register according to their party affiliation before the day of the primaries, are located somewhat further away from the inclusive end. Closed primaries, which are used in several states of the United States,[10] are in the middle – between the category of voters and that of

Utah, and Wisconsin (all three 1960–96), Alaska (1960–6), North Dakota (1968–86), Vermont (1972–96), Hawaii (at least since the 1960s), and Idaho (since 1976) (Kolodny and Katz 1992; Goodliffe and Magleby 2000; State of Hawaii; Idaho Secretary of State).

[7] In the research literature, this type is sometimes labeled "semi-open." We prefer the semi-closed label because the main difference between closed and open primaries is that in the former the voter needs publicly to affiliate with a party. In semi-closed primaries, the voters still need to publicly announce in which party primaries they will participate, even if at the last moment.

[8] The Democratic and Republican parties of the following states used semi-closed primaries (in parentheses are the time periods for which we have reliable data): Alabama, Arkansas, Georgia, Illinois, Indiana, Mississippi, Missouri, South Carolina, Tennessee, Texas, and Virginia (all in the 1980s and 1990s), Arizona (since 2000), California (since 2002) (Goodliffe and Magleby 2000; Arizona Constitution; California Secretary of State).

[9] It should be noted that what are called "open" primaries outside the United States is different from what the Americans call open primaries. Outside the United States, open primaries are a candidate selection method in which nonmembers can participate. In the US open primaries, voters can participate without publicly exposing their party affiliation. We thus place the non-American open kind together with the semi-closed American primaries.

[10] The Democratic and Republican parties of the following states used closed primaries (in parentheses are the time periods on which we have reliable data): Florida (1960–2008), Arizona (1960–98), California, Connecticut, Delaware, Kentucky, Maine, Maryland, Massachusetts, Nebraska, Nevada, New Hampshire, New Jersey, New Mexico, New York, North Carolina, Ohio, Oklahoma, Oregon, Pennsylvania, South Dakota, West Virginia, and Wyoming (all from 1960 to 1996) (Kolodny and Katz 1992; Goodliffe and Magleby 2000; Florida Department of State). Some of these states allow the parties to conduct semi-closed primaries if they wish; that is, to allow unaffiliated voters to take part in their primaries. Yet, the default alternative is still a closed primary method.

party members. The level of inclusiveness of the selectorate of the Democratic Progressive Party in Taiwan (1998–2001) also places it at this middle point. It used a unique weighted selectorate that combined the results of both a party members' vote and a public opinion poll (Baum and Robinson 1999; Fell 2005).

The open convention, which allows any voter to take part in a candidate selection meeting, is probably the less inclusive version of the most inclusive family of selectorates. While it allows any voter to take part in a selection meeting without any need to prove party affiliation or even to preregister, it is still quite a demanding system, as it requires the voter to attend a meeting at a certain date, time, and location. This kind of selection – which is similar to some of the American caucus systems (Marshall 1978) – was used in the past in Canada, especially in the 1920s–1950s period, before the parties started to institutionalize their membership (Engelmann and Schwartz 1975; O'Brien 1993).[11]

### *Party members*

We now move into the party members' zone, but at its inclusive end, closer to the general electorate. Here we have the case of the Dutch Democrats 66 in the 2004 European elections, which held meetings where both party members and all voters could participate, but then allowed only party members to make the final decision through voting via postal ballots (Depauw and Van Hecke 2005; Hazan and Voerman 2006). We also have the case of the Taiwanese Kuomintang (2001–4) that weighted the voting of party members with public opinion polls (Fell 2005). Another example is the Argentine Peronist (Justicialista) Party and the Radical Civic Union, who in some districts (1983–2001) allowed party members and independents to participate in their primaries (De Luca, Jones, and Tula 2002; Jones 2008).

In the middle of the party members' zone we find the typical European closed primary (Newman and Cranshaw 1973), which – as opposed to American closed primaries – usually means "party primaries" (Gallagher 1988c: 239–40) in which the selectors are party members, not merely registered adherents. From this point on in the selectorate continuum we exclude the party supporters. Over the years, usually in an incremental fashion, more and more Western democracies allotted their members a significant role in candidate selection (Scarrow, Webb, and Farrell 2000; Bille 2001; Kittilson and Scarrow 2003). The "purest" type of party primary is where the party members' votes alone decide the composition and rank of the candidates. Several parties, across a wide spectrum of time and space, have used party primaries, albeit not consistently over time and not necessarily in all districts. Among them are the following examples: the Australian Labor Party

---

[11] Scarrow (1964) described the dynamics of such a selection process taking place in 1962 in the Liberal Party in Ontario.

(Epstein 1977*b*); the Belgian ECOLO (Deschouwer 1994); the German Social Democrats, Christian Democrats, and Greens at the single-member district level (Borchert and Golsch 2003; Schüttermeyer and Strum 2005); the major Icelandic parties – Independence Party, Social Democratic Party, Progressive Party, People's Alliance (Hardarson 1995; Kristjánsson 1998, 2002); the major Israeli parties – Labor, Likud, and Kadima (Hazan 1997*a*, 1997*b*; Rahat and Sher Hadar 1999*a*, 1999*b*; Rahat 2008*a*; Rahat Forthcoming); major Mexican parties – the Institutional Revolutionary Party and the Party of the Democratic Revolution (Baldez 2007; Langston 2006, 2008; Wuhs 2006).

When party members have a dominant or significant role in candidate selection – but they are not the sole selectors and other, more exclusive party actors take part in the selection of candidates – we are still in the party members' zone but are moving toward the party delegates' area. The cases here involve multistage methods. For example, in several of the Danish parties, from the 1970s until the twenty-first century, central party agencies could veto or change the selection made by the party members (Bille 1994, 2001; Pedersen 2002). In the Kuomintang in Taiwan in 1988–9, the party's executive could ignore the members' vote, yet chose to respect their verdicts in 90 percent of cases (Baum and Robinson 1999). In Finland, the election law states that party organizations have the right to change up to one-fourth of the candidates selected by the members' vote.[12] In Canada, national party leaders have veto power over the party members' selection, although they usually refrain from exercising it (Cross 2002, 2004),[13] while in Ireland the national party leadership kept and even enhanced its veto power in those parties that adopted a membership vote (Galligan 2003; Weeks 2007).

The right that party agencies (typically national executives and/or party leaders) possess is rarely used because it can cause conflicts within the party, with allegations that the oligarchy does not respect the more popular democratic will. This is why party agencies are more influential vis-à-vis the members when the order is reversed – when the party delegates (or even the party elite) screen the potential candidates, and the party members make the final decision.

---

[12] Section 117 of the Election Act of Finland states:

> On the recommendation of the party board, the result of the vote by the members can differ no more than one fourth from the number of candidates nominated by the party (*right of change*). Even then at least half of the candidates of the party must be persons who have received most votes in the vote by the members. (Ministry of Justice, Finland [Italics in original])

[13] In 1970, with the law that required the printing of party labels beside candidate names in federal ballots, party leaders were given the power to veto candidacies. In 1992, the Liberal Party granted its leader the right to appoint candidates, thus enhancing his powers as a selector, though most candidates at most times were still selected by party members at the constituency level (Carty and Eagles 2003).

When party agencies can filter the candidates, who are then put to a membership vote, we are getting close to the middle between the party members and the selected party delegates zones. If the screening process still leaves a large and viable pool of candidates from whom party members can make the final decision, then we are still on the party members' side. In Israel, the Meretz Party in 1996 produced a sizeable "panel" of candidates from which the members chose the final list (Hazan 1997a; Rahat and Sher Hadar 1999a). The Social Democrats and the Liberals in Britain did much the same (Criddle 1984, 1988; Norris and Lovenduski 1995; Rush 1988), as did several of the parties in Belgium in some of the districts, especially the Belgian Socialist Party during the 1960s (Obler 1970, 1974).

When equal weight is given to the party delegates and to the party members, then we are in the middle between these two categories. In Taiwan in 1995–6, the Democratic Progressive Party used a weighted method in which the vote of the members was equally weighted to the vote of the party representatives (Baum and Robinson 1999). British Labour's use of a multistage method since 1997 – where candidates were screened by party agencies, selected by party members, and could still be vetoed by the National Executive Committee – can also be seen as a middle-of-the-road example (Quinn 2004). The same seems to be the case for the Democratic Party of Botswana in 2002, where party members selected candidates after a national party agency screening (Ohman 2004), and for both Dutch Labor (1960–4) and the Pacifist Socialists (1957–73) that allowed their national executives to propose the list of candidates, yet let the members then vote and alter both the rank and the composition of these lists (Koole and van de Velde 1992).

The "party members" selectorate can be further distinguished according to the restrictions on party membership, the additional requirements that are placed on members with a conditional right to take part in the party selectorate, and the level of accessibility of the selector to the selection procedure. For example, one rule that could restrict membership, or just the right to participate in candidate selection, is the rate of membership dues. Members' participation may also be restricted by the requirement of a minimal party membership period prior to candidate selection, proof of party activity, etc. The Mexican Party of National Action is a good example of a party that placed barriers on membership participation. A member could take part in candidate selection only after six months of membership, and in order to keep this right had to pay party dues and take part in party gatherings (Langston 2008).

Accessibility may also be an important factor in distinguishing between such selectorates. Levels of accessibility and inclusiveness are higher if a party adopts postal ballots[14] or e-voting.[15] Spreading polling stations all over the country is less

---

[14] Postal ballots were used by the Dutch D66, the British Labour Party, and by several Danish parties.

[15] In 2000 in Arizona, the Democratic Party conducted its primaries online (Alvarez and Nagler 2001).

accessible.[16] A much less accessible yet inclusive method is an all-member party convention, as is usually the case with candidate selection in the Canadian parties and some of the Irish parties over the last decade. While all members can attend such a meeting, it requires more effort on their part.

### Selected party delegates

When party members have less of an impact than selected party delegates, the selectorate is still located between these two zones, but is closer to the latter. Here, for example, the members can ratify or reject a list of candidates drawn up by the party agency, as was done by the French Socialists in 1986 (Thiébault 1988). Also in this category is a multistage process where the members are only one stage in a process that is more than two stages. Since the 1980s, the British Conservatives used a multistage method, which started with a screening by a nonselected national party agency, followed by a local selected party agency screening, and ended with a party members selection meeting (Norris and Lovenduski 1995).

We move slightly further toward exclusivity when the candidates are produced by a wide delegate convention – when the ratio of members to delegates is in the low range of one delegate for each three to four members – as was the case in Ireland with the Fianna Fail, Fine Gael (until it adopted membership ballots in the 1990s), and Labour parties (Gallagher 1980, 1988b). Another example is selection by a party agency that might be followed (or preceded) by a membership ballot, as was the case in the Swedish Communist/Left Party (Pierre and Widfeldt 1992).

When the selectorate is an agency of the party, we are in the middle of the continuum. Inside the party the relative size of each agency is a sign of its inclusiveness: conventions are usually larger than central committees, which in turn are usually larger than executive bodies, such as bureaus. As the size of the particular party agency gets smaller, we move closer to the exclusive pole of the continuum. The terminology used in each country is not necessarily equivalent, and hence one must be cautious when inferring the extent of inclusiveness based solely on what a particular party calls a specific agency. In addition, the more inclusive party agencies contain delegates selected by party members, while the more exclusive ones include representatives who were selected by such delegates. The use of party delegates is widespread. Since the 1950s, the major German parties used delegate conventions at the single-member district level, preferring them in most cases over the alternatively more inclusive selectorate prescribed by the party law – selection by the members themselves (Borchert and Golsch 2003; Roberts 1988). This was also the typical selectorate in Australia (Epstein 1977b; Norris et al. 1990). Several Israeli parties (National Religious Party 1996–2006,

---

[16] Primaries conducted in the United States involve the spreading of polling stations across the particular state.

Shinui 2003, Herut 1977–88, Likud 1992, 1999–2006) used their central committees to select candidates (Barnea and Rahat 2007; Rahat 2008*a*). From the 1920s to the 1950s, this was also one of the methods that was used by the Canadian parties (O'Brien 1993). Even in those countries where more inclusive selectorates are now the norm, or already were before, we still find the use of delegates to select candidates from time to time in certain parties, or in certain constituency organizations. Such cases include the occasional use of delegate conventions by both Belgian and Argentine parties (De Luca, Jones, and Tula 2002; De Winter and Brans 2003; Jones 2008; Obler 1970).

When a nonselected party agency, such as a nomination committee, has an influence on the selection of candidates, alongside the selected party agency, we move toward less inclusiveness (or more exclusiveness), but remain within the selected agency zone. One example is the assorted system used by both the Party of National Liberation and United Social Christian Party in Costa Rica, where most candidates were chosen by a selected party agency, but several were nominated by the party's president (Taylor-Robinson 2001). There are many examples of multistage methods when both directly and indirectly selected party agencies take part in candidate selection, as in the Austrian Socialist Party 1945–90 (Müller 1992); the Dutch Christian Democrats 1986, Christian Historical Union 1960–79, and Radical Political Party 1973–89 (Koole and van de Velde 1992); the British Conservatives from the 1950s to the 1970s and Labour from the 1950s until 1987 (Denver 1988; Lovenduski and Norris 1994; Ranney 1965; Rush 1969). Yet another example is a weighted method where both nominated and selected delegates choose the candidates, such as in the New Zealand Labour Party since the 1950s (Catt 1997; Milne 1966; Mulgan 2004; Vowels 2002).

We are in the middle, between the selected party delegates and the party elite, when there is a relative balance of power between the selected and the nonselected party agencies. This was the case with the multistage methods used in the 1980s in the Union for French Democracy (Thiébault 1988), the Dutch People's Party for Freedom and Democracy from the 1960s to the 1990s (Koole and van de Velde 1992), and the Spanish Socialists from 1979 to 1998 (Field 2006). The Norwegian parties, in most cases, from the 1920s and until 2002, followed such a system, according to a law that allocated funding to political parties that selected their candidates in a (selected) delegate convention at the level of the multimember constituency. In practice, a nomination committee submitted a list of candidates, and the selected delegates either ratified or changed the list, position by position (Valen 1988; Valen, Narud, and Skare 2002). Candidate selection at the Land level in Germany also belongs here. Although party delegates are the final decision makers at this level, the selection is made on the basis of a recommended list that is designed by the Land party elite (Borchert and Golsch 2003; Porter 1995).

## Party elite

This category includes nomination committees that are formed for the sole purpose of selecting the party's candidates, as well as nonselected party agencies (typically small executive boards) that are entrusted with several different tasks including the selection of candidates.[17] Nomination committees are usually composed of a few party leaders, their representatives, or aficionados. Their composition, as well as their decisions, is many times ratified *en bloc* by more inclusive party agencies. The composition of both nomination committees and nonselected party agencies can be regarded as slightly more inclusive if it is indirectly selected, or somewhat more exclusive if it is not.

When the selection power of the party elite is stronger than that of the selected party agency, we move into the party elite zone and are squarely within the exclusive part of the continuum. Here we have cases of multistage methods that involve various selected and nonselected (or highly indirectly selected) party agencies, with more influence to the latter. For example, the French Rally for the Republic in the 1980s allowed a nominating committee to select its candidates, but afforded some influence to other directly and indirectly selected party agencies (Thiébault 1988). The Italian Communists from 1956 to 1986 allowed for the involvement of a selected party agency, but the final word over candidate selection was given to an indirectly selected party agency (Bardi and Morlino 1992). The Chilean Party for Democracy and National Renovation allowed their national board and national council, respectively, to be involved, but the final decision was made – because of the constraints set by the binominal electoral system – by negotiations between the party leaders (Navia 2008). In the Japanese Liberal Democratic Party during the 1950s–1990s period, the last stage of candidate selection was also in the hands of an exclusive national committee that consisted of fifteen senior leaders (Fukui 1997). When, for example, the selected party agency is only asked to ratify a decision made by the nomination committee, we are still leaning slightly toward the inclusive side of the party elite zone. This was the case in the Taiwanese Kuomintang in 1995 (Baum and Robinson 1999), and in the Israeli Mapai from 1949 to 1955 (Brichta 1977). In the Greek Pan-Hellenic Socialist Movement, local and relatively inclusive agencies were consulted in the early stages of the selection process, but the final list of candidates was determined by a committee that was appointed by the party leader. In 2006, the process was democratized when it was decided that the selection committee would be chosen by the members of the party's National Council. This is clearly a more inclusive selectorate, which moves the party to the "selected delegates zone" yet leaves it in an exclusive position within that zone because the delegates are not selected directly by party members (Ashiagbor 2008).

---

[17] We include in this category small party agencies (not more than a few dozen members) that are composed of people who were selected indirectly or nominated by other (possibly selected or indirectly selected) party agencies.

When only a nonselected party agency/group is involved in candidate selection, then we are squarely in the middle of the party elite area. This is the kind of selectorate that seems to reflect Michels' (1915) notion of party politics. That was the case in the Venezuelan Democratic Action Party in the 1990s (Coppedge 1994); the Italian Christian Democrats from 1957 to 1984 (Bardi and Morlino 1992); the Mexican Institutional Revolutionary Party before 2000 (Langston 2001); the Chilean Independent Democratic Union from 1989 to 2001 (Navia 2008); in a significant number of constituencies in several of the main Belgian parties, especially since 1968 (De Winter 1988; Deschouwer 1994); the Indian Congress Party in the 1950s and 1960s (Graham 1986; Kochanek 1967); the Danish Peoples Party in 1998 (Pedersen 2002); and in the Argentine Peronist and Radical parties in some districts in Argentina (De Luca, Jones, and Tula 2002; Jones 2008).

We move toward the single-leader pole with such exclusive selectorates as a gathering of the party founders in a new party, or an informal group of factional leaders in older parties. Israel's ultra-religious parties serve as an example of such highly exclusive selectorates. In one party, Shas, a Council of Sages – a small body of Rabbis headed by a highly influential spiritual leader – formed the candidate list (Rahat and Hazan 2001).

## A single leader

The extreme end of the exclusive pole is defined by a selectorate of a single individual. If the leader does not have complete control over candidate selection, then we are close to the exclusive end of the selectorate continuum, but not at its pole. In Forza Italia, in the 1990s, founding leader Silvio Berlusconi chose the candidates in cooperation with the party's regional coordinators (Hopkin and Paolucci 1999). Jean-Marie Le Pen, the French National Front leader, together with its general secretary, chose the party's candidates, with some influence given to nonselected forces (Thiébault 1988). Winston Peters, New Zealand First's founder, was also given almost complete control over candidate selection (Catt 1997; Miller 1999; Mulgan 2004).

Similar to the party elite, a single leader will lean more toward the inclusive side if the leader is selected, and more to the exclusive pole if it is a nonselected leader. Once again, some of the Israeli parties serve as examples of such an extremely exclusive selectorate. In 1988–96, in one ultra-religious party in Israel, Degel HaTorah, a single rabbi was authorized to decide the composition and order of the party list (Rahat and Sher-Hadar 1999*a*). In 2005, Prime Minister Ariel Sharon quit his party (Likud), formed a new one (Kadima), and also called for new elections. He alone was to choose its list of candidates (Hazan 2007).[18]

---

[18] After suffering a stroke in the middle of the election campaign, the leadership of the new party was taken over by his deputy, Ehud Olmert, who singlehandedly completed the list of candidates.

## CLASSIFYING PARTY SELECTORATES ALONG
## THE SELECTORATE CONTINUUM

Figure 3.3 illustrates the levels of inclusiveness of the selectorates using a twenty-five-point scale (0–24). It is based on the continuum in Figure 3.1. Indeed, every six points along the scale relate to one selectorate, or category, along the continuum that appears in Figure 3.1: single leader (0), party elite (6), party delegates (12), party members (18), or the voters (24). Its additional property – designed to deal systematically with the challenge of complexity – is a distance of six points between each category. This distance is needed in order to allow the categorization of those cases where we deal with more than a single selectorate (the assorted, multistage, and weighted candidate selection methods). To demonstrate the usefulness of this continuum we located examples of cases that were mentioned in the previous section at most of its points.

The six-point distance allows us to illustrate four possible scenarios:

1. A single selectorate is responsible for candidate selection, in which case the classification falls clearly into one distinct category (0, 6, 12, 18, or 24).
2. Two selectorates (located near each other) have equal weight in the selection. Each selectorate may choose only one-half of the candidates, or their influence is equal in a weighted or multistage method. In these cases classification falls in the middle, between the two selectorate categories (3, 9, 15, or 21).
3. Two selectorates (located near each other) are involved in candidate selection, both have a significant role, yet one is either somewhat more important than the other or clearly dominant compared to the other. For example:

   (a) If in an assorted system, one selectorate selects two-thirds of the candidates and the other selectorate the remaining third; if in a multistage method, we estimate the influence of one selectorate to be higher than the other; or if in a weighted system, the weight of one selectorate is around two-thirds, while the other is about one-third. In these cases we are no longer in the middle, between two categories, but leaning closer to one category (2, 4, 8, 10, 14, 16, 20, or 22).

   (b) If in an assorted system, one selectorate selects 80 percent of the candidates and the other the remaining 20 percent; if in a multistage method, we estimate the influence of one selectorate to be much higher than the other; or if in a weighted system, the weight of one selectorate is around 80 percent, while the other is about 20 percent. In these cases we are much closer to one category than the other, but not clearly in that category alone (1, 5, 7, 11, 13, 17, 19, or 23).

After considering several options – using a continuum with less or with more resolution – we concluded that the twenty-five-point continuum is the most appropriate. Beyond the cross-national comparison exhibited in Figure 3.3, it

Scale (top): Single leader — Party elite — Party delegates — Party members — Voters

Inclusive ←————————————————————————————→ Exclusive

24  23  22  21  20  19  18  17  16  15  14  13 **12** 11  10  9  8  7  **6**  5  4  3  2  1  **0**

|  |  |
|---|---|
| 24 | USA – Democratic and Republican parties of Washington (since 1938) |
| 23 | USA – Democratic and Republican parties of Hawaii (at least since 1960s) |
| 22 | Iceland – some parties in some districts (since 1970s) |
| 21 | USA – Democratic and Republican parties of Florida (1960–2008) |
| 20 | Netherlands – D66 (1990s) |
| 19 | Argentina – Justicialista Party and Radical Civic Union in some districts (1983–2001) |
| 18 | Israel – Labor Party (since 1992) |
| 17 | Finland – all parties (since 1975) |
| 16 | Belgium – the Belgian Socialist Party (1960s) |
| 15 | Taiwan – Democratic Progressive Party (1995–6) |
| 14 | UK – Conservative Party (since the 1980s) |
| 13 | Ireland – Fianna Fáil (1950s–2007) |
| 12 | Germany – all parties in most cases in the single member districts (since 1950s) |
| 11 | Costa Rica – National Liberation and United Social Christian Party (2000) |
| 10 | New Zealand – Labour Party (since the 1950s) |
| 9 | Norway – all parties in most districts (1920–2002) |
| 8 | Italy – Italian Communist Party (1956–86) |
| 7 | Japan – Liberal Democratic Party (1950s–1990s) |
| 6 | India – Congress Party (1950s–1960s) |
| 5 | - |
| 4 | - |
| 3 | Israel – Shas (1984–2006) |
| 2 | Italy – Forza Italia (1990s–2000s) |
| 1 | Israel – Degel HaTora (1988–96) |
| 0 | Israel – Kadima (2006) |

FIGURE 3.3. The party selectorates continuum

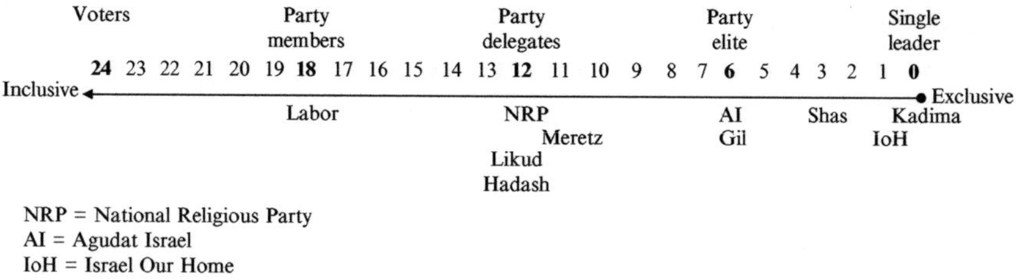

| Voters | | Party members | | Party delegates | | Party elite | | Single leader |
|---|---|---|---|---|---|---|---|---|

```
              24  23 22 21 20  19 18 17 16 15 14  13 12 11 10  9   8  7  6  5  4  3  2   1  0
Inclusive  ◄──────────────────────────────────────────────────────────────────────────────►  Exclusive
                               Labor              NRP                AI         Shas   Kadima
                                                  Meretz             Gil               IoH
                                                  Likud
                                                  Hadash
```

NRP = National Religious Party
AI = Agudat Israel
IoH = Israel Our Home

FIGURE 3.4. Party selectorates in Israel 2006 – high variance within the same party system

affords both synchronic and diachronic comparisons. First, we can get a clearer perspective on the difference in candidate selection methods across parties in one country at a specific time, as shown in Figure 3.4, which exhibits the variance in the inclusiveness of party selectorates prior to the 2006 general election in Israel.

Second, such a continuum also allows an examination over time of shifts – both large and small – as exemplified in Figure 3.5. Israel's Labor Party and its predecessor, Mapai, show a linear pattern of democratization, one that starts with small steps taking place over three decades (moving from 7 to 10), and ends with a great leap (from 10 to 18) in 1992. Likud and its precursor, Herut, also democratized, but at a different pace of greater leaps up to 1996, then returned to a less inclusive selectorate from 1999 to 2006, and finally redemocratized in 2008.

Using a scale with lower resolution, for example a thirteen-point scale, would place two examples next to each other, leading one to conclude that the differences are minor, when their differences are actually critical. For example, a multistage method in which the party delegates select a short list while the party members make the final selection (located at 8 on a thirteen-point scale, such as the Meretz Party in Israel in 1996), as opposed to a multistage method in which the order is reversed – the party members select the shortlist while the party delegates make the final selection (located at 7 on the thirteen-point scale, such as the Tsomet Party in Israel in 1996), are too distinct to be placed right next to each other. Clearly, *ceteris paribus*, the selectorate with the final say is the more important one (if the list of candidates is long enough, e.g., it exceeds the number of realistic positions) because it can move candidates into, or away from, the realistic positions. The Meretz Party's selected agency (a central committee) produced a shortlist of thirty candidates, at a time when the party had only twelve representatives in the parliament – the list thus contained more than twice the number of realistic positions. The party members then ranked the candidates, which gave them the more important role. Tsomet, on the other hand, allowed its members to pick twenty-three candidates out of thirty-eight – the remainder was comprised of the four sitting representatives and nine picked by a small committee. Ostensibly, the membership played an important role, picking almost two-thirds of the candidates.

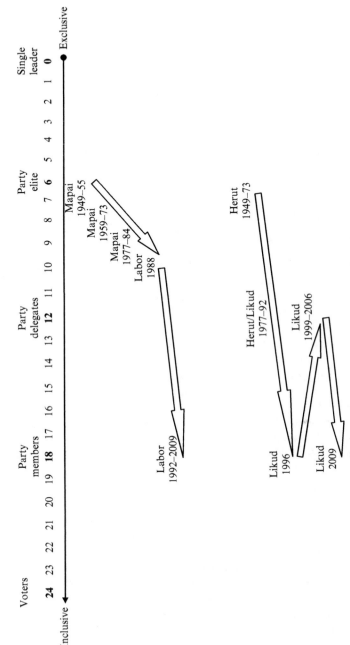

FIGURE 3.5. Party selectorates in Israel's major parties, Mapai/Labor and Herut/Likud, 1949–2009 (years under party names refer to the election years in Israel)

However, when the selected party agency ranked the candidates, the four sitting representatives came first, followed by two nominated by the small committee, and only then did it rank the first candidate chosen by the members. However, since the party had only five seats in the outgoing parliament, this was not only a completely unrealistic position, but all the realistic positions were given to the incumbent representatives. Placing these two at 8 and 7 on a thirteen-point scale would locate them too close to each other, while the gap between them on a twenty-five-point scale (16 and 13, respectively) is both more conceptually appropriate and empirically necessary.

The twenty-five-point scale is also sensitive enough to identify small yet significant changes. For example, in 1949–55, Israel's Mapai used a highly exclusive nomination committee composed of a few party leaders to decide both the composition and the ranking of its candidate list, thus supposedly placing it at 6 on the scale. The only reason that its final location is slightly different, position 7, is the fact that the composition of the nomination committee, and also its decisions, were usually ratified by wider party agencies. Subsequently, prior to the 1959 elections, Mapai decided to select its candidates through a two-stage process that involved additional selectorates. In the first stage, twenty-five candidates were named by a nominating committee and twenty-five by the party's eleven regional councils. In the second stage, the nominating committee ranked these candidates in positions 1–50 on the candidate list. While the nominating committee remained the dominant selectorate, the regional councils effectively influenced the composition of the list, because Mapai always had more than twenty-five realistic positions (Barnea and Rahat 2007). This is reflected by placing it in position 8, which clearly signifies the dominance of the party elite yet alludes to the secondary but significant role of the regional selected party agencies.

A continuum with a higher resolution would be too demanding, and one with lower can always be produced by simply collapsing the points into fewer categories. We, therefore, believe that the twenty-five-point scale is optimal, but not necessarily ideal. There are still problematic cases that require making rough estimations because the simple rules given above do not apply, for example in cases where three or more selectorates are effectively involved in the selection process, or even those cases in which two selectorates are involved yet they are not close to each other in terms of inclusiveness (or party elites and party members). We may end up with an estimation of inclusiveness at 12 on the selectorate continuum, not because party delegates chose the candidates but rather because the weight of both the party members and the party elite in the selection was equal. Nevertheless, this price is unavoidable if we need to operationalize inclusiveness in order to conduct a large $N$ analysis, and want to avoid creating multidimensional models that produce almost as many categories as empirical cases.

## DEMOCRATIZING THE SELECTORATE

As we conclude our discussion of the selectorate, there are two issues that need to be addressed. The first looks back at candidacy, which was discussed in the previous chapter, while the second looks forward at two dimensions that we discuss in the next chapters – decentralization and voting.

Table 3.1 integrates the two dimensions of candidacy and the selectorate, presenting each party's candidate selection method according to its level of inclusiveness or exclusiveness. In the American case, when candidacy and the selectorate are inclusive, the party hardly has a say when it comes to candidacies under its label. Scarrow (2005: 9) describes one of the more well-known cases:

> A notorious instance of what happens in a party without such a safeguard occurred in the U.S. state of Louisiana in 1991, when voters in a Republican primary nominated David Duke as the party's gubernatorial candidate. Party leaders could personally repudiate the candidate, an outspoken white supremacist and former Ku Klux Klan member, but they had no way of denying him the use of the party label.

We find no example for the opposite case, where both candidacy and the selectorate are exclusive, and while this is no evidence that there is indeed no such case, its rarity is quite logical: Why would a party elite limit its pool of candidates if it is in full control by being the exclusive selectorate?

A high level of inclusiveness on one dimension combined with a high level of exclusiveness in the other would mean that the party leadership, or the party apparatus, retains control over the process. For example, the Italian Communist Party included nonmembers as candidates, but this was done under the supervision of an exclusive selectorate (Wertman 1988). In a similar way, the Israeli ultrareligious parties have no formal rules regarding candidacy, yet the highly exclusive selectorates ensure that all selected candidates will be ultra-religious men. This seems to be a pattern also in the leader-dominated extreme right and populist right European parties, where anyone can be a candidate – their selection is based on the leader's predisposition toward them. An opposite case, with the same logic

TABLE 3.1. *Inclusiveness in candidacy and in the selectorate*

|  |  | Inclusiveness in the selectorate | |
| --- | --- | --- | --- |
|  |  | Low | High |
| Inclusiveness in candidacy | Low | — | Belgian Socialist Party (1960s) |
|  | High | Italian Communist Party (1976) | US Republican and Democratic parties (since the 1920s) |

of retaining control over those selected, is the Belgian Socialist Party in the 1960s, which frequently used the most inclusive selectorate among the Belgian parties to select its candidates but ensured their cohesion through very exclusive candidacy (Obler 1970). These days, however, the significance of candidacy requirements is low as politics becomes less partisan and ideological, and more personalized and electoral. When candidacy is highly inclusive, *de jure* and especially *de facto*, the significance of the level of inclusiveness of the selectorate increases.

Democratization of the candidate selection process is expressed as a widening of participation in the process; that is, when the selectorate following a reform of the candidate selection method is more inclusive than previously. Adopting only more inclusive candidacy requirements (the first dimension in the analytical framework), implementing decentralization (the third dimension), or shifting from appointments to a voting system (the fourth dimension) may be labeled democratization, but they are not. They are facilitating variables only and neither define nor exhibit democratization. More inclusive candidacy requirements may be adopted, yet the same limited selectorate could still have control over the final results, thereby curtailing the impact of democratization. Decentralization could mean only that control of candidate selection has passed from the national to a local oligarchy. Indeed, if the selectorate is decentralized from a national party congress of several thousand participants to a handful of local executive committees each consisting of a dozen party notables, the overall selectorate may have actually become more exclusive. Voting procedures may replace appointments, but the vote itself could be restricted to a very exclusive body. In other words, it is the inclusiveness of the selectorate that is the necessary variable for democratizing candidate selection methods. Sartori (1973: 19–20) appropriately equated democratization with the "massification" of politics, because the hitherto excluded masses are now allowed to enter. The consequences of such intraparty democratization can be curtailed if the party can still exert power through exclusive candidacy requirements. On the other hand, if both the selectorate and candidacy become more inclusive, then the party will experience more of the political ramifications associated with democracy within parties.

The nature of the selectorate, along the inclusiveness–exclusiveness continuum, is important because it allows us not only to classify candidate selection methods, to assess the political consequences of each selectorate, and to analyze differences along the continuum and their ramifications, but also to uncover trends over time in one country and across countries. Such trends are fairly evident, and their consequences are the focus of the second part of this book. However, before moving to the political consequences of democracy within parties, there are two more dimensions which need to be discussed – decentralization and voting versus appointments.

# 4

# Decentralization

Several of the most prominent scholars who pioneered the research on candidate selection chose to devote substantial consideration to the degree of centralization of the candidate selection method. Ranney (1981) proposed centralization as the first of three dimensions for measuring the variation among candidate selection methods; only afterward does he mention inclusiveness and finally direct or indirect participation. Gallagher (1988a) chose three main aspects in order to describe candidate selection: the first was centralization, followed by participation (i.e. what we label inclusiveness), and then the qualities required of aspirants. Marsh (2000) picked centralization as the first dimension of two, the second being participation, as do Narud, Pedersen, and Valen (2002a, 2002b, 2002c). Centralization, these scholars argue, is the extent to which the national level influences candidate selection, as opposed to the weight of the regional and/or the local levels. This is, we will argue, only one aspect of centralization – centralization need not be only territorial, it can also refer to nonterritorial aspects such as gender and minorities.

Marsh (2000) was correct when he stated that his two chosen dimensions – centralization and participation – are not entirely independent of each other. Indeed, more centralized selection methods are usually more exclusive, and vice versa. The national party's involvement is typically that of relatively small executive agencies, while regional and local involvement is typically that of selected delegates or even party members. However, as Gallagher (1988a: 4–5) stated, "Even knowing that selection is made by constituency agencies, of course, still leaves open the question of how widely party members and voters are involved." We argue that most scholars do not make this distinction as clear as it needs to be, even those who recognize that inclusiveness of the selectorate and centralization can vary widely. Generally the more decentralized candidate selection is, the greater the possibility for individual party members to play a role – but this is an inclination and not a rule. Decentralization, therefore, deserves to be addressed on its own.

Candidate selection methods may be seen as decentralized in two senses, territorial and social, parallel to the concepts Lijphart (1999) proposed when he dealt with the division of power in federal and unitary democratic regimes. It is territorial when local or regional party selectorates nominate party candidates, as opposed to national party selectorates. However, regardless of the extent of decentralization, each territorial category can vary in its level of inclusiveness. For example, a decentralized selection method would be one in which the local level has the power to decide, but this power can be held by a local leader, a party branch committee, all party members, or even all the voters in an electoral district.

Decentralization based on territorial mechanisms, in order to ensure regional and/or local representation, is rather straightforward. In many European cases, the selectorate at the district level plays the crucial role in candidate selection. The Norwegian case, where the national party agencies cannot veto candidates who are determined at the district level,[1] and territorial representation is taken into account inside each district, is an example of territorial decentralization (Valen 1988; Valen, Narud, and Skare 2002).

Decentralization of the selection method can also be social or corporate; for example, it ensures representation for representatives of groups that are not defined territorially, such as trade unions, women, minorities, or even subgroups within these groups. Nonterritorial decentralization can be found in many parties that are closely connected to interest groups. In many socialist parties there is significant representation for union representatives while in right-wing parties there is, many times, representation for business and farmers' associations. Probably one of the most prominent examples is the role of the trade unions in the British Labour Party. In the 1950s–1960s, the trade unions controlled approximately one-fifth of the candidacies and one-third of its legislators (Ranney 1965; Rush 1969). In Belgium, legislators not only kept close ties with interest groups, but maintained their interest group positions after being elected because it was via these organized interests that they were selected. De Winter (1997) states that interest groups in Belgium had an important role in the selection or removal of candidates, and at times even a monopoly over candidate selection. These decentralizations are not likely to be found in the parties' regulations or their constitutions, but are rather phenomena that express the power of these groups within the parties.

When candidates are selected exclusively by a national party selectorate, with no procedure that allows for territorial and/or social representation – be it a nonselected leader, a national party agency, the entire party membership, or even the national electorate that selects all candidates from the whole nation – then we have a method that is located at the centralized pole (Figure 4.1). At the decentralized poles, candidates are selected exclusively by local party selectorates and/or intraparty social groups.

Once again, we have to determine and weigh the impact of different selectorates at different levels in the case of a mixed selection method. A case in point is that of

---

[1] The Norwegian Nomination Act of 1920, which was revoked in 2002, stated that candidates were to be selected at the level of the constituency, and that the center did not have the power to alter this decision (Narud 2003).

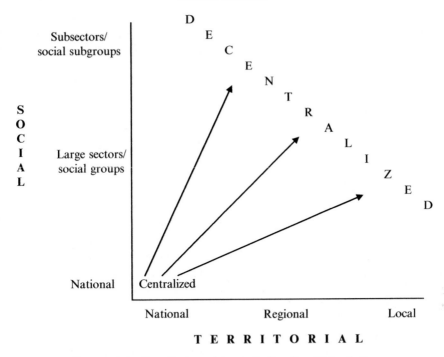

Subsectors/
social subgroups

S
O
C
I
A
L

Large sectors/
social groups

National | Centralized

National     Regional     Local

**T E R R I T O R I A L**

D E C E N T R A L I Z E D

FIGURE 4.1. Centralization and decentralization of candidate selection

the Italian parties in the 1980s, in which central, provincial, and local selectorates took part in a multistage candidate selection process. According to Wertman (1988), the provincial level party agencies played the main role in candidate selection vis-à-vis the center and the district level selectorates. Thus, the Italian parties of the 1980s are in the middle area of the territorial continuum. Still, there were differences between the parties, which placed the Italian Communists, for example, closer to the centralized pole than their Socialist counterparts. Similar calculations might have to be made for weighted and assorted candidate selection methods.

Territorial centralization is not a direct consequence of the national electoral system, although the latter does influence the former. Federal systems do have an inclination toward decentralized candidate selection methods, but there are many exceptions – candidate selection in Austria, a federation, is more centralized than that of a unitary state like the United Kingdom. Both India and the United Kingdom use single-member district plurality electoral systems, but candidate selection in India – at least in the 1950s and 1960s – was highly centralized, and in the UK it was decentralized. While both Israel and the Netherlands use a single, national constituency in their general elections, local branches and regional agencies played a significant role in the selection process in many of the Dutch parties, but much less so in Israel where the process is very centralized.[2] Moreover, the fact that various parties in one country, at a specific point in time, use different candidate selection methods underlines this distinction, which is buttressed by the more frequent changes to candidate selection methods by parties while the electoral system remains intact. Other, party-specific factors – such as party age, size, and ideology – may be associated with the extent of centralization, but they are far from supplying general, universally applicable rules. For example, ideology may have an impact, yet both centralized and decentralized candidate selection methods can be found in parties of the left as well as those of the right.

If we have to generalize, then it would be correct to say that in most parties the selectorate at the electoral district level plays a significant, and even a dominant role in candidate selection, while other nonnational levels (local or regional) play secondary role and the central party leadership usually supervises the process to some degree (Ranney 1981: 82–3). It is difficult to point to any recent trends regarding the balance of power between the center and the lower regional and local levels. Marsh (2000) argues that in recent years political developments that have strengthened the party leadership have also led many parties to try to increase the degree of centralization. This could be tied to developments such as the "presidentialization" of politics (Poguntke and Webb 2005), the increase of public financing and "cartelization" of parties (Katz and Mair 1995), and the professionalization of ever more capital-intense election campaigns. Krouwel's (1999) study of parties from 1945 to 1990 concluded that the dominant trend in the selection of parliamentary candidates in Western Europe was one of increased centralization. However, a study of candidate selection procedures across Western Europe from 1960 to the 1990s by Bille (2001) reached the opposite conclusion: There is no movement in the direction of more centralization, and if there is any evident trend it is toward increased decentralization.

The centralization of candidate selection also has its own contentious political consequences. One school argues that if the candidates have to appeal to the central party leadership in order to be selected, then the party's representatives in parliament are more likely to toe the party line. Alternatively, candidates whose selection is decided within the constituency will respond to the demands of their local base and might be willing to rebel against the national party leadership more often. Another school argues that it is possible to give the local level significant or even exclusive control of candidate selection while maintaining high cohesion and discipline, either because the local agencies see these qualities as important, such as in the United Kingdom (Ranney 1968), or because there is a division of labor between the local

---

[2] The large parties in Israel employed a mechanism for territorial representation, but a clear advantage was given to the center. For example, between 1959 and 1988, Mapai, and its successor Labor, allowed regional and local party agencies to select about one-half of its candidates for approximately the first fifty positions on the list, yet the national party organs decided their final positions on the list.

and national levels – the former selects while the latter governs – such as in Canada (Carty 2004). This issue will be elaborated and developed in Chapter 9.

## DEMOCRATIZING VERSUS DECENTRALIZING

While an inclusive selectorate and a constituency-based selection method seem to go hand in hand, they must be theoretically and analytically distinguished from each other, as shown in Figure 4.2, and may be divorced in practice. In Denmark, for example, the selectorate became more inclusive, marked by the adoption of members' postal ballots in four parties, but the level of decentralization remained unchanged (Bille 1992). In the United Kingdom, the selectorate became more inclusive over the years, with the adoption of a membership vote for selecting candidates who were screened by party agencies at the national and constituency level. At the same time, the role of the central party agency in screening candidates, and its general involvement in the process, increased (Norris and Lovenduski 1995). Many scholars have not made this distinction, while others who have done so still mix both dimensions.

Bille (2001: 365–6) correctly states, "The phenomenon of decentralization is related to democratization . . . although in addition to decentralization, *true* democratization requires reforms that make both the candidacy requirements and the selectorate more inclusive at the local level" [emphasis added]. In other words, decentralization does not necessarily entail the transfer of power from an exclusive national oligarchy to a more inclusive local leadership. If the centralized process was based on a membership ballot, and decentralization shifted power to 5, 50, or even 500 exclusive regional or local nomination committees, fewer people might end up being involved in the process rather than more. Gallagher's (1980: 500) study of the Irish case leads him to conclude, "The important decisions, then, are taken at local level, but this does not of itself mean that the candidate selection process is any more democratic in Ireland than elsewhere. Local parties can be controlled by elites in the same way as national parties." Thus, decentralization may be seen as a contingent step in the direction of democratization, but only if the decentralized selectorate is more inclusive than the earlier centralized selectorate.

Bille himself, after making the distinction between decentralization and democratization, then mixes up the two dimensions when he attempts to measure democratization based on six categories, the first five of which focus on national versus subnational control of candidate selection rather than on a more inclusive selectorate – his sixth category.[3] A similar mix can be found in Kittilson and

---

[3] Bille's (2001: 367) first five categories include: complete national control over the selection of party candidates, subnational organs propose and national organs decide, national organs provide a list from which subnational organs decide, subnational organs decide but subject to the approval of the

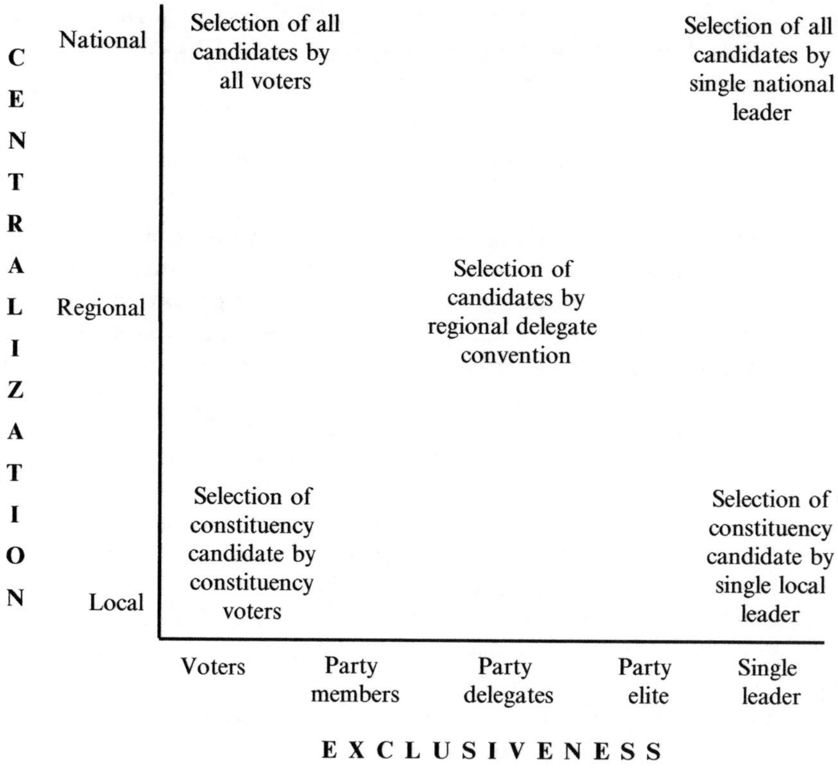

|  | | Voters | Party members | Party delegates | Party elite | Single leader |
|---|---|---|---|---|---|---|
| **C E N T R A L I Z A T I O N** | National | Selection of all candidates by all voters | | | | Selection of all candidates by single national leader |
| | Regional | | | Selection of candidates by regional delegate convention | | |
| | Local | Selection of constituency candidate by constituency voters | | | | Selection of constituency candidate by single local leader |

**E X C L U S I V E N E S S**

FIGURE 4.2. Exclusiveness and centralization as separate dimensions

Scarrow (2003), whose first three categories of inclusiveness (out of five) also focus on national versus local selectorates.[4] Gallagher (1988c: 236) also presents aspects of inclusiveness alongside those of centralization – under a category that clearly lumps them together ("The selection process: centralization and participation").[5] Janda (1980) devotes a chapter in his book on political parties to the centralization of power, defining it as the number of participants in the decision and their location in the organizational hierarchy, which brings together two

---

national organs, subnational organs control the selection of candidates. Only his last category alludes to what he earlier called "real" democratization – the introduction of a membership ballot.

[4] Kittilson and Scarrow's (2003: 70) categories are: national leadership, regional delegates, local party selectorate, members can vote, nonmembers can vote.

[5] Gallagher's (1988c: 237) categories are: party voters, party primaries, subset of constituency party members, national executive, interest groups, national faction leaders, party leader.

dimensions that need to be separated.[6] Hence, as Janda (1980: 111) wrote, " . . . the more restricted the privilege to participate in candidate selection, the more highly centralized is the party." Norris (2004: 27) divides between the degree of centralization and the breadth of participation in her analysis, but then merges them when she concludes, "In the most decentralized processes, nomination decisions in each local area rest in the hands of all grassroots party members who cast votes in closed primaries, or even the mass public in open primaries." Krouwel's (1999) study assesses internal party democracy using a scale of centralization that combines these two dimensions.[7] An incomplete overlap between inclusiveness and decentralization is to be found in Lundell's (2004) study of the determinants of candidate selection. Lundell's scale of centralization combines these two dimensions, but does not allow inclusiveness to vary independently within many of the centralization categories. For example, the centralized end of the scale allows inclusiveness to fluctuate widely from selection by the party leader to primaries at the national level, whereas selection at the more decentralized district level covers only a selection committee, the executive district organ, or a delegate convention.[8] The overlap is almost complete with Ohman's (2004) scale of the centralization of candidate selection. For example, the only difference between the two most decentralized categories is that the extreme one allows all or most party members to vote while the next-most extreme is a delegate conference.[9] In other words, both

[6] Janda's (1980: 111) categories are: nominations are determined locally by vote of party supporters, for example in a direct primary; selection is made by local party leaders whose selection must be ratified by party members; selection is made by local leaders with little participation by members; selection is made locally, but the selections must be approved by the national organization; selection is made by associations affiliated with the party or regional associations, but the selection must be approved by the national organization; selection is done by the national organization, but the selection must be approved by local or affiliated organizations; selection is determined by a national party congress or caucus; selection is determined by a national committee or party council.

[7] Krouwel's (1999: 94) categories are: incumbent national leader, party central office or national executive, interest or other external groups, parliamentary delegates, national convention or congress, select group of local party members, party members.

[8] Lundell's (2004: 31) categories are: selection at local party meetings, by local selection committees or by primaries open for all party members; selection at the district level by a selection committee, by the executive district organ, or at a convention by delegates from the local parties; the same as the first two but regional or national organs exercise influence over the selection; the same as the previous categories but local, district, or regional organs exercise influence over the selection; selection by the party leader, by the national executive organ, by a national selection committee, or by primaries at the national level.

[9] Ohman's (2004: 48) categories are: selection at the local level by all or most party members through a direct vote, with no or only nominal confirmation by other party agencies; selection by a constituency-level delegate conference, with no or only nominal confirmation by other party agencies; the same as the previous category, but with confirmation from central party agencies; selection by regional bodies, or by a national conference, where delegates from all parts of the country decide on all candidates without confirmation by higher levels; selection by national party leadership subject to confirmation by lower levels; selection by the party leadership without confirmation by lower levels.

are constituency level decisions, with no or only nominal influence by other party agencies, and what varies is the extent of inclusiveness. Ohman (2004: 12) clearly combines the two dimensions when he states that, "The most decentralized method would allow all eligible voters in the country to take part in the selection of the candidates, even if they are not members of the party in question. The other extreme would be when a single individual chooses all candidates for the parliamentary elections."

Contrary to what the aforementioned scholars contend, inclusiveness, as it was defined in Chapter 3, focuses on the extent of participation in the process and should be distinct from centralization. This may be what Denver (1988) alluded to in describing the British political parties as being centralized but with decentralized selection; that is, the selection process was characterized by high territorial decentralization yet also by small selectorates. Ranney (1981), for example, proposed three dimensions for analyzing candidate selection – centralization, inclusiveness, and direct or indirect participation – and clearly distinguished between the first two. Centralization is described along a six-point scale made up of the following purely territorial elements: selection by national agencies with occasional suggestions by subnational agencies; selection by national agencies after serious consideration of suggestions by subnational agencies; regional selection with national supervision; regional selection with no national supervision; constituency selection with national supervision; constituency selection with regional supervision; constituency selection with no supervision (Ranney 1981: 82).

Ware's (1996) five dimensions of candidate selection also distinguish between the extent of centralization (his second variable) and the degree of participation (his third). He acknowledges that they are not independent of each other, but he does not mix between them. An interesting step toward differentiating the democratization of candidate selection from decentralization is given by Scarrow, Webb, and Farrell (2000). They raise two separate hypotheses concerning candidate selection: the first concerns its transfer over time to the party members; and the second is that the national party elite maintains or obtains the right to veto the decision made by local party members. In other words, what we see here is first democratization, and second centralization. The local party elites are weakened by democratization, while the party's national elite does not lose power because candidate selection is simultaneously being centralized. In their words, "... parties' decision-making processes will display movement toward ... greater centralization *and* greater inclusiveness" (Scarrow, Webb, and Farrell 2000: 137, emphasis in original). The two hypotheses are validated by the data, but not equally. The democratization of candidate selection received limited empirical support; that is, more countries have expanded their selectorates than have curtailed it. Clearer support is given to the centralization hypothesis, yet this does not display a trend but rather an existing situation. While there are cases where the party center has gained power – such as Australia, the two main parties in Ireland, the Liberal Party in Canada, and British Labour – the interesting element is that in most cases the existing power has not been cut. This shows that an expansion of the selectorate does not need to go hand in hand with decentralization, and that these two could also move in opposite directions at the same time.

Narud, Pedersen, and Valen (2002*a*: 13) clearly delineate between their two main dimensions of candidate selection – centralization and inclusiveness – and show that there does not have to be an apparent connection between them:

> In combination, these two dimensions include four distinct varieties of nomination systems. At one extreme is found an inclusive, yet central, process: Participation is open to many individuals, though the outcome of the process is decided at the central level – not in the local branches of the party. An alternative nomination system is one that is decentralized and open at the same time. But we may also envisage decentralized and closed systems, where the decisions are made in the local party branches by a small group of "gatekeepers." A fourth type would be one with centralized nominations restricted to a few party members.

## DEFINING AND MEASURING TERRITORIAL DECENTRALIZATION

Territorial decentralization, which focuses on the local–regional–national dimension, is quite a clear concept. If the party's local base has the full power to decide who its candidate will be, then we are at one end of the spectrum. If the national party is in full control of candidate selection, then we are at the opposite end. In the middle we find examples where candidates are decided at a level higher than the local, but lower than the national. Or, alternatively, if both the local and the national levels share power in the selection of candidates, then we are also near the middle, the exact balance of power determining how close to which end.

There is, however, another way to look at territorial decentralization, and that is from the perspective of the candidates. Candidates are selected either by a selectorate that is theirs and theirs alone (defined territorially or socially), in which case we are at the decentralized pole, or by the same selectorate as all of the other candidates, in which case we are at the centralized end. If some, but not all, of the candidates share the same selectorate, then we are in the middle of the dimension. This new and different, not to mention unconventional, perspective on the decentralization of candidate selection requires further explanation.

While some researchers address candidate selection at the national level, and most scholars – including the authors of this book – prefer to assess this topic at the level of each separate party at a specific point in time, when it comes to decentralization we can empirically design a framework for classification by looking at candidate selection from the perspective of the individual candidate. There are two questions raised by the individual candidate:

1. How distinct is/are the selectorate(s) involved in my selection?
2. If there are two or more selectorates involved in my selection, what is their relative weight in the process?

The answer to the first question shows us the degree of decentralization for each selectorate. The answer to the second question tells us where exactly to classify candidate selection along the subsections of the dimension.

Consider a country divided into single-member districts where candidate selection is decided by the party at the electoral district, without any influence exercised at any other level. This means that each individual candidate will be selected by a selectorate – of the particular party in a single constituency – that is different from all the other selectorates. That is, in each constituency the selectorate is different, for each party. The United States is an example where voters in the primaries of each constituency cannot participate in selecting candidates in any constituency other than their own. In other words, each of the 435 Congressional districts produces different selectorates for each party, and hence for each of the party candidates in the constituency. From the candidates' perspective, their particular selectorate is made up of people who can only select a candidate in his or her own constituency, and are not involved in the selection of candidates in any another constituency. Two adjacent constituencies will thus have no overlap in their selectorates; they will be mutually exclusive. This is a picture of complete decentralization: a distinct selectorate makes the decision over who will be the party's *one and only* candidate.

Now consider a country that has a single, national electoral district, and where candidate selection for the party lists is decided at the national level, without any interference from lower levels. In this case, each individual candidate will face exactly the same selectorate – of the national party – as each of the other candidates. Israel is an example of a country where the parties produce national lists for which all of the candidates must compete. In most cases the selectorate (and even the selectorates) for each and every candidate within a particular party is identical. From the candidates' perspective, they must face a selectorate that will choose all of the party's candidates. The exact same selectorate is involved in the decision concerning each and every one of the candidates. This is a situation of complete centralization: a single unified national selectorate makes the decision for *all* of the party candidates.

The interim case is a country with multimember districts, where each party produces a regional list of candidates. The candidates here must face a selectorate that is similar to that of all the other candidates in the district, but different from that of all the other districts. Iceland's six electoral districts each send nine representatives to the legislature.[10] Each candidate in a multimember district,

---

[10] Nine additional representatives, for a total of sixty-three, are elected in a second tier based on the results in the six districts.

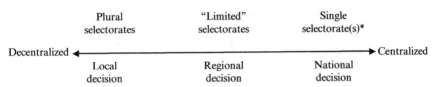

F IGURE 4.3. Decentralization and the number of selectorates per candidate
* Complex candidate selection methods can produce several national-level selectorates
that are involved in the selection of *all* the candidates.

will face a selectorate that chooses eight other candidates, and there will be six such separate selectorates. This is a case of neither complete decentralization nor absolute centralization, but somewhere in the middle. Between the two poles of singular versus plural selectorates, as shown in Figure 4.3, the middle can be labeled as limited in the number of selectorates. In the most decentralized case, the number of selectorates would be equal to the number of legislative seats (or two and even three times that number, if several selectorates at the same level are involved in the selection). The most centralized case will involve a single selectorate, or possibly a few selectorates as long as they are all at the national level.

What must be emphasized is that the question of how many selectorates exist in general – whether each candidate will be selected by his or her own distinct selectorate – divorces the issue of decentralization from that of inclusiveness. A singular selectorate can be either inclusive (national primaries) or exclusive (the national party leader). Exactly the same holds true for plural selectorates: they may involve the entire party membership within each constituency, or can be limited to the party oligarchy in the districts. This also follows for the interim case of a limited number of selectorates, and for all the possibilities along this dimension.

The second question focuses on the number of selectorates involved in the selection of a particular candidate, rather than in general. This question assesses the complex cases of candidate selection, specifically where a selectorate at one level can influence the choice made at another level. The answer to this question will influence the location of each party along the continuum in Figure 4.3.

For example, if the national party leadership is allowed to create a shortlist of potential candidates from which the local party at the constituency level can choose its candidate (such as in the United Kingdom), then selectorates at two levels are involved in the process.[11] This is, therefore, not a clear case of centralization or decentralization, but somewhere in-between. The exact placement of the party along the decentralization dimension depends on the relative strength of the central party vis-à-vis the constituency party. Alternatively, the availability of a

---

[11] It should be noted that in the UK several selectorates are involved in candidate selection at the local level. They are all local, yet they vary in their levels of inclusiveness, from small exclusive party agencies to larger more inclusive party agencies to party members.

veto for the national party, after a candidate is chosen by the constituency (such as in Canada), is a similar case of two selectorates influencing the decision. In-between cases can also exist, such as a combination of the interim case of a limited number of selectorates and selectorates from either of the two poles. If a regional selectorate has to take into account the demands of the separate territorial elements within the region (such as in Norway), or a regional selectorate at the multimember district level can be influenced by the national party (such as in Austria), then we are close to one of the two ends of the dimension, but we are not at the end.

This framework for classifying territorial decentralization has its drawbacks, particularly when it comes to parties that employ more than two stages of candidate selection or when we encounter either assorted or weighted candidate selection methods. However, regardless of these complexities, the attempt to classify decentralization by looking at the individual candidate and his or her selectorate(s) achieves several goals. First, it clearly delineates the extent of decentralization using empirical data that should be relatively accessible, resulting in a simple dimension that can provide researchers with an easy and valid way to categorize and operationalize decentralization. Second, it unmistakably separates between decentralization and democratization of candidate selection. There is no mixing or combining of the centralization and the selectorate dimensions, and one does not vary from the other interdependently. This should, we hope, result in a dimension that scholars will no longer confuse with inclusiveness. Third, it is a flexible dimension, allowing parties to shift based on a change in their method of candidate selection, or in the relative power of one selectorate versus another vis-à-vis the individual candidate.

## MECHANISMS OF DECENTRALIZATION

Two mechanisms can be used for ensuring territorial and social representation via decentralization. The first mechanism used to ensure territorial and social representation is the establishment of separate territorial, sectarian, or social group districts, where the candidates and the selectors live in the same region, or are identified as or are members of the same sector or social group. The second is the reserved place mechanism, which guarantees a minimum number of positions on the list (or a minimum number of realistic seats in the case of single-member districts) for candidates representing specific localities or regions, or belonging to a distinct sector or social group. Establishing quotas for women, a practice adopted by many parties, is one example. If decentralization based on territorial mechanisms is usually ensured by using districts, reserved places are often used for ensuring social decentralization.

We have already discussed the issue of territorial districts, so here we will address the sectarian or social group district, where the candidates and the selectors are members of the same sector or social group. Unlike the territorial district, it is not built on a parallel electoral district, and it is thus no wonder that it is quite a rarely used mechanism. This mechanism decentralizes *both candidacy and the selectorate*, because the candidates not only need to be different from other candidates, but they also compete only against similar candidates and are selected by a distinct selectorate. A social group district in the candidate selection process is similar to the kind of social group constituencies found in the general elections in New Zealand, where members of the Māori minority are asked to decide if they wish to vote in the general district where they reside or in specific Māori districts. Israel's two main parties adopted such mechanisms of social decentralization in the mid-1990s. Both Labor and Likud allowed all their dues-paying members to participate in the selection of candidates, and each member was asked to choose from two lists: one composed of candidates who ran nationally and one made up of constituency candidates. The latter were somewhat fictitious, since Israel has no districts and employs a single, nationwide electoral constituency. The parties, however, established internal districts, both territorial and social. Labor, for example, had four social districts: kibbutz members (collective settlements), moshav residents (cooperative settlements), minorities (i.e. Arabs), and Druze.[12] Party members had to belong to a social district, a specific social group, in order to run and in order to vote in the district. Specific positions were reserved on the party list for these social districts, alongside reserved places for women, immigrants, and the territorial districts (Hazan 1999*a*). In those cases where parties allocate candidacies to affiliated social groups, and let them decide who will be their representative, we see the de facto creation of a social district in which the selectorate and the candidate are defined as belonging to the same group. For example, the allocation of specific candidacies to union representatives in the Japanese Socialist Party can be seen as the de facto creation of a district in which the union is the selectorate (Shiratori 1988; Youn 1977).

Belgium also supplies us with examples of both of the representation mechanisms, which were used at the (territorial) district level. In the Belgian Christian Social Party in 1961, the reserved place mechanism was used when it was decided that in some Brussels districts, Flemish and Francophone candidates would alternate seats on the party list.[13] In 1965, separate intraparty subdistricts were actually established when Francophone and Flemish party members in these districts selected, separately, Francophone and Flemish candidates for parliament (Obler 1974).

---

[12] A religion that split from Islam and is found mainly in Israel, Lebanon, and Syria.

[13] In 1961 and 1965, reserved places were also allocated to German candidates in a constituency with a large German-speaking minority.

The reserved place mechanism – securing a minimal number of realistic positions on the party list, or a minimal number of realistic seats in the case of single-member districts, for candidates belonging to a distinct sector or social group – implies the decentralization of *candidacy alone*. That is, unlike the case of districts, the selectorate is not defined along territorial or social lines. In some cases, candidates who are eligible for reserved places compete for their place on the list against *all* of the other candidates. The reserved representation mechanism is implemented in these cases only if the candidates do not attain the reserved position or higher ones. In other cases, the candidates compete against candidates like themselves for the predetermined positions only. Establishing quotas for women, a practice adopted by many parties, is one example.[14] Here, women are allotted a certain percentage of seats on the party's list, or women are the party's candidates in a specific percentage of constituencies, yet they are selected by men and women alike.[15]

In order to make this kind of social decentralization more actual than virtual, women have to be given positions high enough on the party list so that a substantial number can be elected. In other words, the parties should seek a specific number of women representatives, not a symbolic percentage in nonrealistic positions low on the party list. One way of doing this in a list system is "zipping," creating a zipper on the party list where every position is alternatively a man or a woman, such as in the German Green Party since 1990 (Davidson-Schmich 2006), the South African National Congress Party (Ashiagbor 2008), and the Dutch Labor Party in 2002 (Andeweg and Irwin 2002), or in which one member of each gender must appear in every set of three candidates, as is the case of the party lists of the Mexican National Action Party (Ashiagbor 2008).

The challenge in countries with single-member districts is different. It is not about locating women in realistic positions on the list but rather about ensuring that women are the party's candidates in realistic seats – safe, marginal, and targeted seats – rather than in those that the party expects to lose. This is quite difficult to achieve, as it means the active involvement of the center in coordinating the use of these mechanisms in the face of likely resistance at the district level. Such involvement is easier when the party is in opposition for a long time and when the adoption of such mechanisms is accepted as part of the recovery strategy. Indeed, prior to the British election of 1997, the Labour Party (after spending eighteen years in opposition) implemented all-women short lists, from which women candidates were selected in about one-half of the vacant Labour districts

---

[14] There are several online databases that show the proliferation of quotas for women, allowing scholars to distinguish between those set at the state level and those established by the political parties. See, for example, Global Database of Quotas for Women (2009).

[15] In many cases the quota is gender neutral, in the sense that it determines a minimum or maximum share of the candidacies for each gender without explicitly relating to women, although the aim is to ensure their representation.

and in marginal ones where the gap in the previous elections was under 6 percent (Criddle 1997).[16] It is also easier to adopt such mechanisms when incumbents are not involved. In the first Scottish and Welsh legislative elections in 1999, the Labour Party used a mechanism called "twinning" in which every two constituencies had to present a male candidate in one and a female candidate in the other (Bradbury et al. 2000; Edwards and McAllister 2002; Squires 2005).

The goal of enhancing representation through the use of mechanisms of social decentralization may be achieved through adherence to quotas established via legislation, thereby circumventing the parties. This is the case in about fifty countries (Htun 2004). In other cases, parties voluntarily establish quotas (Kittilson 2006). The more effective are the quotas with clear rules concerning ranking or district placements, and sanctions for noncompliance (Dahlerup 2006; Krook 2009; Mateo-Diaz 2005; Tremblay 2008).

Beyond the most outstanding and well-researched mechanism of social decentralization – women's quotas – these mechanisms can be, and have been, applied to regional, ideological, age, and occupational groups, among others. For example, in one German Land, the Social Democrats allocated 10 percent of its list positions to those under thirty-five years old (Scarrow 1999*b*). British Labour comes somewhat close to this in ensuring the representation of minorities. If one or more minority candidates (black, Asian, or other minority) are nominated by the branches or another local party group, then the resulting shortlist must include one minority candidate (Ashiagbor 2008).

There is a connection between territorial and social decentralizations, in that the former has an impact on the latter. If candidate selection is decentralized along territorial lines, it becomes more difficult for the party leadership to implement the mechanisms of social decentralization. Matland and Studlar (1996) argued that more centralized candidate selection methods allow the party leadership to respond to pressures for increasing the diversity of representation, such as in the adoption of gender quotas. Moreover, centralized methods enable the party to intervene in order to ensure that quotas are applied. In contrast, more decentralized candidate selection lowers the influence exercised by the central party organs. Therefore, a party might need to centralize in order to increase the influence of the party center in candidate selection, and thus to decentralize socially. In other words, without central control, candidate selection could prove to be a barrier for social groups that is as difficult to overcome as the obstacles raised by majoritarian electoral systems.

The main obstacle to increasing the representation of women in the selection of candidates in single-member districts is the incumbents – most of them men whose political future is threatened when quotas are used. That is, they have to give up

---

[16] The British Conservative Party, after ten years in opposition, adopted mechanisms for enhancing women's representation, after it had strongly objected to these for decades (Ashiagbor 2008).

their seat (rather than moving to a lower position in a candidate list, which can still leave some hope for reelection). Indeed, in the United Kingdom, the greatest breakthroughs in women's representation were achieved when there were no incumbents – when the new parliament of Scotland and the new Welsh Assembly were elected (Bradbury et al. 2000; Mitchell and Bradbury 2004; Squires 2005). Another opportunity is when the party is in opposition and the number of incumbents shrinks.

## CONNECTING BETWEEN DECENTRALIZATION AND ELECTORAL SYSTEMS

It is intuitive to say that candidate selection is influenced by the electoral system. Aspects of the electoral system, such as the electoral formula, the district magnitude, and the availability of preferential voting have significant consequences on the political parties' choice of candidate selection methods. At the most basic level, if a country has a single nationwide district, the parties need to choose only a list of candidates. If, on the other hand, the country is divided into single-member districts, the parties must choose individual candidates to stand in each district. Mixed-member electoral systems force the parties to produce individual district candidates alongside a party list. Here the parties must employ different criteria in each selection process, yet the two processes are not isolated, especially if some of the same candidates are allowed to run in both the districts and the list. The more intricate the electoral system, the more constraints are placed on the parties' candidate selection methods.[17] In short, the connection between the electoral system and the candidate selection process is not only intuitive but also rather apparent.

Moreover, the impact of a change in the electoral system on candidate selection might be substantial, forcing the parties to adapt their internal nomination procedures. For example, in the 1990s, both New Zealand and Japan reformed their electoral systems and adopted mixed-member systems, and the parties, for the first time, had to walk through unfamiliar territory in selecting candidates for a list that in the case of New Zealand reached fifty-five places. Adjusting to these changes is not only a major organizational undertaking for the political parties, it also undoubtedly involves political consequences – district nominations in both

---

[17] For example, the unique Chilean electoral system, based on two-member proportional districts, coerces the party alliances to make complex strategic calculations of their candidacies in the general elections. This makes the involvement of exclusive national party elites a necessity, and limits the significance of the selection of either more inclusive or decentralized party selectorates (Siavelis 2002, 2005).

countries were more prized than list places, especially by incumbents, which led to fierce battles within some of the parties (Hazan and Voerman 2006). Also in the 1990s, when Italy shifted from proportional representation to a mixed system, the parties there had to produce individual constituency candidates for the first time – a no less daunting or politically significant challenge. In 1917, when the Nether- lands adopted proportional representation, the parties' candidate selection proce- dures faced similar upheavals that included intraparty political ramifications.

Decentralization of candidate selection, largely in its territorial sense, can and should be assessed in relation to the electoral system of a particular country.[18] For example, if we are dealing with a case of single-member district elections, it is both interesting and important to assess whether the candidate selection methods of the particular parties are less decentralized or the same as the electoral system. In countries with somewhat centralized electoral systems, such as multimember regional districts, we should gauge decentralization in the parties' candidate selection methods in regard to whether they are more decentralized, more cen- tralized, or similar to the national electoral system.

It is quite likely that decentralized electoral systems, such as single-member districts, will influence the parties to adopt more decentralized candidate selection methods. However, as with other aspects of decentralization, this is not always the case. The British electoral system is more decentralized than that of Norway, but the candidate selection method is more influenced by the central party organs – such as in the production of approved candidates lists – in Britain than it is in Norway. What does seem to be clear is that the more inclusive a candidate selection method is in terms of the selectorate, and the more territorially decen- tralized it is, the more there is a need for representation correction mechanisms to ensure social representation.

As long as we are able to distinguish clearly between the extent of candidacy requirements, the level of inclusiveness of the selectorate, and the degree of decentralization – both territorial and social – we are closer to having a more comprehensive and precise picture of candidate selection methods. What remains is to assess the appointment or voting method (or a mix of the two) used in the process of candidate selection, in order to complete our framework for assessing candidate selection methods. Only after this last dimension is explained can we pursue our inquiry into the political consequences of different candidate selection methods.

---

[18] Lundell (2004) found no evidence of a relationship between the electoral system and the degree of decentralization of candidate selection methods. However, his findings are questionable because he mixes centralization and exclusiveness.

# 5

# Appointment and Voting Systems

If candidate selection is considered to be the "secret garden of politics" (Gallagher and Marsh 1988), then this last dimension – appointment and voting systems – is the hidden flowerbed within the secret garden. Studies of candidate selection ignore this dimension altogether.[1] While the study of electoral systems – which focuses on the consequences of various electoral formulas – is highly developed (see, e.g., Rae 1967; Lijphart and Grofman 1984; Grofman and Lijphart 1986; Taagepera and Shugart 1989), intraparty voting systems are largely ignored or, at best, treated as merely a "logistical consideration" (Ashiagbor 2008). An interesting universe of voting systems – which includes methods that are not and cannot be used at the national level[2] – is ignored, largely due to problems of accessibility to data.

When selecting their candidates, parties use an appointment system, a voting system, or a mix of the two. In a voting system, votes alone determine the candidates' positions on a list in the case of multiple candidacies, or which specific contender will be the party's candidate in the case of a single candidacy. A voting system requires at least two people, but preferably more, to determine candidacies. However, a selection method is not considered a voting system – but rather an appointment – unless two conditions are filled:

1. The candidate's votes must be the sole determinant of their candidacy.
2. The voting results must be used to justify and legitimize the candidacy.

When one or more of these conditions are not fulfilled, then we are dealing with an appointment system, or with a mixed appointment voting system (Rahat 2009). For example, the case in which an agreed-upon list is ratified *en bloc* by unanimous or majority vote cannot be considered a "voting system"; instead it is a mixed appointment-voting system, with much more weight given to the appointing selectorate than to the one that merely ratifies.

---

[1] The exceptions are researchers who have compared plurality and runoff primaries (Engstrom and Engstrom 2008; Glaser 2006).

[2] For example, the elimination vote, which requires several voting rounds until one candidate gets a majority of the votes, cannot be used in general elections because it is too demanding in the technical sense: it requires the voters to repeat voting until there is a winner, which can take long hours of voting.

## APPOINTMENT SYSTEMS

When the selectorate is a single party leader then, by definition, we have an appointment system. When the selectorate is more than one person, then we can have either an appointment system or a voting system. However, an appointment system is unmanageable when the selectorate includes more than a certain number of people. The most inclusive selectorate that could use an appointment system is a small selected party agency, or a nominating committee that is composed of no more than a few dozen delegates.

Appointment is usually a procedure that is characterized by deliberation among a limited number of people, and wherein decisions are reached through wide consent. When the selectors represent particular groups within the party – for example, factions or social groups – they will try to obtain the best candidacies for their groups through negotiations and bargaining with the representatives of the other groups. While these procedures are exclusive in terms of participation, they enable both serious deliberations concerning the candidates' qualities and a high level of coordination that creates an opportunity to balance candidacy in factional and social terms. In other words, representation correction mechanisms are not as crucial for ensuring representation as they are when only the aggregation of votes determines candidacies.

Pure appointment systems are less widespread these days than in the past, and this is related to the tendency to expand the inclusiveness of selectorates. Today, pure appointment systems are found especially in those parties where there is a significant source of traditional or charismatic authority. These include religious parties, such as the ultra-orthodox Israeli parties, alongside right-wing parties with charismatic leaders, such as Berlusconi's Forza Italia, and also several of the extreme right-wing parties in Scandinavia. Other possible scenarios that could lead to the adoption of a pure appointment system are: new parties, especially when they lack a clear base within society; a split from an existing party that does not have enough time to create a solid institutional base; or parties that have merged and need to ensure that all of their components will have their fair share of representation in the newly amalgamated party.

## VOTING SYSTEMS

In almost all cases, intraparty voting systems are about selecting individuals rather than teams of candidates. A notable exception is the primaries conducted in Argentina's two large parties, where competition is between lists of candidates rather than between individual candidates (De Luca, Jones, and Tula 2002).[3]

---

[3] In Uruguay, parties conduct their internal selection during the general elections, according to a system which ensures that intraparty competition does not lead to a loss of votes; voters vote for alternative candidate lists within the same party (Moraes 2008).

Where ranking is relevant – in closed and semi-closed list systems, as well as in open list systems where the candidates appear in an order arranged by the party – then voting also determines the ranking of the candidates. We wish to look at the main differences among voting systems – including the number of voting rounds, the voting formulas used, and the ballot structure – followed by a discussion of the significance of the differences in the voting, and the counting, of the selectors' votes.

### Single-round versus multi-round systems

In a single-round voting system, all candidates for realistic positions are selected at one time. In a multi-round system, on the other hand, realistic positions on a list, or realistic candidacies in the case of single-member districts, are gradually selected. For example, a party that expects to win five seats in a specific multimember district might select all of them at once, using a single-round system, or it might select the candidates one by one, round by round, from the first position down to the fifth. The multi-round system allows the selectorate some control over the composition of candidacies. If a certain person who surprisingly failed to get selected is considered to be important for the party, or if it seems that there is a problem of representation – for example, there are not enough women/minorities/ laborers – the multi-round system provides an opportunity to fix this. Of course, this could be seen as a vice rather than a virtue, since it can be argued that it infringes on the principle that competition among all candidates should be conducted under equal conditions of uncertainty. It should also be noted that multi-round systems are much more demanding, and we can therefore expect them to be used by more exclusive and more dedicated selectorates, such as party delegates.

In Norway, a regional delegate convention uses a multi-round voting system when it votes, position by position, on the list that a nomination committee predesigned (Matthews and Valen 1999). This is also the way that the German parties select their candidate lists in the delegate conventions at the Land level (Porter 1995; Roberts 1988; Wessels 1997). In the United Kingdom, there is a de facto multi-round selection, as each constituency selects its candidate at a different time, some more than a year or two before elections and others only a few months or weeks before. This allows candidates who lose in their initial bid to try their luck in other constituencies, like candidates in a multi-round system where a list is selected gradually from top to bottom. It also gives the national party an opportunity to try to balance candidacies.

### Voting systems: From majoritarianism to proportional representation

We now enter into the truly hidden universe of voting systems. This universe includes systems that have received serious systematic treatment in the research

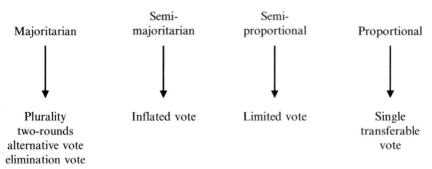

| Majoritarian | Semi-majoritarian | Semi-proportional | Proportional |
|---|---|---|---|
| ↓ | ↓ | ↓ | ↓ |
| Plurality two-rounds alternative vote elimination vote | Inflated vote | Limited vote | Single transferable vote |

FIGURE 5.1. The four main types of intraparty voting systems

literature only from those who focus on their theoretical properties (Brams and Fishburn 2002), rather than those who employ empirical treatment. Figure 5.1 presents the various categories of voting system that are in use by political parties around the world. They are divided into four categories, ranging from majoritarian to proportional representation (PR), with two categories in-between.

*Majoritarian systems.* In a majoritarian system, the number of votes for each selector is equal to the number of realistic candidacies to fill. That is, if there is only one position to fill – for example, one party candidate in a single-member constituency – then each selector has just one vote. If there are fifteen realistic positions on a party's list, then each selector has fifteen votes.

The plurality method determines the victory of a particular candidate (in case of a single candidacy), or the ranking of the candidates on a list, on the basis of a comparison of the number of votes. When dealing with a single candidacy – in the case of single-member districts, or in cases of multiple candidates when candidates are selected one by one in a multi-round system – the candidate with the highest number of votes is the winner. When more than one candidate is to be ranked on a list, then the candidates with the highest number of votes equal to the number of realistic positions are selected. For example, if ten candidates compete for six list positions, then the six with the highest number of votes are selected. Such a system was used in the party primaries of the Finnish Social Democrats, where each selector had a number of votes equal to the number of seats the party held in the district (Kuitunen 2002). A similar voting system was used in the Israeli Likud primaries of 1996 (Rahat and Sher-Hadar 1999*a*, 1999*b*). In 1997, the Kenyan African National Union used a system called *Mlolongo* – party members in the constituency were called to stand in line behind the candidate they supported, and the candidate with the longest line won (Ohman 2004). In some of the provinces of Argentina, party primaries in the two large parties are determined by plurality vote; that is, the list with a plurality vote wins all of the candidacies (De Luca, Jones, and Tula 2002).

Interestingly, many parties in countries with plurality electoral systems use candidate selection methods that require a majority, rather than a mere plurality. There are several kinds of majoritarian system that require a candidate to have the support of more than 50 percent of the selectors in order to be selected. One way of doing so is the runoff system. In a case where no candidate wins a majority of the votes in the first round, a second round is conducted between the two candidates with the largest pluralities. Such a system was, and still is, in use in primaries in several US states (Engstrom and Engstrom 2008; Merriam and Overacker 1928).[4] In the past, when the southern part of the United States was dominated by the Democratic Party and the primaries were the place to look for real competition, the Democratic Party in almost all of the southern states used the two-round system. This was a way to legitimize the selection and to ensure that competition was kept within the party, thus preserving its dominance (Key 1949). Later, Democratic dominance disappeared, yet in some states the system was preserved (Engstrom and Engstrom 2008; Glaser 2006). Parties in Germany also used a runoff system when selecting candidates for single-member districts (Porter 1995), and sometimes a two-round system whereby selection in the first round required a majority while in the second round a plurality was sufficient (Szabo 1977).

The scant literature focusing on the political consequences of voting methods in the context of candidate selection deals with the use of plurality versus a two-round system. This literature is a testimony to the potential of such research, and the likely debates that will follow such studies. Glaser (2006), for example, attributed much significance to the two-round systems and supplied evidence for their being more competitive – in terms of the number of candidates and the vote distribution. He also claimed that those cases where a candidate did not win a plurality in the first round, but did win in the second round – admittedly, a minority of the cases – justified conducting a second round. Engstrom and Engstrom (2008) argue the opposite, claiming that the evidence does not support the conducting of a second round in candidate selection for several reasons: in a majority of cases candidates do win a majority in the first round; in most of the remaining cases candidates win a large enough plurality in the first round to decide the race; and, in most cases with a second round, the candidate that won a plurality in the first round also won the second round.

The second option for a majoritarian system is the alternative vote. In this case, selectors rank the candidates according to their preferences. If no candidate wins a majority of first preferences, then the second preferences of the selectors of the candidate with the fewest first preferences are revealed and divided among the remaining candidates. This procedure is repeated until a candidate accumulates a majority. This system is in use in several parties in the United Kingdom (Denver 1988; Norris and Lovenduski 1995; Shepherd-Robinson and Lovenduski 2002).

---

[4] In some states, the threshold was lower than 50%, and required a second round only if no candidate won 40% or 35% of the vote.

TABLE 5.1. *Elimination vote — an example*

| Candidate | Round 1st | 2nd | 3rd | 4th | 5th | 6th |
|-----------|-----------|-----|-----|-----|-----|-----|
| Sarah     | 22        | 22  | 24  | 26  | 30  | 51  |
| Abraham   | 24        | 24  | 26  | 32  | 43  | 49  |
| Leah      | 25        | 25  | 25  | 27  | 27  | —   |
| Jacob     | 10        | 13  | 13  | 15  | —   | —   |
| Rebecca   | 12        | 12  | 12  | —   | —   | —   |
| Rachel    | 4         | 4   | —   | —   | —   | —   |
| Isaac     | 3         | —   | —   | —   | —   | —   |
| TOTAL     | 100       | 100 | 100 | 100 | 100 | 100 |

The third option is the elimination vote. Here, if no candidate wins a majority of the votes, then the candidate with the fewest votes is ousted and all of the remaining candidates compete again.[5] This procedure is repeated until one candidate gains a majority. Table 5.1 provides an example of competition among seven candidates according to the rules of the elimination vote. The example intentionally points to the special dynamics of such a selection method, as the winner in the sixth concluding round is a candidate who never led in any of the previous rounds.

This procedure is time consuming – as its alternative name, the exhaustive ballot, indicates. It is thus typical for selection meetings in which all of the selectors gather to choose the candidates. Parties in Britain (Denver 1988; Norris and Lovenduski 1995; Rush 1969), Australia (Norris et al. 1990), New Zealand (Jackson 1980; Stephens 2008), Canada (Erickson 1997; Williams 1981), and the Irish Fianna Fail (Gallagher 1988*b*) have used this voting system in their candidate selection processes, in gatherings of either delegates or party members.

*Semi-majoritarian systems – inflated vote.* In a semi-majoritarian system, the number of votes for each selector is higher than the number of realistic candidacies. That is, if there are five realistic positions on a list, then each selector has more than five votes. We call this method an "inflated" vote. A semi-majoritarian system creates different incentives than a majoritarian system in which the number of votes for each selector is equal to the number of positions to fill. In a majoritarian system, for example, it is rational for groups of candidates (when we deal with more than a single candidacy) to organize and jointly ask for the selectors' votes. This, in turn, could result in a situation whereby a plurality of the selectors – or a majority, in the event that a majority is needed – can win all of the candidacies.

---

[5] According to one version of the elimination vote system, more than one candidate is eliminated when the sum of the votes of the last candidates is lower than the number of the votes of the candidate who is ranked immediately above them (Paterson 1967; Rush 1969).

An inflated vote system requires much more sophisticated efforts of coordinating the vote, because beyond asking selectors to vote for a group of candidates equal in size to the number of realistic candidacies, those who are trying to organize the vote also have to ask the selectors to split their other votes among various "straw" candidates. Such a system was used by the Belgian Socialist Party, which usually allotted its members a number of votes equal to its number of incumbents in the multimember district, plus one (Obler 1970). It can also come into being when a party whose electoral fortunes decline does not bother to update the number of votes it allots to each selector.

*Semi-proportional representation systems.* In a semi-proportional representation (semi-PR) system, the number of votes for each selector is lower than the number of candidacies to fill. That is, if there are twenty realistic positions on a list, then each selector will have less than twenty votes. This system is known as the "limited vote" system. The Labor Party in Israel used this system when it allotted its party members a number of votes lower than its expected seat share in selecting the party's national list. Indeed, parallel to its electoral decline since 1992, Labor has allotted its party members a declining number of votes, from a maximum of fifteen in 1992, to eight in 2008. In some of the provinces in Argentina, the logic of semi-PR is adhered to in the allocation of positions on the party list: the candidacies are divided in the party primaries between the list with the plurality vote (it wins a majority of the candidacies) and a minority list that gets every third or fourth candidacy as long as it passes a certain threshold (De Luca, Jones, and Tula 2002).

*Proportional representation systems.* PR within parties can be conducted in two ways. One way is a competition among lists, similar in its rules to list PR electoral systems. In some of the provinces in Argentina, candidacies are divided in party primaries according to PR rules, among candidate lists that pass a certain threshold (De Luca, Jones, and Tula 2002). The second way is to use a personalized PR system – the single transferable vote (STV). In this system, selectors are asked to rank the candidates. The preferences of the voters are revealed from top to bottom. Candidates are selected if they achieve a certain quota. If they achieve more than the needed quota, their surplus second preferences are divided among the other candidates and any candidates who now have more than the required quota are selected. If there are still candidacies to fill after this procedure, the candidate with the lowest number of first preferences is eliminated and the second preferences of his selectors are allocated to the other candidates who are still in the race. This procedure is repeated until all of the positions are filled.

Not surprisingly, the STV system was used by the parties in the country that is known for the use of this electoral system – Ireland. The Irish Fine Gael, Labour, and the Progressive Democrats used the STV voting system in their candidate selection meetings for a long time (Gallagher 1988*b*), and Fianna Fail started using it more recently, prior to the 2002 and 2007 elections (Galligan 2003; Weeks 2007). The shortlist in the British Labour Party – which is later presented to party members for the final selection of candidates – is also selected using the STV system (Shepherd-Robinson and Lovenduski 2002).

### Ordinal versus categorical voting systems

The distinction between ordinal and categorical systems is one more way to look at intraparty voting systems. In a categorical system, the selector is either expressing support for a specific candidate or candidates, or refraining from doing so. In ordinal systems, voters are allowed to express preferences concerning the candidates they choose – who is their first choice, their second choice, and so on.[6]

Among the majoritarian systems that are aimed at selecting a single candidate, plurality, runoff, and elimination votes are categorical while the alternative vote is ordinal. In addition, a system in which selectors are asked to rank a number of candidates that is equal to the number of realistic positions is considered a majoritarian-ordinal system. Yet, the fact that not all votes are equal – a higher preference is worth more than a lower one – means that we also have a different type of competition. For example, it is harder to build an organized group of candidates when there is ordinal voting because there is a need to agree not just on the candidates themselves, but also on the rank of each candidate.

The same is true concerning those methods that we label semi-majoritarian and semi-PR systems. These can be based on either categorical or ordinal voting. In these cases, selectors are asked to select or rank a certain number of candidates that is different from the number of realistic positions – higher in the case of the semi-majoritarian system and lower in the case of the semi-PR system. While members of the Belgian Socialist Party were sometimes asked to rank a number of candidates equal to the number of incumbents in their multimember district plus one, there were differences in the counting methods. In some constituencies a points system was used, in which each position had a "negative" score, based on one point given to the first candidate ranked, two for the second, and so on. In this case, the lower the number of points that a candidate had, the higher their rank. In other constituencies preferences were revealed from top to bottom. The candidate with the highest number of first preferences won the first position. Among the candidates who were left, the candidate with the highest number of first and second preferences won the second position. The candidate who was selected for the third position was the one with the highest number of first, second, and third preferences among those that were left, and so on (Obler 1970).

---

[6] In the Labour and Conservative parties of the United Kingdom, shortlists are designed using ordinal systems (Shepherd-Robinson and Lovenduski 2002).

In 2003, every member of the Reform Party in Estonia was allowed to rank the top thirty positions on the national list. The results were calculated according to a formula where the first position received 40 points, the second 36, the third 33, the fourth 30, the fifth 28, the sixth 26, the seventh 25, and so on. In another Estonian party, Res Publica, members ranked the candidates at the national level, and each rank received one point more than the one that followed: 20 for the first, 19 for the second, and so on (Kangur 2005). It should be noted that the differences in the number of points allotted to each position may not only lead to different results, as will be demonstrated later in this chapter, but can also influence the strategy of the competitors.

In the case of a PR voting system that selects individuals rather than a list, we have only an ordinal system, STV. It is impossible to implement a proportional allocation of positions in a personalized voting system without the possibility of transferring preferences.

The way that votes are counted is what distinguishes between ordinal voting systems. Some systems count preferences, from top to bottom. The candidate with the highest number of first preferences is selected for the first position; then, among the remaining candidates, the candidate with the highest number of first and second preferences is selected, etc. For example, the Swedish Social Democrat Party adopted the following system:

> After a general vote the candidates are placed on the ballot paper according to the following rules. The first place is occupied by the candidate who has received most valid votes for this place. The second place is occupied by the candidate who totally has received most valid votes for the first and second places. The third place is occupied by the candidate who totally has received most valid votes for the first, second and third places. The following places are filled with the same method of counting as above. (Constitution of the Swedish Social Democratic Party 2001: 32)

In an STV system, counting is different and is based on transferring remainder preferences from the selected candidates along with the lower preferences of those selectors who gave their first preferences to weak candidates. Because STV is based on a different method of revealing preferences, it can lead to a different translation of votes into candidacies.

Other counting methods reveal all preferences at once, allotting a specific number of points for each position. In this case, the victorious candidate in the case of a single candidacy, or the candidates' positions in the case of a party list, is the result of the number of points that he (they) accumulated. A simple allocation is based on giving one point to the lowest preference of each selector and adding one point for each higher preference. A more sophisticated point system would combine the logic of categorical and ordinal voting, giving all selected candidates a certain number of points, and then adding one point for each higher preference. The Israeli National Religious Party used such a system, whereby each selector ranked seven candidates: the candidate ranked seventh received four points, the candidate ranked sixth got five, and so on up to the first preference who received ten points (Rahat and Sher-Hadar 1999*b*). Other parties prefer a different logic of giving the highest ranks a bonus, as in the case of the Reform Party in Estonia mentioned above.

### On the significance of the difference between voting systems

Tables 5.2 through 5.5 present hypothetical results of voting by 100 selectors who are asked to rank five competitors. Such voting may determine a single candidacy (in a single-member district, or a candidacy for a specific position on a list) or the rank of several candidates on a list. Our aim is to use these results to clarify the different political consequences of various ballots and of different counting methods. The examples allow us to analyze various categorical ballots (one vote, three votes – in Table 5.2) and ordinal voting with three different counting methods (top to bottom, simple point system, sophisticated point system – in Tables 5.3–5.5), all based on the same distribution of votes or preferences.

A look at the example in Table 5.2 clarifies the potential differences between a single-vote and a multivote system. In both competitions, the candidate who wins, or those candidates who win higher positions on a list, is (are) the candidate(s) who is (are) preferred by a plurality. However, when three votes are allotted to each selector, candidates who are the second and third preferences of most of the selectors can actually win the top positions. Candidate A wins a plurality in a single-vote contest, but is last when we count three votes – the selectors either like him or hate him. Candidate E is someone few selectors dislike but few also prefer over all the others. She wins in the three-vote contest, although only one-tenth of the voters see her as their first preference. To sum up, we can see that the result of a categorical voting system, which ignores the selectors' preferences, can still be influenced by their preferences once the number of votes that each selector is allotted is higher than one.

TABLE 5.2. *Ranking three preferences with five candidates — a single vote versus three votes of equal weight*

| Candidate | 1st preference (single vote total) | 2nd preference | 3rd preference | Multi-vote total |
|---|---|---|---|---|
| A | **30** | 5 | 5 | 40 |
| B | 25 | 15 | 21 | 61 |
| C | 20 | 20 | 30 | 70 |
| D | 15 | 30 | 10 | 55 |
| E | 10 | 30 | 34 | **74** |
| Total | 100 | 100 | 100 | 300 |

Bold = winning candidate.

We now turn to the different ways that preferences can be counted and their impact on the selection results. Table 5.3, using similar results to Table 5.2, shows the consequences of a counting system that reveals preferences from top to bottom. The first position is filled by the candidate who wins the highest number of first preferences, the second is filled by the candidate who wins the highest number of first and second preferences combined, and the remaining positions are determined by the combined number of first, second, and third preferences. Candidate A wins the first position as a result of a plurality of first preferences, similar to the outcome when each selector has a single vote. Yet, the candidates who win lower positions are different than those who won them in either a single- or a three-vote plurality competition. Following the majoritarian counting logic, the second position goes to candidate D, who was ranked low (fourth) when we ignored preferences using the single- and the three-vote system.

Unlike the previous systems, the two following systems reveal all the preferences of the selectors at once. They differ in that they give the ranks different weights. In our example, the simple point system (Table 5.4) allots three points for each first rank that a candidate wins, two points for a second, and one point for a third. The more sophisticated point system (Table 5.5) allots five points for each first rank that a candidate wins, four points for a second, and three points for a third. The simple point system gives more weight to a candidate's rank than the sophisticated vote system. In the simple point system, a single first rank equals three third ranks and one and one-half second ranks. In the sophisticated system, the differences are much more moderate; a first rank equals 1.67 times a third rank and 1.25 times a second. These differences also produce different winners and losers, and are likely to generate different behaviors by the competing contestants. The higher the bonus that one achieves from a higher rank, the lower is the incentive to cooperate with other competitors.

TABLE 5.3. *Ranking three preferences with five candidates — revealing preferences from top to bottom*

| Candidate | 1st preference | 1st + 2nd preferences | 1st + 2nd + 3rd preferences |
|-----------|------------|-----------------|---------------------|
| A | 30 [1] | 35 | 40 |
| B | 25 | 40 | 61 [5] |
| C | 20 | 40 | 70 [4] |
| D | 15 | 45 [2] | 55 |
| E | 10 | 40 | 74 [3] |
| Total | 100 | 200 | 300 |

Brackets = final rank of the candidate.

TABLE 5.4. *Ranking three preferences with five candidates — simple point system*

| Candidate | 1st preference points | 2nd preference points | 3rd preference points | Total points |
|---|---|---|---|---|
| A | 90 | 10 | 5 | 105 [5] |
| B | 75 | 30 | 21 | 126 [2] |
| C | 60 | 40 | 30 | 130 [1] |
| D | 45 | 60 | 10 | 115 [4] |
| E | 30 | 60 | 34 | 124 [3] |
| Total | 300 | 200 | 100 | 600 |

The number of points follows simple rules: 1st preference = 3 points; 2nd preference = 2 points; 3rd preference = 1 point.
Brackets = final rank of the candidate.

TABLE 5.5. *Ranking three preferences with five candidates — sophisticated point system*

| Candidate | 1st preference points | 2nd preference points | 3rd preference points | Total points |
|---|---|---|---|---|
| A | 150 | 20 | 15 | 185 [5] |
| B | 125 | 60 | 63 | 248 [3] |
| C | 100 | 80 | 90 | 270 [2] |
| D | 75 | 120 | 30 | 225 [4] |
| E | 50 | 120 | 102 | 272 [1] |
| Total | 500 | 400 | 300 | 1200 |

The number of points follows sophisticated rules, 3 points for being selected plus one for each higher position: 3rd preference = 3 points; 2nd preference = 4 points; 1st preference = 5 points.
Brackets = final rank of the candidate.

Table 5.6 presents a summary of the different final ranks according to the various voting methods and counting alternatives, and clearly shows that each system translates votes into candidacies differently. This is what is known in the electoral system literature as the mechanical effect of electoral systems (Duverger 1954; Taagepera and Shugart 1989). Voters, and candidates especially, are aware of these effects and adapt their voting and campaign behaviors to the different systems, which thus adds a psychological (or behavioral) effect. As Brams and Fishburn (2002: 177) put it, "Common voting procedures used in selecting between two candidates are essentially strategy-proof, but most procedures involving three or more candidates are not." Those candidates who understand the system can gain by playing according to its rules – if it is a zero-sum game (one-vote system) or a system that also provides payoffs for cooperation.

One example of the psychological impact of the voting system involves the nature of competition, whether is it a zero-sum game or if it also rewards

TABLE 5.6. *Ranking three preferences with five candidates — results according to different voting and counting methods*

| Final rank | Single vote | Three votes of equal weight | Preferences revealed from top to bottom | Simple points system | Sophisticated points system |
|---|---|---|---|---|---|
| 1 | A | E | A | C | E |
| 2 | B | C | D | B | C |
| 3 | C | B | E | E | B |
| 4 | D | D | C | D | D |
| 5 | E | A | B | A | A |

cooperation. A single-vote system does not supply incentives for cooperation, as all candidates fight on their own for a single prize. A multi-vote system creates a reason to cooperate, as candidates can strike deals with other candidates for their mutual benefit. The type and importance of such cooperation is influenced by the way that votes are counted. For example, the exposure of preferences from top to bottom and the simple points system give less incentive to cooperate than the sophisticated voting system in the example above, because the two former methods put more weight on the rank of the candidate than the latter system. In short, voting systems matter.

## MIXED APPOINTMENT-VOTING SYSTEMS

As already elaborated in previous chapters, candidate selection is often conducted by several selectorates. In a multistage system, sometimes one or more selectorates use an appointment system while another one or more selectorates use a voting system. For example, in Norway a nominating committee develops a recommended list, taking into consideration the need to balance representation in terms of geography, gender, age, occupation, etc. This recommendation is then voted on, not *en bloc* – a way that would give the appointing selectorate a clear advantage – but position by position, thereby allotting roughly equal influence to the appointing and the voting selectorates (Matthews and Valen 1999). The multistage system in the Conservative Party in the United Kingdom also involves appointments by small selectorates, at both the national and the constituency levels, and voting by wider selectorates at the constituency level (Norris and Lovenduski 1995). In Belgium, the Christian Social Party used a variety of systems similar in their logic to the general, semi-open electoral system. These systems allowed members either to ratify a predetermined candidate list – a list designed by a nominating committee or by party delegates – or to vote for individual candidates. Votes for the list were weighted in various ways with the individual votes, which led in most cases to a de facto ratification of the proposed list (Obler 1970). Thus, while each selectorate may use either an appointment or a voting system, the overall process may involve mixing them and also giving them different weights in influencing the results of the selection process.

## DEMOCRATIZATION AND VOTING/APPOINTMENT SYSTEMS

Voting is perceived as more democratic than appointment because the democratic norm dictates summing up the secret votes of individuals rather than conducting group negotiations. A party that replaces appointment with voting, or even adds voting to a process that was formerly conducted through appointment, is democratizing its selection method. Appointment will likely take place in small bodies that allow for deliberation, while voting enables larger audiences to express the aggregated wills of the individuals. That is, the adoption of larger, wider, more inclusive selectorates necessarily leads to the adoption of voting systems. However, such democratization is not likely to lead to results that are more representative. It is easier to ensure representative candidacies when there is more control over the selection results and greater ability to coordinate the selection, rather than simply aggregating individual votes (Rahat, Hazan, and Katz 2008; Rahat 2009).

Not all voting systems, however, have a similar potential to create unrepresentative candidacies. The adoption of multi-round systems allows selectorates to coordinate selection and thus fix misrepresentation. The adoption of non-majoritarian systems allows for the representation of minorities within the parties. It is very hard to ensure heterogeneity of candidacies when the selection is majoritarian (Denver 1988).

Candidate selection is a form of intraparty competition that can deteriorate into a conflict that will threaten the cohesion of the party exactly at the time when it needs to present a united front vis-à-vis the other parties (that is, on the eve of the general elections). Appointment systems can help parties keep their internal peace because they allow them to balance the representation of different forces within the party. Yet, because of the low democratic legitimacy of appointment systems, it is easier for those who lost to justify their unwillingness to accept the results, and maybe even to split and establish a new party, or to run as independents where possible. Voting systems, on the other hand, are more likely to create legitimate democratic results, but because they lack the element of negotiation they are more likely to create unbalanced representation. Among the voting systems, the more proportional ones are more likely to enable the balancing of group representation.

In this chapter, we turned our attention to the most neglected dimension in candidate selection and pointed to the existence of an interesting variety of intraparty voting systems. We hope that this will both tempt and encourage scholars to delve deeper into this hidden field and undertake systematic empirical study of this still uncharted world. The end of this chapter also completes the first part of the book: the four dimensions used for the classification of candidate selection methods. After developing a framework for distinguishing between the various candidate selection methods, we now turn to analyze their political consequences.

# Part II

## The Political Consequences of Candidate Selection Methods

Part II focuses on the political consequences of candidate selection methods through an analysis of four democratic dimensions: participation, representation, competition, and responsiveness. All of these dimensions are part of our basic understanding of modern representative democracy – a regime in which the citizens *participate* in choosing among parties or candidates who *compete* with each other in an attempt to be the *representatives* of the people, and who are expected to demonstrate *responsiveness* to their demands after they are elected. However, modern representative democracy is implemented at the national level. What happens within parties? The answers are not the same as they are for the national level, because parties are – as their name suggests – part of a democratic whole, not the democratic system but a subsystem within it.

Our analysis mainly involves the relationship between the level of inclusiveness of the selectorate and these four dimensions. We would have liked to address other relationships, and to analyze such intriguing issues as the influence of exclusive candidacy requirements on representation (do strict candidacy requirements breed unrepresentative candidates?); the impact of decentralization on turnout (does decentralization increase turnout in candidate selection, especially in the cases of the more inclusive selectorates?); and the effect of the intraparty voting systems (is it similar to the national level, where proportionality encourages participation?). Such questions, and many others, can be asked only in the future, after candidate selection is sufficiently researched to the point that scholars will have enough comparative data to begin answering them. We hope that this part of the book will ignite enough interest to lead down such a path.

# 6

## Participation

Participation is a central dimension of democracy. In a modern representative democracy, the entire adult citizen population has the right to elect the representatives who will govern them. Democracy at the national level requires universal participation, that is, maximum inclusiveness. But what about participation at the intraparty level? In this chapter we address this issue, looking at participation as inclusiveness and as turnout, as well as the question of the quantity versus the quality of participation within parties.

In many democracies, candidate selection methods are becoming more inclusive (Bille 2001; Hazan 2002; Kittilson and Scarrow 2003; Scarrow, Webb, and Farrell 2000). If in the past most party selectorates were composed of party delegates – standing agencies such as national or local committees and congresses, or special nomination or selection conventions – today more and more parties give rank-and-file members the right to influence candidate and leadership selection. This general trend makes analyzing the expansion of the selectorate – particularly the adoption of the highly inclusive method of party primaries – relevant for virtually all democracies, whether they are moving in a similar direction or if their political actors are contemplating such a shift.

Although there is much debate over the extent of the decline in party membership and its interpretation, its occurrence – indicated by both absolute and relative measures – is a clear empirical finding (Mair and van Biezen 2001; Scarrow 2000). In light of this phenomenon, one of the ways that citizens are brought back in by political elites is through increasing their role inside parties (Scarrow 1999*b*). This is often expressed by giving rank-and-file party members influence over important intraparty decisions, among them candidate selection. While this phenomenon is recognized in the research literature, its political consequences are still in need of systematic evaluation.

In this chapter, we are concerned with the actual impact of democratizing candidate selection methods on patterns of political participation – specifically the political consequences of expanding the selectorate from an exclusive to a more inclusive body of participation. For example, what are the ramifications of a party's decision to shift its selection of candidates from a small nominating committee to a larger group of party delegates? Or alternatively, what is the effect of shifting from the latter to party primaries? In party primaries, the focus of this chapter, party members' votes decide who the party's candidate will be in a single-member district or the candidacies (and often the ranking of candidates) on the party list for general elections. However, before analyzing the political consequences of intraparty democracy for participation, we must distinguish between two very different concepts related to participation: inclusiveness and turnout.

## INCLUSIVENESS VERSUS TURNOUT

Candidate selection methods can be distinguished according to the four dimensions outlined in the earlier chapters. This chapter focuses on the party selectorate – the body that selects the party candidates. Party selectorates are classified according to their level of *inclusiveness*. At one extreme, the selectorate consists of the entire electorate of the nation; that is, all citizens who are eligible to participate in general elections. At the other extreme, the selectorate – or rather the selector – is a single party leader. Between these poles, we can find various alternatives, from a relatively inclusive body of party members, through party delegates, and up to a small, exclusive nominating body that is composed of just a few leaders.

A completely different concept is that of *turnout* in the candidate selection process, which ranges from very high to very low, regardless of the size of the selectorate. A very inclusive selectorate, such as that of all party members, can produce either high or low turnout. By the same token, a relatively exclusive selectorate may also shift along the turnout continuum. The United States provides a clear example of how inclusiveness and turnout can vary independently of each other (Norrander 1986). Turnout increases in those primaries where there is competitiveness and decreases in those where the race is not even close, regardless of the level of inclusiveness – even across states or time where this level is constant. In those states where one party clearly dominated, and the primaries determined the eventual winner of the general election, turnout for selecting the candidate was sometimes even higher than in the general election (Key 1949). In addition, variables such as education, age, income, and profession influenced the level of turnout across similar candidate selection methods, even more than they affected turnout in general elections (Crittenden 1982).

One can envision the inclusiveness–exclusiveness dimension as the horizontal axis and the level of turnout as the vertical axis. These two can vary independently, since expanding the amount of people who are allowed to take part in the candidate selection process does not require them to actually participate. While it is quite likely that the *absolute* number of people participating will be higher in the more inclusive candidate selection methods, it is likely to be *relatively* lower than in the more exclusive arenas. We can predict this negative correlation between inclusiveness and participation by following Olsonian logic: the more potential participants there are, the weaker the incentives are to participate actively (Olson 1965). Indeed, Tan (1998) and Weldon (2006) found that the larger a party is (in terms of membership), the less active its members are. Evidence that is presented later in this chapter points in the same direction – turnout tends to decline as we move from an exclusive selectorate to a more inclusive body.

## INCLUSIVENESS

Israel's experience with the democratization of several of the parties' candidate selection methods is a case in point. In the pre-state years, and in the first decades after independence (1948–73), the parties used highly exclusive selectorates, such as nomination committees composed of a few leaders, to select their candidates. In the 1970s and 1980s, many parties transferred candidate selection to their wider and more representative institutions, composed of party delegates. This was the first step toward expanding participation, which was followed in the 1990s by several parties further opening up with the adoption of inclusive party primaries. The absolute selectorate figures clearly show that Israel's main parties underwent a dramatic increase in political participation when selectorates ranging from 1,269 (Labor's Central Committee delegates in 1988) to 3,153 (Likud's Central Committee in 1992) were replaced by those ranging from 178,852 (Likud's membership in 1996) to 261,169 (Labor's membership in 1996). This was the essence of the adoption of party primaries. In this sense, absolute political participation increased dramatically. Moreover, since the Israeli electoral system is a national closed-list system, which gives no say to the voters as to the composition of party lists, the party primaries provided an important new venue for increased participation.

In the 1992–2009 period, the average ratio of dues-paying members (those who were eligible to participate in party primaries in the main parties in Israel) to party voters stood at 1:5.3 (Table 6.1). In the nine cases of party primaries in Israel to date, between one-third and one-ninth of the main parties' voters – that is, the potential population of party members, if one assumes that a party member is likely to be a party voter – chose to register as members. Of these, an average 57.6 percent turned out to vote in the primaries, which means that on average approximately 1 in 9.8 party voters (10 percent) took an active part in the candidate selection process. These figures indicate the creation of a new, significantly more inclusive arena of political participation.

Did the more inclusive candidate selection methods, such as party primaries, bring citizens back into party politics? Rahat and Hazan (2007) analyzed the Israeli case and concluded that primaries brought about only a provisional

*Democracy within Parties*

TABLE 6.1. *Number of party members, participants in party primaries, party voters, and their ratios in Israel's main parties, 1992–2009*

| Party | Year | Number of party members | Number of participants in candidate selection | Number of voters in general elections | Ratio members: voters | Ratio participants: voters |
|-------|------|------------------------|-----------------------------------------------|--------------------------------------|----------------------|---------------------------|
| Labor | 1992 | 164,163 | 118,197 (72.0%) | 906,810 | 1:5.5 | 1:7.7 |
| Labor | 1996 | 261,169 | 194,788 (74.6%) | 818,741 | 1:3.1 | 1:4.2 |
| Labor | 1999 | 163,044 | 101,087 (62.0%) | 670,484 | 1:4.1 | 1:6.6 |
| Labor | 2003 | 110,988 | 58,783 (53.0%) | 455,183 | 1:4.1 | 1:7.7 |
| Labor | 2006 | 116,948 | 68,331 (58.4%) | 472,366 | 1:4.0 | 1:6.9 |
| Labor | 2009 | 59,025 | 31,789 (53.9%) | 334,900 | 1:5.7 | 1:10.5 |
| Likud | 1996 | 178,852 | 91,907 (51.4%) | 767,401 | 1:4.3 | 1:8.3 |
| Likud | 2009 | 98,492 | 48,458 (49.2%) | 729,054 | 1:7.4 | 1:15.0 |
| Kadima | 2009 | 79,649 | 35,125 (44.1%) | 758,032 | 1:9.5 | 1:21.6 |

Year indicates the year of the general election prior to which the primaries took place.

*Source*: Data from the political parties and newspapers.

resurgence in party membership.[1] Israel's experience with trying to meet the challenge of declining party membership by empowering party members is quite common. Research on participation and activism in German parties in the 1960s found that party members did not take advantage of the participation mechanisms that were available to them (Gunlicks 1970). Nevertheless, in the 1980s and 1990s, the veteran German parties adopted additional participatory devices, including member participation in candidate and leadership selection, as a reaction to declining membership and electoral losses, and in response to demands for more direct political participation. Scarrow (1999b, 2002) concluded that reforms meant to bring about more inclusive parties did not succeed in bringing more citizens into party politics, but did empower those who were already members. The German Green Party institutionalized a series of organizing principles inspired by grassroots participatory ideals, but still failed to attract large numbers of party activists. Poguntke (1992) argued that those people who could be expected to be active in party participatory democracy are loyal to specific policies and not to a party organization. They can be mobilized for the promotion of specific goals, but not for continuous partisan activity.

In addition to the cases of Israel and Germany, Britain (Webb 2002), France (Knapp 2002), the Scandinavian countries (Sundberg 2002), and Ireland (Murphy and Farrell 2002) all provide examples of parties that expanded and empowered their selectorates. Yet in these cases too, their efforts failed to enlarge the number of members significantly.

---

[1] More recent data on membership in 2006 and 2009, included in Rahat (Forthcoming), substantiates these findings.

The parties' adoption of more inclusive participatory arrangements in their candidate selection methods seems to have had only partial success in combating declining membership and in engaging citizens to participate in party politics. Attempting to be modest in our expectations, we can indeed argue that adopting more inclusive candidate selection methods, such as party primaries, resulted in two positive developments for participation, and therefore for democracy: First, although it did not bring about a serious and sustained increase in party membership that brought citizens back into party politics, it did stem the decline in the number of party members, or at least slowed it down. Second, a new arena for political participation was created wherein citizens could influence aspects of politics that they were unable to before, which was especially important in those institutional settings where voters previously lacked such influence (Cross 2008).

## TURNOUT

The average turnout of party members in Israel's party primaries is 57.6 percent, ranging from 74.6 percent in Labor in 1996, to 44.1 percent in Kadima prior to the 2009 election (Table 6.2). Turnout in Labor has declined over time, while in both Likud and Kadima it never reached high levels – with more recent figures at around 50 percent or below. Table 6.2 shows that in Israel there were differences in the rate of participation between the parties, and also for the same party at different times. One is tempted to argue that such political variables as competitiveness, the party's being in government, or the party's public support affect the rate of member participation. Yet, it appears that the best predictor for turnout rates is the relative distribution of voting stations. This explains the higher levels in Israel's

TABLE 6.2. *Turnout in party primaries for selecting the candidate lists compared to general elections in Israel, 1992–2009 (in percentages)*

| Year | Labor | Likud | Kadima | General elections |
|------|-------|-------|--------|-------------------|
| 1992 | 72.0 | — | — | 77.4 |
| 1996 | 74.6 | 51.4 | — | 79.3 |
| 1999 | 62.0 | — | — | 78.7 |
| 2003 | 53.0 | — | — | 68.9 |
| 2006 | 58.4 | — | — | 63.5 |
| 2009 | 53.9 | 49.2 | 44.1 | 64.7 |
| Average | 62.3 | 50.3 | 44.1 | 72.1 |

Year indicates the year of the general election prior to which the primaries took place. Voter turnout in general elections is from the Central Elections Committee (http://www.knesset.gov.il/elections18/heb/history/PercentVotes.aspx), last accessed 24 February 2010.

*Source*: Data from the political parties and newspapers

Labor Party compared to Likud; and the decrease in participation in Labor primaries over the years is correlated to the adoption of a more frugal policy concerning the spread of polling stations. The fact that this "technicality" is the best predictor for turnout stands in contrast to the turnout rate in party congresses, which take place in one location yet manage to draw participation of more than 90 percent. When one remembers that members pay for the right to participate in these party primaries, turnout seems quite low.

Similar, and even lower, rates of membership turnout in candidate selection were recorded in other countries. Obler (1970) reports – on the basis of data from fifty cases – that turnout in the Belgian party primaries in 1958–65 was 58.9 percent on average; in only 16 percent of the cases was it more than 60 percent. Membership turnout in candidate selection in Canada was between one-third and one-half (Cross 2002, 2004). In Finland, it stood at 39–45 percent prior to the 1979 elections, while prior to the 1995 elections the averages for the four largest parties in the various districts were between 20 percent and 63 percent (Helander 1997; Kuitunen 2002). In 1999, two-thirds membership turnout was recorded in Fine Gail (Gallagher 2003). In Taiwan, the turnout in the Kuomintang primaries stood at 45.1 percent in 1989, 29.1 percent in 1991, and 29.6 percent in 1992 (Wu and Fell 2001), while in the Democratic Progressive Party in 1989 it stood at 70 percent (Fell 2005). In Denmark, membership participation through postal voting – in those parties in which voting is not just consultative – was between 53 percent and 76 percent (Pedersen 2001).[2] In the more inclusive cases, turnout was lower. In Iceland's party primaries, turnout in 1983 was 26 percent, and in 1987 it was only 16 percent (Hardarson 1995). In Argentina, between 1989 and 2003, the Peronist Party had an average of 14 percent of registered voters participating in its "open" primaries, and only 7 percent when it used closed primaries, while the Radical Civic Union experienced even lower figures – 5 percent and 2 percent respectively (Jones 2008). In the United States, turnout for the primaries for the House of Representatives in twenty-four states with closed primary systems stood at 27–37 percent of those voters who registered as Democrats and Republicans (Ezra 2001).

The turnout statistics given above reflect various countries and parties in diverse settings (from voting in a meeting to voting through the mail), which allows us cautiously to propose two conclusions: First, overall turnout of party members is somewhere around 50 percent, or somewhat lower, with a wide range of 20–75 percent. Second, turnout is lower in the more inclusive cases where participation is open to all voters. In order to give these turnout statistics more meaning, we now compare them to turnout in general elections and to turnout in the more exclusive selectorates.

---

[2] Participation rates for events other than candidate selection are similar. For example, rates of participation in mayoral candidate and leadership selection in German parties were between 34% and 57% (Scarrow 1999*b*). Weldon's (2006) data on party members' activities in general, based on surveys, is similar.

If we evaluate turnout in party primaries in Israel vis-à-vis turnout in the general elections, we see that in all cases the latter is higher than the former (Table 6.2). While party members invested more than the voters in securing their right to vote (they even paid dues in order to become members), they still demonstrated lower turnout levels. As far as we can tell, this is true for practically all political parties in the democratic world, even those where selection was the true election.[3] If we follow Olsonian expectations based on the size of the selectorate (assuming that rewards are equal), then we would expect a higher turnout among party members than among regular voters. We can thus conclude that the incentives for participating in party primaries are perceived as lower than those in general elections, somewhat similar to second-order elections in which such levels of turnout are quite common.

A comparison of turnout in party primaries to turnout in the more exclusive selectorates composed of party delegates tells us that Olsonian logic works well when the return is similar – that is, turnout in candidate selection among party delegates is much higher. Data collected in Israel are revealing because although they do not systematically cover all cases – due to the poor levels of documentation in intraparty selection – the picture is clear. For example, while turnout in Likud primaries in 1996 and 2009 was around 50 percent, turnout in its central committee selection was 92 percent in 1992 (first selection round); 88 percent in 1999; and 91 percent in 2006. In 1988, the only time that Labor selected most of its candidates using its central committee, turnout was 98 percent (first round), compared to 53–75 percent recorded in the primaries. Turnout in the cases of selection by party agencies in other Israeli parties was also similar: 79 percent, 87 percent, and 89 percent turnout in Meretz in 2003, 2006, and 2009, respectively; 92 percent in the National Religious Party's central committee in 2003; and 92 percent in Hadash in 2009.

A comparison with data from the United Kingdom reveals a similar picture. The British Conservative Party used a general meeting of party delegates in the last stage of choosing its candidates for the European Parliament in 1979. Turnout was higher than 70 percent in two-thirds of the cases, and over 90 percent in one-quarter of cases. At the same time, the Liberal Party used party primaries in some constituencies, and turnout was quite low – the highest turnout was only 34 percent (Holland 1981).[4]

The Kuomintang in Taiwan used two selectorates at the same time: party activists (cadres) and party members. These two selectorates, each with a

---

[3] The exception is the southern United States, where turnout in the primaries was higher than the general elections during the hegemony of the Democratic Party (Key 1949).

[4] The Labour Party also used party delegates in the final stage, with somewhat lower turnout. Compared to the Conservatives, where only 5% of cases had a turnout of lower than 50%, in Labour it was 10% of cases. Regardless, the two parties combined show that the lowest level of turnout for party delegates – even after the vast majority of candidates had already been filtered out – was almost the same as the highest turnout exhibited by the more inclusive party primaries of the Liberal Party.

different level of inclusiveness, showed a large gap in turnout prior to the 1991 and 1992 elections – just under 30 percent among the party members, but almost 70 percent among the party activists (Wu and Fell 2001: 32). Data on turnout in leadership selection in several countries paints a similar picture. Turnout in the exclusive selectorate of the parliamentary party is higher than turnout among party delegates; turnout among the latter is, in turn, higher than turnout in the more inclusive selectorate of party members (Kenig 2007).

Turnout among party members is lower in comparison with turnout in general elections and in candidate selection among party delegates. This might not be a surprise since candidate selection is seen as less significant than general elections and party members are expected to be less committed, or less motivated, than party activists. If inclusiveness was expected to produce a new and more involved arena for participation, then this expectation was not met. If the expectation was more modest, such as the creation of just one more arena for participation, then it could have been fulfilled if we would have been able to avoid the problems presented in the next section.

## QUANTITY VERSUS QUALITY: THE PATHOLOGIES OF INCREASED INCLUSIVENESS

Beyond the positive desire to expand participation, for whatever reason, there are political consequences that need to be taken into account by parties before they become more internally democratic. The inability to retain an increase in membership (if there was any such increase), and to convince new members to indeed turn out in higher numbers, are two indicators of problems resulting from expanded participation, but there are more phenomena that must be considered.

The overarching question, which will be assessed here on several levels, is: Does adopting more inclusive participatory methods of candidate selection influence the quality of party participation?

We now look beyond the overall numbers to analyze the question of the quality of membership and its meaning. Duverger's (1954: 90–116) taxonomy of degrees of participation in political parties (Figure 6.1) sets reasonable expectations of party members. It is built from concentric circles of increasing affiliation and participation. The widest circle is that of voters, citizens who merely vote for a given party. The next is that of supporters, voters who also acknowledge that they favor a particular party and may occasionally speak on its behalf. The third circle is the party members, who are at minimum supporters who are formally registered with the party, and a minority of whom actually takes an active part in party activities (Selle and Svåsand 1991; Heidar 1994).

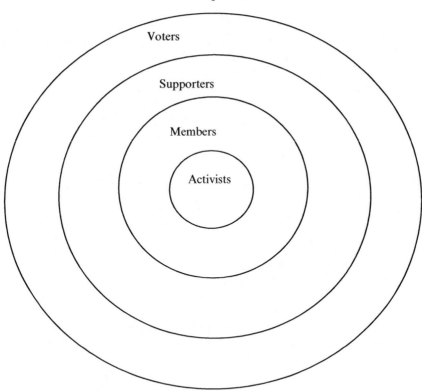

FIGURE 6.1 Degrees of participation in political parties
*Source*: Elaborated from Duverger (1954: 90–1)

Finally, we find the innermost circle of militants or activists, members of the party who see to its organization, operation, propaganda, etc. Following Duverger's taxonomy, and that of other scholars (Seyd and Whiteley 1995), party members are expected at minimum – even when parties intentionally lower the barriers for entrance in order to recruit "supporters" (Scarrow 1994) – to be loyal voters for the party and to be affiliated and engaged with it for more than a short period.

The following discussion points out several disturbing pathologies concerning inclusiveness within parties: the majority of party members might not forge any long-term affiliation with the party, but rather register with the sole purpose of taking part in the more inclusive candidate selection process; many party members might not fulfill even the minimal requirements of being party voters, and the incentives for mass registration may even encourage corruption. In short, primaries may result in instant, opportunistic, and corrupt membership.

## Pathologies of Mass Registration

Over eighty years ago, Merriam and Overacker (1928: 5) pointed out the abuses that arose with the adoption of primaries. "In the first place it soon became evident that there was no guaranty that participation in a party caucus or primary could be confined to members of the party immediately concerned.... Party primaries were invaded and controlled by men of a different or of no political persuasion, and from other districts...." Duverger (1954: 361) described the final stage of candidate selection by the Belgian Christian Social Party in 1949, which included a general poll of the party members on the rolls during the current year. "In certain arrondissements, candidates were known to have organized a member hunt and to have enrolled hundreds of members a few days before the closing date for participation in the poll. Some even tried to buy books of blank members' cards."[5]

The abuses encountered when parties become more inclusive have already received significant scholarly attention across a variety of cases. The most blatant of these is the resulting massive registration drives of party members by the candidates, which produce not only inflated membership figures but also "instant" members who come and go quite rapidly. Instability is another sign of the problematic quality of membership, as it indicates that people join the party, or are recruited, yet do not stay affiliated after the primaries are over. A measure of this is the difference between the number of party members during primaries and the number of members when party primaries are not taking place. Several scholars conducting research on the Canadian parties have provided ample evidence of this. Malloy (2003), for example, states that Canadian party membership is extremely volatile, with cyclical patterns that peak as candidate selection nears due to massive enlistment campaigns, and most do not renew their membership. His description is worth citing in full:

> It is established practice in Canadian politics for potential nominees ... to recruit and transport large numbers of new constituency association members to local meetings solely to support their candidacy, to the point that in 2002 one of the chief concerns ... was disputes over the rules for handling members forms and how many could be copied or distributed at a time. These "instant Liberals," "instant Conservatives," and so on, often have no previous connection to the party and are commonly recruited in mass numbers from ethnic groups, senior citizens, and youth. Most sitting MPs are able to recruit sufficient numbers of local members to overcome any challenger's recruitment efforts, sometimes to ludicrous extents as local associations increase by an average of 300 per cent for nomination meetings. Once they have obtained membership and supported their candidate in the nomination meeting, few renew their membership or otherwise participate in the party. (Malloy 2003: 126)

---

[5] Duverger cites an administrative report of the General Secretary to the party congress.

In the elections of 1993, in 84 percent of the Canadian constituencies with competition, the winning candidate reported enlisting new members into the party; and in one-third of the constituencies with competition, the number of new members enlisted by the candidates more than doubled the existing membership (Erickson 1997). Carty, Cross, and Young (2000) reported an increase in party membership of 60 percent and 70 percent, and up to 300 percent in some instances, prior to candidate selection. These new members enlist only in order to take part in candidate selection and do not renew their membership (Carty and Cross 2006). While instant membership doubles the number of party members in Canadian parties, within two years it returns to the earlier figure (Carty and Eagles 2003).

Moreover, not only did the candidates conduct a massive enlistment of members into the party, some candidates also paid the membership dues (Cross 2006). The problem of instant members has brought about the creation of internal and external committees in the Canadian Liberal Party to look into the matter, but many of their proposals have not been implemented (O'Brien 1993).

Registration campaigns in Israel prior to the primaries led to an increase of between 59 percent and 332 percent in the number of party members (Table 6.3). When there were no primaries on the horizon, the number of members dramatically decreased back to former levels. It would appear, therefore, that most of the members joined the parties – or were recruited – with the sole intention of participating in the more inclusive candidate selection process, and not in order to create a significant link between themselves and the party.[6]

TABLE 6.3. *Membership at the beginning and at the end of registration campaigns in Israel's main parties, 1991–2008*

| Party | Year | Number of members at beginning | Number of members at end | Growth rate from beginning (%) | Decline rate till next beginning (%) |
|---|---|---|---|---|---|
| Labor | 1991–2 | 80,000 | 164,163 | 105 | −51 |
| | 1995–6 | 80,000 | 261,169 | 226 | −73 |
| | 2001–2 | 70,000 | 110,998 | 59 | −57 |
| | 2005 | 48,000 | 119,717 | 149 | −50 |
| | 2007 | 60,000 | 103,568 | 73 | — |
| Likud | 1992–3 | 50,000 | 216,000 | 332 | −58 |
| | 1995–6 | 90,000 | 178,852 | 99 | −44 |
| | 2001–2 | 100,000 | 305,000 | 205 | — |

*Source*: Data from the political parties and newspapers

[6] Another indication of the problematic nature and quality of party membership is the phenomenon of "double registration," the simultaneous enrolment of citizens in more than one party. While this is usually not against the law, it might be prohibited by particular parties (such as the New Democratic Party in Canada). In Israel, it stands not only against the rules set in the parties' constitutions, but is also against the Parties Law. Regardless, the cross-referencing of party members' names conducted in 1996 revealed that 8% of Labor members and 12% of Likud members were also members of another party (Israel, Party Registrar, 13 March 1996).

Scherlis (2008: 587) describes the Argentine experience with primaries as follows:

> Soon, party primaries became blatant clashes between electoral machines. Victory in primaries depends on the capacity to mobilize clienteles. This entails significant spending for a variety of goods and services, from the salaries of the local brokers, who establish the link with the clients, to the funds for buses, taxis and drivers needed to transport voters to the polling stations. In these primaries ideological issues are not at stake, nor do the contestants' backgrounds matter. Hence, who wins is solely determined by the resources at their disposal and their efficient use.

In Taiwan's Kuomintang Party, whoever succeeded in enlisting more new members to take part in candidate selection won (Fell 2005), while in the Progressive Party members were recruited and their fees were paid, and there was even bribery (Baum and Robinson 1995).

The adoption of one-member–one-vote party primaries in British Labour resulted in pressure for the massive registration of members – for example, the party's National Executive Committee (NEC) reported that 800 out of 4,000 members in four constituencies in Birmingham were not even registered as voters. Another example is that of 217 membership forms received with a single personal check; and after a two-year investigation, the NEC decided to accept only nine as members – the other 208 either did not want to be members or did not exist (Criddle 1997: 192–3). Party primaries also produced massive ethnic registration – for example, Asians in Labour by Asian candidates – a phenomenon that also took place in Canada (Carty and Cross 2006). These could be perceived as channels for marginalized groups to influence politics, but in reality they are better captured as classic patron–client relations.

An examination of the 1996 Israeli election results uncovered thirteen towns in which the number of Labor Party members was larger than the actual number of voters (Rahat and Sher-Hadar 1999a). A shared characteristic of most of these towns – low socioeconomic standing – indicates that media allegations concerning patron–client methods in the registration campaigns were evidently grounded in reality. Back and Solomos (1994) argued that in the British Labour Party, candidates paid membership dues, members were enlisted without their knowledge, and often registration was based on patron–client relations. Intraparty democratization in Mexico also encouraged the creation of patron–client relations between members enlisted from weaker socioeconomic strata and the candidates and their affiliates (Combes 2003).

In 2005, the Israeli Labor Party decided to nominate a committee, headed by a former judge, to ensure that all new registered members were recruited according to the law – that is, that they voluntarily joined the party, paid their membership dues, and were not members of other parties. As a result, almost one-half of the 90,000 new memberships were canceled on legal grounds. We argue that a similar

Pandora's box is likely to be opened elsewhere, and that parties around the world choose to ignore these problems, just as they do in the case of the financing of intraparty selection (Hofnung 2006).

It appears that many citizens register with a party in order to select a particular candidate, with no intention of voting for this candidate's party in the general election. In some Icelandic districts, the number of participants in the primaries outnumbered the total number of party voters – in one district the former was 140 percent of the latter (Kristjánsson 1998, 2002). Hardarson (1995: 163–4) examined which percentage of those who took part in the Icelandic primaries also voted for that party in the general elections. The results were between 75 percent and 90 percent, depending on the party, for the 1983 and 1987 elections, with the overall average being 81.1 percent in 1983 and 82.5 percent in 1987. This means that almost one out of five who took part in a particular party's candidate selection process did not vote for that party at the subsequent election.

These phenomena do not result from the adoption of primaries per se, since such occurrences are also evident in parties that do not hold primaries – for example, in the massive registration of members prior to the selection of delegates for positions in a party agency. However, they provide an indication that the quality of empowered membership is problematic and may even decline following the strong incentives that such a system creates to register a large quantity of new members, regardless of their quality.

## Uninformed and passive members

In Israel, many who were recruited in massive registration campaigns were uninformed to the point that they did not know that by registering to take part in the party's internal contest they became party members (Rahat and Sher-Hadar 1999*a*).[7] This is but one indication of the problematic nature of the relationship between the parties and their newly empowered members. Kristjánsson (2004) showed a similar gap between the number of party members listed by the parties in Iceland (just over 50,000 – which is one-quarter of the electorate) and the result of a survey from which one can conclude, on the basis of the respondents' answers, that only about 34,000 considered themselves to be party members. He concluded that 40 percent of the members listed by the parties "entered the party, without any feeling of attachment, in order to vote in the party's primary" (Kristjánsson 2004: 65).

Taking into account Duverger's (1954) taxonomy (Figure 6.1) – together with the fact that many registered members joined, or were recruited, only for the sake of the primaries – we would expect the members' participation rate in party

---

[7] A survey prior to the 1996 elections in Israel (Arian and Amir 1997) found a relative gap of almost 50% between those who declared that they were party members (9%) and those who declared that they participated in the party primaries (13%).

primaries to be somewhere between the level of participation in candidate selection by party agencies (activists/delegates) and participation in general elections
(voters). That is, party members should be less motivated than party activists, but
more so than the average citizen. However, as already shown, the average turnout
rate for primaries appears to be lower than for the general elections.

Parties, as voluntary associations, must have the ability to use selective incentives
in order to reward their activists and encourage them to continue to work for the
party organization. From this perspective, the adoption of party primaries – which
can bring about mass registration on the eve of intraparty elections – is damaging for
the party. Registration that suffers from the pathologies outlined above does not
serve the party, but rather the immediate personal needs of the candidates. Enhanced
and equivalent inclusive political participation in candidate selection damages the
differential structure of rewards in parties – the privileges of long-time loyal
activists are equal to those of new, temporary, and unfaithful registrants.

### The strategic few and the passive many

With the adoption of a more inclusive selectorate, all interested players – the
candidates, the members, and the parties – place an emphasis on the quantitative
side of the registration campaign rather than the qualitative. They interpret numbers
as political power, and seek to reap the immediate rewards vis-à-vis each other,
concentrating on both the intraparty struggle and the forthcoming general election.
The phenomenon of instant, opportunistic, corrupt, and unobligated (and sometimes
even uninformed) membership, together with the fact that approximately one-half of
party members do not bother to participate in party primaries, indicates that most
members are not strategic actors who decide to take advantage of the opportunity
that party primaries grant them. On the contrary, the new party members play the
game as relatively passive participants, and this is despite holding positive attitudes
about the new participatory devices and calling for further reforms in this direction
(Young and Cross 2002). The gap between idealistic stands concerning democracy
within parties and real-life abuse of these participatory opportunities is a result of the
interactions between a few interested strategic actors – such as interest group
leaders, vote contractors, and the competing candidates – and a largely passive
and uninterested public. Many party members do not join a party at their own
initiative, but rather are mobilized by these few strategic actors.[8]

---

[8] An interesting counterexample, showing what party membership could be like in the off-years
when there are no primaries and the "hard core" of party members is what remains, can be seen in a
survey conducted in Israel (Citizens' Empowerment Center in Israel 2007). In 2007, when the Likud
Party did not have primaries, its party members responded that 50% of them had been members for over
a decade; 77% were sure they would remain members; their reasons for joining were mainly due to
identification with the party platform and to advance certain public policies, while support for a
particular candidate was far behind.

Von Beyme (1996: 147) called parties in the postmodern era "omnibus parties," where "people enter the vehicle, are carried for a while and drop out when they do not see any reason to go further." This concept is carried even further in the case of party primaries. Kitschelt (1988: 130) encapsulated the major points of our argument when he claimed, "The very emphasis on individualist, participatory norms and ideologies is likely to create unexpected perverse effects in the parties' behavior, such as a lack of activists' commitment to party work, high turnover, and the rise of informal party elites." Candidate selection in an inclusive selectorate may thus become a personal enterprise rather than a partisan matter, an enterprise of instant members recruited by individual politicians, and not one of attracting new active members. When parties do not make a serious effort to control registration, and prefer to focus on recruiting more members than any other party – what Scarrow (1994: 46) calls to "improve membership statistics" – the demonstration of their public "credibility" could prove to have perverse long term political consequences.

## WHAT CAN BE DONE?

Various solutions can be suggested for the problems of membership quality that stem from the adoption of party primaries. The first is to adopt the logic of "if you can't beat them, join them," implying a further opening of the parties, which would enable even nonpartisans to participate in party events, such as policy decisions and candidate selection (Poguntke 1992). In this case, increased participation is seen as an end in itself, with no aspirations for enhancing the power of parties as collective associations. As Dalton (2008) argues, we may have less participation per event, but more participatory events. This direction could lead to the Americanization of politics – parties becoming arenas, rather than associations with a substance of their own.

Another solution (Teorell 1999) might be to reject the participatory democracy model as too demanding (and maybe too naïve), leaving no room for the choice not to participate. Instead, parties should adopt the model of deliberative democracy – a model that does not reject representative government, yet suggests adding aspects that the "competitive model" lacks and that go beyond the electoral process. Leaders, members, and supporters would be linked by a deliberative poll – for example, a statistically representative sample of supporters would deliberate with party leaders on policy issues, and a statistically representative sample of members would deliberate on candidate selection. This recommendation seems to solve the problems of quantity versus quality and free-riding, yet is prone to many other problems. The bias of group thinking and the problem of legitimizing the poll in the eyes of most citizens, who never learned the basic rules of statistical probability, are just two such problems.

Other, less sweeping solutions suggested in the literature, or through the experience of parties, include the freezing of membership when the selection process begins (Lovenduski and Norris 1994; Norris and Lovenduski 1995, a step taken by British Labour the Welsh Plaid Cymru).[9] The Canadian New Democratic Party closed registration ninety days before selection, not twenty-one days before (and sometimes even less than that) like the Liberals and Conservatives (Cross 2006). In the Belgian Social Christian Party, candidate selection was open to those who were members for at least one year (Obler 1970). The Irish Fine Gael also limited the right to participate in candidate selection to members who registered at least a year before the selection took place (Galligan 2003). The Progressive Democrats in Taiwan reduced the weight of the members' votes to offset problems of massive membership enlistment and the paying of membership dues by the candidates (Fell 2005). Mair (1987) and Farrell (1994) described a process of centralization of candidate selection in Ireland, in order to offset manipulation and inflation of membership numbers. Over eighty years ago, Merriam and Overacker (1928: 6) poignantly stated the following about the pathologies of a more inclusive selectorate. "In short, the primary election, having become one of the most important steps in the process of government, was open to every abuse that unscrupulous men, dazzled by prospects of almost incredible wealth and dictatorial power, could devise and execute." Following this, they proposed a list of specific recommendations aimed at solving the problems of the American primaries through state legislation.

Our suggestion, which we elaborate in Chapter 10, is to enable the various circles of participation in the party to take part in intraparty politics – that is, meaningful participation should be granted to rank-and-file members – but to maintain a structure of intraparty selective incentives at the same time. In the case of candidate selection, this could be achieved as long as parties involve several party agencies in the process, in a multistaged method, granting the more exclusive circles the ability to screen candidates but giving members the right to decide between a few viable options. This is the current tendency in many European parties, for example in the British parties. It may not save them from a decline in the number of members, nor from some of the pathologies of primaries that were mentioned earlier in this chapter, but it seems to provide an optimal balance between wider participation and the needs of the party as a voluntary association, and to somewhat weaken some of the incentives for misbehavior that are encouraged by pure primaries (Rahat 2009).

---

[9] The rule that determines the freezing of membership in the selectorate when a contest is announced can give an advantage to a retired incumbent in deciding his or her inheritor. That is, incumbents can recruit selectors before they officially announce their resignation (Back and Solomos 1994).

In short, before going too far with the opening up of candidate selection, one should ask whether positive intentions concerning participatory democracy can lead to the demise of meaningful, qualitative participation. In addition, one should inquire whether a more inclusive selectorate has an impact on other aspects of party politics, such as representation, competition, and responsiveness. These issues are the focus of the following chapters.

# 7

# Representation

If there is an agreement in the political philosophy and political theory literature concerning the interpretation of the concept of representation, it is about the multiplicity of its meanings. These meanings are not only different, but at times can even be contradictory. For example, there is the classical and well-known distinction between the notion of the representative as a delegate versus a trustee (Pennock 1968), known also as the mandate/independence controversy (Birch 1993). Beyond these classical notions, scholars have added almost endless distinctions between types of representation. This multiplicity is described as stemming from different philosophical approaches (Birch 1971) and from the historical evolution of the concept (Manin 1997).

In the framework of these theoretical distinctions, the notion of representation as a reflection of society, that is, as representing a microcosm of it (Birch 1993), is only one of several. However, when dealing with representation empirically, rather than theoretically – in the context of recruitment and electoral studies – the notion of representation that is used almost universally and uniformly is that of reflecting the demographic composition of society (or, in the case of parties, reflecting the demographic composition of their voter groups). In the recruitment literature, an institution is considered more representative if it reflects society in terms of gender, class, education, ethnicity, religion, etc. (Best and Cotta 2000b; Norris and Lovenduski 1995; Norris 2006; Patzelt 1999; Putnam 1976). In the electoral studies literature, an electoral system is seen as more representative if it more accurately translates votes into seats – the closer the proportion of votes is to the proportion of seats, the more "representative" the electoral system is considered to be (Gallagher 1991; Lijphart 1985, 1994; Loosemore and Hanby 1971; Rae 1967; Riedwyl and Steiner 1995; Taagepera and Shugart 1989). Studies of recruitment also identify a connection between demographic representation and the type of electoral system that is used. Women's representation was found to be higher in parliaments that were elected by proportional electoral systems than in those parliaments elected by majoritarian systems (Kittilson 2006; Kunovich and Paxton 2005; Matland 2005). However, even parliaments that are proportionally elected are unrepresentative in demographic terms, which leads to the question: Are the parties that select candidates from a large pool of aspirants responsible for this phenomenon?

Because it is party affiliation that influences the voters and gives them a strong cue concerning whom they should vote for – even when the electoral system is highly personal – the decision of the party selectorate(s) concerning who will be the party representative in a realistic seat or list position is often the decisive one. Scholars acknowledge the role of parties in influencing representation, specifically their role in reducing the candidate pool from all (party eligible) aspirants to only the party candidates. Yet, the treatment of candidate selection methods in such studies is rather simplistic. Some who bypass the problem of the lack of accessible data tend to address candidate selection indirectly by linking the nature of the electoral system to the kind of candidate selection method that is in use (Matland and Studlar 1996), thereby overlooking the possibility that the intraparty arenas of competition may independently vary across countries, parties, and time. Others treat candidate selection as an expression of the centralized/ decentralized party structure (Kittilson 2006), and thus ignore the possible consequences of the different dimensions that distinguish between candidate selection methods.

The nature of candidate selection methods is, of course, not the only factor that influences representation, nor is it necessarily the central one. Other factors, as shown by studies of women's representation, may also influence it, such as the low supply of women candidates (Norris and Lovenduski 1993; Shepherd-Robinson and Lovenduski 2002), the financial costs of running a campaign (Cross 2004), or increased primary competition (Lawless and Pearson 2008). Yet even these factors can be linked to the properties of candidate selection methods. The low supply of women may stem from their assessment that a specific method does not give them a fair chance to win, while financial costs are clearly influenced by the level of inclusiveness of the method – the more selectors there are, the more costly an effective campaign will be.

This chapter assesses how responsible the parties' candidate selection process is for representation by analyzing the links between the various aspects that delineate candidate selection methods and representation. It argues that the various dimensions of candidate selection can each have an impact on different aspects of representation. The first section examines representation from a theoretical perspective, links it to the study of candidate selection, raises several methodological issues, and presents two representation indices that are available for cross-national comparative research of party-level representation. Then, the chapter assesses the relationship between each of the four dimensions of candidate selection and representation: the obstacles raised by candidacy requirements, the inclusiveness of the selectorate and the representation of ideas and of presence, the social and territorial tradeoffs resulting from the decentralization of candidate selection, and the nature of the appointment/voting system vis-à-vis representation. Whenever sufficient data are unavailable, we present the little available empirical data. When even this is impossible, we suggest theoretical propositions. The final section discusses the dilemma for those parties that aspire to be both inclusive and representative at the same time.


## REPRESENTATION(S) – THEORETICAL AND METHODOLOGICAL ISSUES

A perspective of representation that is relevant for our study is that of the representation of ideas versus representation as presence. The representation of ideas, as described by Pitkin (1976), sees representatives as reflecting the political beliefs of their voters. Representatives are responsive to their constituents when they support policies that are consistent with the platform on which they were elected. The drawback here is that the representatives do not have to be anything like their constituents. They could be all male, all white, all members of the elite – as long as they act in accordance with a specific set of ideas.

This drawback may be overcome by viewing representation as presence, focusing not on ideas but on descriptive characteristics. In other words, what is important according to this perspective is not what is being represented, but the social identity of the representative. From Lijphart's (1969, 1977) works on consociational democracy, in which stability is said to be attained by guaranteeing a presence for all significant subgroups within society, to Phillips' (1995) comprehensive argument for the politics of presence, this view of representation sees the presence of a representative from a particular group as a crucial element that must be considered in any calculation of representation.

If the representation of ideas could lead to a group of representatives who are quite distinct from their voters, then representation as presence could result in a group of representatives who are unaccountable. If voters choose representatives because of who they are – according to their race, gender, religion, etc. – without an indication of how they are likely to act on the most important issues, then how can accountability be maintained? As Phillips (1995: 24–5) declared:

> While the politics of ideas is an inadequate vehicle for dealing with political exclusion, there is little to be gained by simply switching to the politics of presence. Taken in isolation, the weaknesses of one are as dramatic as the failings of the other. Most of the problems, indeed, arise when these two are set up as exclusionary opposites: when ideas are treated as totally separate from the people who carry them; or when the people dominate attention, with no thought given to their policies and ideas.

Since neither view is truly sufficient, what is needed is a combination of both. Only in the interplay between the representation of ideas and representation as presence will the party become a more representative body, in a politically meaningful way.

We can see expressions of these kinds of representation at the interparty level. Aggregative parties attempt to represent various ideological currents and identities within their ranks, while typical sectarian parties stand for a specific identity (and sometimes also a resulting unitary ideology). In general terms, representation within parties may coincide with notions of representation among parties. That is, both kinds of representation are relevant to candidate selection because parties – in their attempts to address the electorate and to control, or at least regulate, intraparty conflicts – are likely to try to balance their lists of candidates in terms of both notions of representation. A party could strive to have candidates who hold a range of ideological stands that the party claims to represent (representation of ideas) and also a range of identities that the party thinks should be represented (representation as presence). In some parties it is important to give representation to ideological currents (usually defined as the "left" and "right" wings of the party), while in others identity will be seen as central. There are some identities that are important in almost all parties, like gender, and there are identities that have to do with the particular character of the party. A left-wing party may grant more significance to having blue-collar candidates, while right-wing parties may consider it important to have businessmen as their candidates. While the representation of minorities seems to interest many parties around the globe, the identity of these minorities reflects a specific societal context. Furthermore, particular parties may believe that certain nuances are more important than others – aspects that other parties tend to ignore. For example, Shas, an ultra-religious Israeli party, is unrepresentative of its voters in terms of gender and religiosity – it has no women on its list of candidates and its candidates are much more religious than its voters. On the other hand, it is highly representative of the different streams within the ethnic group it claims to represent, and appoints candidates with different backgrounds to realistic positions.

The complexity of the notion of representation and the problems of its assessment are clearly exhibited in its operationalization. First, most studies tend to use representation as presence because it is the cheaper, easier, and more accessible way to operationalize the concept. It is easier to count men and women than to assess the ideological position of each representative. Limited by what the existing literature offers, the lion's share of this chapter is dedicated to representation as presence. Second, because representation as presence is sensitive to national and even intraparty political culture, it is hard to conduct a cross-national comparison, except for the almost universal case of women's representation – and that is what is usually done. Third, when one wants to analyze the influence of candidate selection methods on representation, it is important to look at realistic candidacies rather than at the composition of parliament – which is influenced by electoral results and not only by the selection results. A few studies go beyond looking at the composition of parliaments to analyze the composition of the pool of candidates (Holland 1987; Norris and Lovenduski 1993, 1995). Fourth, when estimating representation, there is a need not only to distinguish realistic candidacies from token candidacies, but also to find a way to measure their relative strength. That is, a list of twenty candidates in which women occupy positions 11–20 is clearly less representative than a list in which women occupy all odd or even positions (Hazan and Rahat 2006; Rahat, Hazan, and Katz 2008).

There are numerous studies which have shown that members of the legislature do not accurately reflect their society in terms of gender, race, religion, education, socioeconomic status, etc. (e.g. see: Putnam 1976; Best and Cotta 2000*b*; Gallagher, Laver, and Mair 2006). There are very few studies, however, devoted to how candidate selection methods affect representation. This chapter aims at filling this gap.

## *Operationalizing intraparty representation*

In order to operationalize representation in candidate selection, we developed two indices designed to measure the level of representation in parties that compete in list electoral systems (Hazan and Rahat 2006). They are sensitive to differences in party size, provide reasonable operational definitions for representation in list systems, and allow for adding data in a weighted manner so as to address parties of different sizes. They can also be used in the case of single-member districts, and can thus serve as useful tools for cross-national comparison.

Our two indices of representativeness take the representation of women as an indicator of the representativeness of the candidate list. The first index relates to the proportion of women in realistic positions on the party list. This is done by measuring the share of women out of the total number of the party's realistic candidates, not those who appear on the list as a whole. The second measure also relates only to realistic positions, but unlike the first takes into account the relative position of women on the list, giving a higher value to higher positions on the party list.

The index of representation (IR) simply calculates the percentage of women in realistic positions on the party list by counting the number of women in realistic positions divided by the number of realistic positions, multiplied by 100. The formula is:

$$\text{IR} = \frac{\sum Wrp}{\sum Rp} \times 100$$

*Wrp* is the number of women in positions equal or higher in rank to the number of realistic positions.

*Rp* is the number of realistic positions (which we defined earlier as the number of seats the party won in the previous election).

An example of the index of representation – in a single selection event – is as follows: Party A won 5 seats in the previous election; women appear in the third and fifth positions in the candidate list for the elections for the next parliament; the index of representation is thus $2/5 \times 100 = 40\%$.

Like the index above, the weighted index of representation (WIR) counts the number of women in realistic positions, but this time takes into consideration their relative positioning. Higher values are given to higher positions on the list. Thus, each position on the list, up to the number of realistic positions, is given a value in descending order – the last position is given one point and each higher one merits an additional point. The formula is:

$$\text{WIR} = \frac{\sum \left[ \left( \frac{Wp}{Vpi} \right) \times Rp \right]}{\sum Rp} \times 100$$

*Wp* stands for the value of the positions won by women in each selection event.
*Vpi* stands for the total value of the positions in the specific selection event.
*Rp* stands for the number of realistic positions available in each selection event.

The example of the weighted index of representation – in a single selection event – is based on the data given in the previous example: First, the sum of values of the positions on the list is calculated. The total value of the list is 5 (for first position) + 4 (for second position) + 3 (for third position) + 2 (for fourth position) + 1 (for fifth position) = 15. Women won position 3 on the list with a value of 3, and position 5 on the list with a value of 1. The sum of these values is $3 + 1 = 4$. The weighted index of representation is thus $4/15 \times 100 = 26.7\%$.

## CANDIDACY REQUIREMENTS AND REPRESENTATION: OBSTACLES AND BARRIERS

The political consequences of candidacy requirements for representation within parties is a topic that has yet to be addressed, and thus our arguments can only be tentative in nature. In the chapter on candidacy, we outlined several common requirements that are imposed by numerous political parties, all of which serve as barriers for potential candidates. Each one of these requirements restricts the possible pool of candidates and thus offsets the possibility that a party will accurately represent the electorate in general, and its voters in particular. For example, a maximum age requirement will exclude the representation of older voters, a membership period of a year or two will hurt the representation of those members who have recently joined the party, a substantial monetary deposit could eliminate the representation of the lower classes, etc. While each requirement above – and the level set by the party – could serve a specific purpose, they will likely impact negatively on representation as presence.

More exclusive candidacy requirements reflect an attempt by the party to control the supply side of potential candidates. This may be due to a desire to maintain party cohesion, so that those who fulfill the enhanced eligibility criteria – and are subsequently both selected and elected – will behave according to party dictates once in office. A party with exclusive candidacy requirements can arrive in office as a cohesive unit, manifesting a patent party culture. But this attempt to ensure party-centered representation might bias representation as presence. Demands for a background of long-time party activity – which can be seen as a sign of loyalty and dedication – obviously work against younger aspirants, who will find it more difficult to prove such a lengthy record. Women and lower-class aspirants may also be hurt if their time resources are lower than those of middle-class men (Norris and Lovenduski 1995, 1997).

If a party adopts more inclusive candidacy requirements – or erases them altogether – where every voter can stand as a party candidate, the party has little to no influence as a gatekeeper for potential candidates. In other words, aspirants for office practically impose themselves on the party, which must accept their candidacy. While this appears to remove the barriers of representation concerning candidacy, it does raise other obstacles that can affect the level of representation. For example, the United States displays some of the most highly inclusive candidate requirements, and as a result politics there have been described as candidate-centered (Wattenberg 1991). Open candidacy has, in turn, brought about an ever-increasing role for financial supporters of prospective candidates, which has negatively influenced the representation of several social groups in American politics. Thus, formal, explicit candidacy requirements can be seen as an attempt to regulate the supply side of recruitment, which has its own biases when there is no such regulation.

Norris (1997*a*, 1997*b*), Patzelt (1999), Best and Cotta (2000*b*), Gallagher, Laver, and Mair (2006), and other scholars found that in most parties the incumbents are not representative of their parties' voters. This means that in order to create a more representative group of party candidates, some incumbents must be replaced by new candidates from those social groups that are underrepresented. Once the obstacle of an existing incumbent is removed, the barrier to representation can be more easily overcome. For example, Burrell (1992) found that in the primaries for the US House of Representatives between 1968 and 1990, women did just as well as men when there was no incumbent candidate.

Thus, a party's treatment of incumbency may also affect representation. It is much harder to transform an unrepresentative group of candidates into a more representative one if incumbents are easily and constantly reselected; it is easier to do so when there is higher, party-controlled turnover. Candidacy requirements, such as automatic renomination, can ease the reselection of candidates, or they can be neutral vis-à-vis incumbents, in which case they will likely continue to limit the ability of the party to enhance representation. Candidacy requirements can also work against incumbents, the best example being term limits, which artificially open up positions or constituencies that can be filled by more representative candidates – but this is not a necessary outcome, and may at times work to the contrary.

A party that offers its incumbents almost automatic candidacy for upcoming elections evidently wants to win those elections – incumbents have already proven their electoral potential. Also, since incumbents already have a base of support in their party or in their constituency, parties – wanting to avoid internal conflict on the eve of a general election – will refrain from exposing their incumbents to internal challenges. This is especially true for candidacies in single-member districts, but also for candidates in multimember districts where the electoral systems in use encourage personal voting (open ballots, single transferable vote, or single nontransferable vote). On the other hand, a party may place restrictions on incumbents in order to ensure some turnover – as is the case with term limits or demanding that an incumbent's candidacy be ratified by a special majority. Such an attempt might be made in order to prevent the creation of an autonomous power center by the party in government, and to keep power in the hands of the extra-parliamentary party. Restrictions on incumbents can also be adopted in order to create opportunities for improving representation. Incumbency can be a major obstacle for parties that are concerned with enhancing representation, and they can cope with this by encouraging turnover. Whatever the intention is, higher turnover creates opportunities to enhance representation.

Parties react in different ways to the dilemma of choosing between incumbency and representation. In general, it seems that the clash between these two is more apparent in single-member districts than in list systems. That is, enhancing women's representation by pushing a male incumbent one position down the list is easier than mandating a woman candidate in a single-member district with an incumbent man. One case in point is France, where the adoption of quotas through legislation failed to lead to a large increase in women's representation at the national level – where single-member districts are in use – but did significantly increase their representation at the local level – where list systems are employed (Murray 2007). Quotas were also effective at the national level in Belgium, where a list PR system is in use (Meier 2004). In Britain, the Labour Party chose to bypass this issue by sticking with its incumbents, but ran all-women shortlists in about one-half of the open seats for the 1997 and 2005 elections (Criddle 1997; Cutts, Childs, and Fieldhouse 2008).

The use of the concepts "closed seat" (a district where an incumbent tries to get reelected) and "open seat" (a district where the incumbent does not compete) in countries that use single-member districts illustrates the preferred status of incumbents. There is no parallel notion of "open" or "closed" position(s) when it comes to party lists. Indeed, incumbents are less safe in list systems (Matland and Studlar 2004). In such systems, incumbents sometimes even face restrictions or rules that place additional requirements on their reselection. In list systems there is more room for maneuver, and representation can be increased significantly without "directly" challenging incumbents. Yet, incumbent men can still lose their safe position if significant gender quotas or zipping – women in every other position – are adopted. This, in turn, leads to struggles over the magnitude of the quotas. Thus, the issue in countries where there are list systems is not that of candidacy requirements (the treatment of incumbents), but rather what we call the level of (social) decentralization. In Israel, for example, incumbent men in both Labor and Likud successfully guarded their interests when most positions that were allotted in the name of representation (territorial or social) – those likely to be taken by newcomers – were not at the top of the list.

It seems that in both single-member districts and list systems, incumbents do not pay the price for the underrepresentation of social groups; it is usually newcomers who have to compete within the confines of the need for representation. Thus, while representation is an ideal to which parties may aspire, its magnitude is often a result of a down-to-earth struggle between incumbents with vested interests in the existing system and newcomers whose interest is to change the rules of the game – concerning candidacy but also other aspects of the selection method – so that they can make room for themselves.

## INCLUSIVENESS AND REPRESENTATION: NEGATIVE FOR PRESENCE, NONLINEAR FOR IDEOLOGY

Smaller, exclusive selectorates are more capable of balancing representation, in both senses (ideas and presence). As Matland (1993:740) puts it, "The power to actually balance the ticket is greater in systems where the nomination process is much more closed than the very open process found in the United States." When selection can be controlled by a party oligarchy that appoints candidates – and to a lesser extent, when voting takes place in a party agency and can be somewhat coordinated – there are more chances that representatives of different social groups (women, minorities, etc.) and ideological currents within the party will capture realistic positions on the party list, or realistic constituency seats. However, when parties allow their members or supporters to produce the list of candidates, the result could be unrepresentative lists, because such a vast selectorate cannot be coordinated or instructed to select a socially (or ideologically) representative group of candidates.

When the parties in Taiwan moved to more inclusive primaries, one of the first problems they encountered was the lack of representation of the various intraparty groups among the selected candidates (Fell 2005). In Iceland, the People's Alliance increased the representation of women from the 1970s, but when it adopted primaries to select its candidates it could no longer do this – that is, the more inclusive primaries became a barrier for the representation of women (Kristjánsson 1998). In Israel – which had one of the highest levels of women's representation in the world in the 1950s – the adoption of more inclusive candidate selection methods over the years decreased the ability of parties to ensure sufficient representation for women. It now has one the lowest levels of women's representation among the established democracies (Rahat, Hazan, and Katz 2008).

The parties themselves, by their behavior, appear to validate the claim that inclusiveness can harm representation. The process of democratization of candidate selection methods in Western Europe took place parallel to increases in the use of representation correction mechanisms. Parties increasingly tend to restrict the choices of their more inclusive selectorates in order to ensure representation, particularly when it is defined as presence and concerns the representation of women. As Norris (2006:106) put it:

> Grassroots members in many European parties have gradually been given greater opportunities to nominate candidates. At the same time selectors are operating within a more constrained scope of decision-making, due to the simultaneous adoption of rules implementing positive action strategies. A wider number of members are therefore able to engage in selection decisions, but they face a more restricted range of choices.

The Dutch Democrates 66, for example, allowed its members a direct role in candidate selection, and as a result produced unrepresentative lists. This led, in 1986, to the formation of a committee that produced a recommended list of candidates for the members. This committee took into consideration several of the candidates' attributes, from social background to media appeal, and produced a more representative list. These candidate lists were usually approved with few changes (Andeweg and Irwin 2002). The Belgian Social Christian Party became disenchanted with inclusive party primaries due to their inability to produce balanced lists of candidates, and its leadership subsequently tried to avoid using them (Obler 1970). In Finland, the same logic of balancing inclusiveness with representation was apparent in the law that both determined that party members would select the candidates and also allowed the party organization in the district to alter one-quarter of the list selected through primaries. Indeed, this type of intervention is often used in order to create a more representative list of candidates (Helander 1997; Kuitunen 2002). According to Narud and Valen (2008), the Norwegian parties' use of exclusive candidate selection methods – which allow the parties to control the process – enabled them to produce more representative candidacies than most other parties elsewhere. An interesting case is Mexico, where in 2002 a law was passed that 30 percent of candidates must be women, unless the party holds primaries to select its candidates (Baldez 2007). This law apparently saw a tradeoff between inclusive participation and representation, and allowed the parties to choose for themselves which principle was more important to them.

The implementation of more inclusive candidate selection methods in large voting entities requires a strengthening of the corrective mechanisms concerning representation of women, other social groups, and geographical peripheries (in the case of multimember districts). From the liberal perspective there is a problem when an advantage is given to the group over the individual (Htun 2004), and the advocates of a free market are also not fond of such mechanisms. Yet, the use of representation correction mechanisms seems to be a norm that has spread, being adopted also by center and right-wing parties, and even at the national level as a norm that obliges all parties. If we adopt the stand that intraparty democracy is not only about enhanced participation, then we should see representation correction mechanisms as a must in those cases where enhanced, inclusive participation is attempted.

There is not much research – beyond the US case of highly inclusive primary systems – when it comes to the relationship between the representation of ideas and the inclusiveness of the candidate selection method. The only research we encountered regarding this relationship outside the United States (Mikulska and Scarrow 2008) found that more open selection methods in the United Kingdom created more congruence between the candidates and their voters on the most salient electoral issue concerning the economy. However, studies of the US primary systems found that this aspect of the relationship between inclusiveness and representation is not linear. When candidate selection is at its most inclusive pole, such as in nonparty and blanket primaries, candidates will pursue positions closer to the median voter (Persily 2001). In somewhat less inclusive methods, such as open primaries, the candidates will be more ideological, due to the likely participation of more principled and strategic voters from outside the party. In more restrictive closed primaries, candidates will be less extreme than in open primaries, but not as moderate as in the semi-open primaries (Kanthak and Morton 2001).

It is very likely that when we move toward the middle of the inclusiveness–exclusiveness dimension, the nonlinear relationship with the representation of ideas will continue. Candidates chosen by party members will be less ideological than those chosen by selected party delegates, for whom loyalty to the party and cohesiveness in office are important concerns (Scarrow 2005). Candidates chosen by the party elite will, in turn, be more ideological than those selected by the party leader, for whom personal loyalty is paramount. These propositions, while theoretically sound, must still be checked empirically.

Scholars tend to analyze, and politicians tend to address, the visible and more easily recognizable distortions of representation as presence, while putting aside the harder to analyze and more complicated representation of ideas. When it comes to representation as presence, the negative relationship is not "accepted" but rather tackled by using correction mechanisms that are designed to deal with the imbalance created by increased participation. Those few who bother to address the relationship between inclusiveness and the representation of ideas usually see it as a byproduct of the system – not as something that can or should be fixed, but rather as something that can vary with changes in the levels of inclusiveness of the selectorate.

## DECENTRALIZATION AND REPRESENTATION: SOCIAL AND TERRITORIAL TRADEOFFS

The decentralization of candidate selection, as defined in this study, can be social or territorial. We analyze each, in turn, vis-à-vis represention. We end this section by addressing the problematic relationship between these two elements – the tradeoffs between social and territorial representation.

As already mentioned in the discussion of inclusiveness, there is a negative relationship between enlarging the selectorate and the resulting representation of different social groups. This tradeoff produces an imbalance that has been rectified, at least partially, by the parties' instituting representation correction mechanisms such as quotas and reserved seats (Dahlerup 2006; Kittilson 2006; Krook 2009; Mateo-Diaz 2005; Tremblay 2008). Factors like party ideology and the power of intraparty groups affect the existence and the scope of these corrective representation mechanisms for the various groups. Moreover, a major factor in deciding to adopt such mechanisms is the electoral appeal that is attributed to the presence of these representatives. Parties tend to ensure representation when it is electorally beneficial, or when they are convinced that ignoring such demands could cost them voter support. Intraparty group demands that are not perceived to be electorally advantageous are often rejected, or answered by symbolic gestures such as allotting them an unrealistic position on a list or a seat in a district with no chance of victory for the party.

In any case, a price (arguably worthwhile) is paid because there is a tradeoff between more inclusive participation and representation. Yet, the very cause of representation might be damaged as a result of unwise use of corrective mechanisms, specifically, mechanisms that may damage the image of those whose representation is being corrected (Bacchi 2005). This is especially likely to occur when small quotas are used for a long period of time. In such a situation, the quota may become a mechanism to ensure the reselection of a specific person, rather than the representation of a social group. Moreover, candidates from the group whose representation was guaranteed will focus their competition on the few positions allotted. If the group competes amongst its own members, each candidate will ask selectors not only for their support but also to refrain from supporting other representatives of the group – in order to increase his or her chances of winning.

In that case – a likely development when quotas are small – the group will gain less votes and there will be an increased need to use corrective measures. The correction mechanism can thus be damaging because it leads to the segregation rather than to the integration of the social group that it is meant to promote. This can perpetuate the group's "competitive inferiority" – which was the rationale for adopting these mechanisms in the first place. A wise use of generous and/or gradually increasing quotas for a predetermined period of time might help over-come this problem.

Territorial decentralization has a positive relationship with territorial represen-tation. If more power in the candidate selection process is given to the regional and/or the local selectorates, at the expense of the national party organization, the likely result will be more candidates chosen who represent the regional and the local levels. They can be seen as territorially representative because they live and run their life in the specific location, or simply because they were selected by a regional or local selectorate.

One should keep in mind that the mere fact that candidate selection is decen-tralized does not mean that interests at a lower level – which also have to be balanced – will necessarily be fewer than those at a higher level. Party officials within the constituency also have to take into account the different groups within the party, and they have many fewer candidacies to play with – and only one in the case of single-member districts.

The most territorially decentralized systems, especially those that produce a single candidate, may achieve optimal representation for the locality, but it will be harder to promote social representation. As Matland and Studlar (1996: 709) argued:

> Centralized control over nominations means that party elites can increase the number of viable women candidates in response to pressure for greater representation. Most single-member district systems tend to have decentra-lized nomination structures; because of this central party organs wanting to increase representation have considerable difficulties in getting their wishes carried out at the local level.

Indeed, in her cross-national comparative study, Kittilson (2006) found that higher women's representation positively correlates with centralized parties. In Germany, for example, since 1953, the ratio of women elected in the constituencies (selected by the more decentralized selectorates) to those elected from party lists (selected by the more centralized selectorates) has varied from 1:3.5 in 1965 to 1:6.5 in 1972 (Roberts 1988: 109).

In Ireland's decentralized system, territorial local representation takes prece-dence over other types of representation, even within the small multimember districts that are used in the general elections. Even where the main parties can choose more than a single candidate to run in the multimember constituencies, the only attempt made to balance the selected candidates is in terms of territorial district interests, rather than according to gender, age, or socioeconomic status (Gallagher 2003; Marsh 2005). The result is that decisions made at these lower levels are independent and do not accumulate to produce a socially representative group of candidates overall, as evident from looking at the low level of women's representation in Ireland.

There is a problem of coordination between the demands and needs of territorial and social decentralization, which can develop into intraparty conflict. This problem is illustrated by the failure of British Labour to coordinate in the 1970s and 1980s for the purpose of increasing women's representation (Denver 1988), and the conflicts between the national center and the local organizations in the 1990s over the implementation of women's representation mechanisms (Mitchell and Bradbury 2004; Quinn 2004). The decentralized selection process used in the Canadian parties was an obstacle to both female and minority candidates in the parties' attempts to increase their representation (O'Brien 1993) and they were able to advance only a limited number of female candidates in vacant constituencies, mainly due to pressure from the national party organization (Cross 2006). This conflict can occur not only in single-member districts, but also in larger districts when the local party has other preferences, or when it feels that its autonomy is affected by the national headquarters' demands for social representation (Valen, Narud, and Skare 2002). In short, the almost unavoidable inherent tension between the interests and values of the local and the national levels is sometimes expressed by conflicts over social representation. The attempt to impose representation correction mechanisms on the lower levels implies some recentralization of the national party's power in the candidate selection process.

Social representation can be ensured by using centralized and exclusive selectorates. For example, the greatest representation of women in Chilean parties in the 2004 local elections was in the most conservative party, the Independent Democratic Union, which used a centralized and exclusive candidate selection method; somewhat lower female representation was achieved in another right-wing party, the National Renewal, which used a decentralized but exclusive selection method. A relatively low number of women were selected in the center and left-wing parties that used decentralized and inclusive methods (Hinojosa 2009). However, while centralization (like exclusiveness) means that that there is more *potential* to ensure social representation, it does not necessarily lead in every case to such as a result (Ware 1996).

Centralization (like exclusiveness) provides opportunities to enhance representation, yet there is still a need to motivate forces within the party to press for the use of these opportunities. In those parties where there are high levels of exclusiveness and centralization, cohesion is also likely to be high, and pressure for representation is less likely to originate from within the party. What might motivate the party elite to address representation are electoral considerations. In those parties where there are high levels of decentralization and inclusiveness, it is more likely that internal pressure for representation will be stronger, but the ability to respond to it will be lower. Correction mechanisms are likely to be the answer in such a scenario. Matland's (1993: 753) account of the high levels of women's representation in Norway identifies an optimal balance between these two options:

> The system of county nomination meetings is sufficiently open to allow organized interests to enter. At the same time the system is sufficiently closed and small enough that a cohesive, well-organized interest can have substantial influence on the choice of candidates, even if they only represent an intense minority within the population as a whole.

## APPOINTMENT OR VOTING AND REPRESENTATION: MECHANISMS AND PREFERENCES

Appointments give the (necessarily exclusive) selectorate the greatest ability to coordinate candidacies and thus to balance representation among different social groups and intraparty (personal and ideological) factions. The output, however, is dependent upon the will of the selectorate (and the pressures on it), as is the case with more exclusive and centralized methods. In those parties where only some candidates are appointed, if the bulk of the candidates selected by a voting system end up being unrepresentative, the remaining appointed candidates can help to balance the overall outcome. Recently, the Canadian New Democratic Party appointed several women, specifically in constituencies where an incumbent party representative had retired, in its attempt to balance representation (Cross 2006).[1] The leader of the Liberal Party also used his powers to appoint several women candidates (Carty and Eagles 2003; Erickson 1997).

Some parties use appointments to increase their appeal to groups outside the party; that is, to project a wider ideological image. In the late 1970s and early 1980s, the Spanish Communist Party appointed candidates from other left-wing parties, and from trade unions, in order to bolster its image (Esteban and Guerra 1985). The Italian Communist Party did the same when it added leftist independents to its candidate lists (Wertman 1988). In Belgium, the leader of the Liberal Party appointed religious candidates in order to change the image of the party and gain support beyond liberal, anticlerical voters (Obler 1973).

As we elaborated in previous chapters, candidate selection is often conducted by several selectorates. In a multistage system, one selectorate can use an appointment system while another may use a voting system, thereby producing a mixed

---

[1] According to Cross (2006), the local organization of the New Democratic Party had to convince the central party that it tried to find a candidate from an underrepresented group if it wanted to appoint someone who was either not a woman or not from a defined minority group.

appointment-voting system. The typical mix is that of starting with appointments by an exclusive selectorate and ending with voting by the more inclusive one. Such an order makes sense, since it is easier to gain democratic legitimacy for early screening than for a veto on the decisions of a more inclusive selectorate. Thus, processes that allow a small selectorate to appoint a list give the party more control over representation, yet give the more inclusive selectorate a chance to democratically legitimize the earlier coordinated process. In Norway, a nominating committee took into consideration the need to balance representation in terms of geography, gender, age, occupation, etc. in designing a recommended list. This recommendation was then voted on (Matthews and Valen 1999). German parties used appointments to the party list – which are ratified by a delegate convention – in order to compensate for the underrepresentation of specific groups among the constituency candidates (Kitzinger 1960; Loewenberg 1966). In Belgium, the use of the model list system meant the appointment of a list that was then ratified (or, rarely, rejected) by party members. The central office agencies of the British Labour and Conservative parties screen candidates; that is, exclusive centralized selectorates actually appoint candidates to a list, and then more inclusive and decentralized selectorates choose the candidates from this list using a voting system. Such systems might be conducive to representation because small selectorates, in order to legitimize their appointments, are likely to respond to the demands of groups within the party for representation (Matland 1993).

When it comes to the voting systems used to select the party candidates, the relationship with representation depends on the specific voting system. While appointment is clearly the easiest way to ensure representation, voting systems differ in terms of their results. The first distinction is between single-round and multi-round systems. The multi-round system – the gradual selection of realistic candidates – allows the selectorate some control over the composition of candidacies. If there is a problem of representation – there are not enough women/minorities/laborers – the multi-round system provides an opportunity to fix it. In a single-round system, all realistic candidacies are filled at once, so there is no chance to fix distortions.

The second distinction has to do with the proportionality of the voting system. A majoritarian voting system, where the number of votes is equal to the number of realistic candidacies, can allow the largest intraparty group to win all of the list positions, or all of the constituencies, and the result will not be representative of different groups within the party. A complete victory for the largest group can be mitigated if the voting rules are not plurality but majority (two-round, alternative, or elimination vote), unless the largest group actually holds a majority within the selectorate. While we do not have evidence of the influence of intraparty voting systems on representation, it would seem logical to argue that as in the case of electoral systems (Matland 2005), plurality and other majoritarian candidate selection methods are more likely to produce less representative party candidacies. That is, we expect social and factional representation to grow with proportionality – from the semi-majoritarian voting system, through the semi-proportional system, to the proportional one.

The choice of voting system can raise obstacles to the largest group's attaining all of the realistic positions. It does not, however, guarantee other aspects of representation. For example, a minority group could win realistic positions under more proportional selection methods, but could select a group of unrepresentative candidates in terms of presence, that is, white-collar, middle-aged, white men from the capital city. Overall representation – beyond possibly that of ideas, if it is ideology that divides the party groups – will be absent. Moreover, if the largest group is interested in advancing representation, adopting more proportional voting systems could actually offset this goal.

An additional factor can be the number of votes allotted to each selector. Matland (1993) found that at the interparty level, the larger the party district delegation is, the greater the representation of women in the district. In a "translation" of this finding to the intraparty arena, we expect that the number of votes for each selector will affect representation. The more votes each selector has, the more he or she is inclined to include representational considerations in voting calculations. Thus, multi-vote systems – whether they are majoritarian or proportional – could produce more representative candidacies than a single-vote system.

More representation can be achieved either through appointments or via a proportional selection method, but this is not necessarily the case. Appointing more representative candidates, or adopting a voting system that allows for a more representative outcome, are only mechanisms that *allow* for representation – they do not *guarantee* it. For more representative candidates to be appointed, representation has to be a significant preference for the party, and especially for its selectorate. The same is true for multi-round and multi-vote selection methods, in which representation can be balanced if this is indeed a priority for the selectorate.


## GUARANTEEING REPRESENTATION


Representation can be conceived in several ways: in terms of ideas; or in terms of presence and its different types – social or territorial. If any kind of representation is a *sine qua non* for a particular political party, then the party must take the necessary steps to guarantee that its candidates are indeed representative – at least of its voters if not of the entire population. Producing a more representative group of candidates can be facilitated by candidacy restrictions imposed by the party, because such barriers can be raised for some (overrepresented) groups and lowered for others. Representation is also connected to the inclusiveness of the selectorate, but not in a positive manner, and thus requires the adoption of correction mechanisms together with the democratization of the selection process. There are conflicting relationships between territorial representation and social representation, which could require some centralization in order to be balanced. Appointment systems, mixed appointment-voting systems, multi-round and multi-vote voting systems, and more proportional voting systems could help produce more representative candidacies than a mere majoritarian, one-round, single-vote selection. Yet, these are all mere mechanisms that can only work if representation is an important principle for the party, or is seen as an electoral asset, and if there are strong groups that promote the cause. Those advancing the principle of representation will have to struggle against the vested interests of most of the incumbents, along with those groups whose representation was already recognized and who have won their share of the representation pie.

The principle of representation presents an uneasy dilemma for democrats. If they opt for what seems to be intuitively a more democratic candidate selection method – an inclusive, decentralized method in which candidates compete for the secret votes of thousands of party members or even supporters – they might end up with the same old candidates, mostly white, upper-middle-class, educated men. Intraparty democracy has to be somewhat limited in order to achieve what they usually perceive as more democratic representation.

Similar to the element of participation, the principle of representation is also perceived as both necessary and positive in a truly democratic society. In order for these goals to be attained, it might be necessary for parties to involve several party agencies in the process, in a multistage method, granting the more exclusive circles the ability to balance candidacies but still giving members the right to decide between a few viable options (Rahat 2009). Opting for a simple, one-stage candidate selection method, removing candidacy requirements, opening up the selectorate, decentralizing, and implementing a pure voting system is unlikely to enable selectors to produce a representative outcome.

# 8

# Competition

In a democracy, we expect to see a free competition of interests, values, and also identities. Parties and candidates present themselves as the representatives of these interests, values, and identities, and from time to time compete with each other for the support of the voters. In the intraparty context, we expect to see competition among candidates for the support of the selectors – be it all voters, party members, party delegates, the party elite, or a single leader. We presume that intraparty competition is important for democracy, especially in those cases where interparty competition is weak – although it cannot serve as a sufficient substitute (Key 1954; Sartori 1976; Turner 1953). Competition – a situation when a plurality of alternatives is presented to the selectors from time to time – is expected to create responsiveness and accountability. That is, incumbents who face competition and who wish to be reselected are expected to be responsive to their selectors, and to be accountable for their actions.

While some competition is both necessary and positive, and no competition is bad for democracy, too much competition may also be problematic. If incumbents think that their efforts will not be rewarded by reselection, why should they bother investing any effort? Moreover, heavy competition might also enhance the importance of money in the campaign and increase the incentives for corrupt practices. High turnover can also affect the ability of the representatives to accumulate experience and thus function better in their legislative and executive posts (Somit et al. 1994). Yet, as a reading of Michels (1915) leads us to expect, it is much easier to identify cases of no and low intraparty competition than cases of excessive competition.

In order to explain what competition is in the context of candidate selection, this chapter will start with an examination of the ways that scholars have operationalized intraparty competition. We then assess the impact of candidate selection methods on competition, beginning with the influence of candidacy. This is followed by a search for evidence of the linkage between the level of inclusiveness of the selectorate and levels of competition. We then show that territorial decentralization is the main explanation for low competition within parties and also examine the impact of social decentralization. Next, we analyze the influences of appointment/voting systems and of multistage methods on levels of competitiveness. We then look into the impact of changing the candidate selection method itself on intraparty competition. We continue by examining the influence of intraparty competition on the fortunes of parties in general elections. The chapter ends with a short summary of what we know about intraparty competition.

## WHAT IS INTRAPARTY COMPETITION, AND HOW CAN IT BE MEASURED?

There are several ways to define intraparty competition between candidates. We start with the simplest distinction between those situations where there is no competition compared to those where competition exists. The definition of noncompetitive candidate selection is that the number of candidates is equal to the number of realistic positions (or lower, although we believe such a shortage is rare). For example, if a party has only a single candidate for a realistic seat in a single-member district, then there is no competition in candidate selection.

In countries with single-member districts – such as the United Kingdom, the United States, Canada, and Germany – there are often districts in which there is no intraparty competition, and scholars use the very occurrence of a contest – that is, having more than one candidate for the party's single seat candidacy – as one indication of competition (Ansolabehere et al. 2007; Borchert and Golsch 2003; Engstrom and Engstrom 2008; Erickson and Carty 1991; Erickson 1997; Norris and Lovenduski 1995; Porter 1995; Szabo 1977; Turner 1953). This lack of intraparty competition seems to apply also for countries in which single or few candidacies are produced in small multimember districts, such as Ireland (Weeks 2007) and Chile (Siavelis 2002, 2005).

When parties produce multiple candidacies for multimember districts, it is more likely that some level of competition exists. We surely have competition when the number of candidates is higher than the number of realistic positions. For example, if a party produces a list of ten candidates for a ten-member district where it can expect five realistic positions, we are likely to see competition – minimally among the incumbents for the higher and safer positions, but also between the weaker incumbents and the stronger challengers for the marginal positions. The case of multimember districts, though, is somewhat more complicated. For example, if a party holds seven seats in a multimember district, and there are only seven contestants, this is low competition rather than no competition. While all contestants will win a realistic position, it is still likely that they will seek to win a higher position on the list, which is safer and can also help them to promote their status within the party and, as a result, in government (Kenig and Barnea 2009). We should still look at the relationship between the number of realistic positions and the number of candidates, but the basic distinction per district will be between high and low competition rather than between competition and no competition, as is the case for single-member districts.

*Number of contestants*

One way to estimate the level of competition – which also distinguishes among those cases where there are more candidates than realistic seats or positions – is to focus on the supply side, examining how many actually ran for candidacy (Norris and Lovenduski 1995). This measure was used to estimate the level of competition in US primaries, for example, by looking at differences in competition between winnable and nonwinnable seats (Standing and Robinson 1958); to estimate the influence of incumbency on competition (Ansolabehere et al. 2007); and to compare contests between runoff primaries and contests in primaries where a plurality is sufficient to win (Glaser 2006).

Similar measures can be used for multicandidacies, assessing the ratio between the number of candidates and the number of realistic positions or the ratio between competing incumbents and newcomers. Such measures are the two aspirants indices (AI1 and AI2; see Hazan and Rahat 2006; Rahat, Hazan, and Katz 2008). The first aspirants index (AI1) divides the number of those who competed for a realistic position on the list (*Crp*) by the number of realistic positions (*RP*). The higher the value of the index, the more competitive the selection process is, which means that the number of competitors for each position is relatively high. The sensitivity of this index to the relative size of the pie in each selection event enables the accumulation of values for the whole population of selection events. The formula is:

$$\text{AI1} = \frac{\sum Crp}{\sum RP}$$

*Crp* stands for the number of candidates who competed for realistic positions.
*RP* stands for the number of realistic positions.
For example, in a single selection event, in party A 30 candidates are competing for 15 realistic positions on the list, and in party B 50 candidates are competing for 20 realistic positions on the list. The value of the first aspirants index for party A is $30/15 = 2$, while the value of this index for party B is $50/20 = 2.5$. Party B is more competitive in this respect.

The second aspirants index (AI2) examines how many nonincumbents were motivated to challenge incumbents by measuring the ratio between "insiders" and "outsiders" competing for realistic positions. The higher the index, the more newcomers were motivated to challenge incumbents. The formula is:

$$\text{AI2} = \frac{\sum Cni}{\sum Ci}$$

*Cni* stands for the number of nonincumbents who competed for a realistic candidacy.
*Ci* stands for the number of incumbents who competed for a realistic candidacy.
A higher value for this index reflects greater competition, which means that the number of nonincumbents who challenged incumbent candidates is relatively

large. The sensitivity of this index to the number of competing incumbents enables us to sum the values in both parts of the equation and to accumulate data for the entire population of selection events that were conducted under similar rules.

For example, in a single selection event, in party A 10 MPs and 20 nonincumbents are competing for positions on the list, and in party B 10 MPs and 40 nonincumbents are competing for positions on the list. The value of the aspirants index for party A is 20/10 = 2, while the value of the aspirants index for party B is 40/10 = 4. Party B is more competitive in this respect.

Both indices are sensitive to developments that can be (but do not need to be) independent from the influence of the candidate selection method itself. That is, voluntary retirement of incumbents might draw high numbers of newcomers and thus inflate both indices. The accumulation of data from many selection events will balance these "noises." Moreover, with the accumulated data, the fact that there are more "voluntary" retirements in the case of specific candidate selection methods only points out its latent impact on competition.

The use of these indices, however, is limited to those cases where we have a clear list of candidates. Such a list is sometimes lacking, especially in cases of appointment by small selectorates in which candidacy is frequently informal and sometimes the party prefers not to make these lists public.

## *Analysis of numerical results*

We propose a group of measures that use numerical results to estimate levels of competition. Such an analysis is limited to those cases where voting occurs and where the results are accessible.[1] Simple distinctions – which are easy to implement when the contest is over a single candidacy – include, first, the definition of those races where the winner won more than a certain percentage of votes as noncompetitive, while defining those where this amount was lower as competitive. For example, in their analysis of primary elections in the United States from 1912 to 2005 for the federal and state houses, Ansolabehere et al. (2007) defined those races where the first-place candidate won 60 percent or less as competitive races. The second distinction is based on definitions of the level of competition on the basis of the margin of victory. Goodliffe and Magleby (2000: 11), for example, defined a competitive primary as one in which "the difference in vote percentage between the first- and second-place candidates was less than 20 percent." Third, there are more sophisticated measures which take into account the number of candidates and their share of the votes. Such measurements are proposed by Kenig (2009*b*) to

---

[1] For example, when we asked for the results of the candidate selection contests from the Irish Fine Gael, we were told that "usually the results would remain confidential from the candidate." (Personal communication with Vincent Gribbin, Head of Internal Communication, Fine Gael Headquarters, Dublin, Ireland, 26 January 2009.)

analyze leadership contests, but can also be used to analyze any contest for a single candidacy.

Analyzing results of a contest for multiple positions requires more sophistication and caution than the straightforward case of competition for a single candidacy. A measure for analyzing the results of a multi-vote selection method is the vote concentration index (VCI; see Goldberg 1992). This index examines the number of votes concentrated on the candidates at the very top of the list. The more these votes are dispersed among the candidates, the more competition there is in the selection process. The formula is:

$$\text{VCI} = \frac{\sum\left[\left(\frac{Vnv}{Vt}\right) \times Nv\right]}{\sum Nv}$$

*Vnv* stands for the number of votes won by the candidates in the top positions on the party list that is equal to the number of votes allocated to each selector in a selection event.

*Vt* stands for the total number of votes cast.

*Nv* stands for the number of votes allocated to each selector.

The formula weights each selection event according to the number of votes that were cast. The higher the value of this index, the less competition there was because the votes were concentrated on fewer candidates.

For example, in a single selection event, in party A 100 selectors took part in candidate selection and each was allowed to vote for 10 candidates. The vote total is $100 \times 10 = 1,000$. The top ten candidates together won 650 of these votes. The vote concentration index is thus $650/1,000 = 0.65$. In party B 200 selectors took part in candidate selection and each was allowed to vote for just one candidate. The vote total is $200 \times 1 = 200$. The top candidate won 120 votes. The vote concentration index is thus $120/200 = 0.6$. According to this index, competition in party A was slightly greater than competition in party B.

The vote concentration index can be used in cases where selectors have a single vote or multiple votes. This measure, however, needs to be developed further since in its current form it is sensitive to influences that can bias results, such as the number of contestants.

### Incumbents versus nonincumbents

Another way to look at competition is to assess the success rate of newcomers in their attempts to challenge incumbents. The selection of newcomers indicates that even after a candidate was selected and elected in the last election, there is a chance that in the next election their position or seat will be lost. Such an analysis can be conducted in voting as well as in appointment systems. There is also no crucial need here for lists of the candidates who took part in the contest – although it can help in distinguishing between retirement and defeat – because the focus is not on the overall pool of candidates, but rather on the party's actual candidates for office in the general election.[2] It should also be noted that significant intraparty turnover – which can serve as a sign of competitiveness – may not reflect genuine democratic competition but rather power that resides in the hands of local "party bosses" who replace incumbents so that no alternative power center is created (Field 2006).

In single-member districts, counting the number of deselections is straightforward, as candidates are either in or out. Indeed, many scholars of US primaries, like Key (1967), look at the rate of incumbent success to compare levels of competition across cases. The analysis of candidate lists is more complicated because incumbents have to compete with each other, not just with newcomers, and as a result may move up or down the list (not off it).[3]

We suggest two indices to analyze the success of nonincumbents in either single- or multicandidacy contests (Hazan and Rahat 2006; see also Rahat, Hazan, and Katz 2008). The first is the nonincumbents winning index (NIWI), which weights the nonincumbents' share of positions at the top of the list (top is defined as the number of incumbents in the specific contest). The second index is the nonincumbents ranking index (NIRI), which weights the relative positions of nonincumbents at the top of the list. A high share of the top positions captured by nonincumbents along with high rankings indicates a high level of competition. These measures can be used in contests with both single and multiple positions, and as such can be useful for cross-national comparisons.

The nonincumbents winning index measures the "success" of new candidates according to whether or not they won "an incumbent's position." Thus, if 20 incumbent MPs competed for positions on the party list, the entrance of a new candidate in any of the top 20 positions would be considered a success. The definition of incumbent is any candidate who was elected to the previous legislature. The formula is:

$$\text{NIWI} = \frac{\sum Wni}{\sum Ci}$$

*Wni* is the number of nonincumbents who won a position on the list that is equal or higher in rank to the number of competing incumbents in each selection event. *Ci* is the number of incumbents competing in the selection event.

For example, let us assume that in a single selection event five MPs compete for a position on the list of candidates for the next parliament. They win the first, second, third, fifth, and seventh positions on the candidate list. This means that one

---

[2] Moreover, even when there are such lists, it is still possible that several incumbents predicted that they were going to be defeated and retired; and since we do not count them as defeated, the analysis might point to a somewhat lower rate of incumbent defeat.

[3] The rare occasions when incumbents face each other in selection contests for single-member districts usually occur after redistricting (Herrnson 1997).

nonincumbent won (the one who won the fourth position on the list). The non-incumbents winning index is therefore $1/5 = 0.2$.

Where selection is by party delegates or party members, those incumbents who appeared on the intraparty ballot – from which either party delegates or party members select their candidates – are considered as trying to win a realistic position. Where there is a more exclusive selectorate, such as a nominating committee, usually there are no such ballots or formal lists of candidates. The task of distinguishing the losers from those who willingly retired requires the construction of a small bio-graphical profile for each MP who either disappeared from the official candidate list produced by the party or appeared in an unrealistic position. Newspaper accounts from the time of the selection, biographies and autobiographies, intraparty material, and historical studies can help to accomplish this complex task.

The second index, the nonincumbents ranking index, counts the number of nonincumbents who won "an incumbent's position," taking into consideration the relative position that they won and giving higher values to winning higher positions on the list. That is, each position on the list, up to the position that is equal to the number of competing incumbents, is given a value in descending order – the last position is given one point and each higher position is "worth" an additional point. The formula is:

$$\text{NIRI} = \frac{\sum \left[ \left( \frac{Vpni}{Vpi} \right) \times Ci \right]}{\sum Ci}$$

*Vpni* stands for the value of the positions won by nonincumbents in the selection event.

*Vpi* stands for the total value of the "incumbent's positions" in the specific selection event.

The value of the victory in each selection event (*Vpni/Vpi*) is then multiplied by the number of incumbents competing in the selection event (*Ci*). We then sum all the selection events and divide the product by the sum of the number of incum-bents competing in all selection events.

For example, let us assume that in a single selection event, five MPs compete for a position on the list of candidates for the next parliament. They win positions one, two, three, five, and seven on the list. The total value of the list is five (for the first position) plus four (for the second position) plus three (for the third position) plus two (for the fourth position) plus one (for the fifth position) $= 15$. The single nonincumbent won position number four on the list which has a value of two. The value of the index (for an example with a single selection event) would thus be $2/15 = 0.133$.

The "sophomore surge" is another type of measure that focuses on incumbency. It is calculated as the gap between the percentage of votes a candidate gets when first selected and his or her second bid (this time for reselection) as an incumbent (Ansolabehere et al. 2007). This measure can also be used in contests with multi-candidacies (such as a contest for several positions on the list), although its sensitivity to the influence of a change in the rules, such as the number of votes allotted to each selector, calls for caution and improvement.

## *Summary of the indices*

Each index of competitiveness has its advantages and weaknesses. Each stresses a specific aspect of competition and ignores others. Some may prefer specific indices, pointing to their strengths over others from a theoretical point of view. All scholars, however, will be constrained by the type of data they have and by the ability of the measures to be adapted to a wide variety of selection methods. It should also be noted that the results of these measures are not independent from each other. For example, a high supply of candidates could point to a particular interpretation of competition – indicating that the candidates estimate that there is a chance for success – but this might actually reduce the values of other measures of competition. This is the case, for example, if we use turnover, or incumbency defeat, as a measure of competition. That is, a high number of competitors might benefit incumbents in their attempt to be reselected. When there is an incumbent competing, he or she is likely to be well known, and thus voting will largely be for or against the incumbent. The more challengers there are, the more these "negative" votes could be spread out, and the lower the plurality needed in order to win. Thus, being more competitive in one aspect (number of candidates) may lead to being less competitive in another one (defeat of incumbents).

The optimal strategy for analyzing competition is to employ several indices, taking into consideration the possible covariance between them. The menu of indices for analyzing single candidacy contests is quite long. A comparative study of multiple candidacy contests requires an improvement in the existing measures and the development of additional ones.

## THE IMPACT OF SELECTION METHODS ON COMPETITIVENESS

The high success rates of incumbents in their bids for reselection and reelection are well documented (Somit et al. 1994). Indeed, "deselection *appears to be* a relatively rare phenomenon, the norm being that incumbents desiring to run for reelection are renominated" (Matland and Studler 2004: 97, emphasis in original). The advantage of incumbents results from their being recognized and known; the resources they have as members of the legislature to sustain visibility and their link with their constituency; and their ability to present achievements rather than promises, which gives them an edge in recruiting votes and other resources for their campaign (Gallagher 1988c). Yet, we also know that beyond the universal claim that incumbents have an advantage, there is significant variance in the rates of incumbent reelection (Somit et al. 1994). Much less, however, is known about the weight of candidate selection in the reselection and deselection of incumbents, and even less about the differences (if there are any) among the various candidate selection methods. In this section we look at the available analyses and data in order to analyze how candidate selection methods affect competition.

It is not easy to identify the influence of candidate selection methods on competition because there is no systematic cross-national comparison, and even cross-party comparisons in which there is a significant variance – beyond the American differentiation between types of primaries – are rare. We thus base this section on a collection of data from various democracies, and the few attempts to actually identify the link between competition and candidate selection methods.

### Candidacy and competition

Our democratic instincts are likely to lead us to think that the more inclusive candidacy requirements are, the more competitive the system is. After all, more exclusive requirements will limit the pool of candidates and will curtail the right to be selected. However, as already noted above, a wide-open field for candidacies might actually help incumbents retain their seats or positions. That is, as long as candidacy requirements do not shrink the field too much – up to the point where the selectors have no choice – they might actually enhance competition.

The treatment of incumbents is another issue we must examine here, especially if we consider nonincumbent victories in candidate selection as an indicator of a high level of competition. Some parties privilege their incumbents. This was a fiercely fought-over struggle in the British Labour Party (Young 1983). At the beginning of the 1980s, it was determined that incumbents would have to stand for reselection after they served for three years or more. Yet, they still enjoyed the rule that determined that they must be included automatically in the shortlist (Norris and Lovenduski 1995). The cancellation of the automatic readoption of incumbents in Labour did not bring about significant levels of turnover, and there were contests in fewer than a third of seats (Ware 1996). In 1993, the rules were changed in favor of incumbents and determined that they would have to face challengers only if they were not nominated as candidates by two-thirds of the nomination bodies in their constituency (branches, unions, and other partisan groups). Later, the requirement was decreased to one-half (Quinn 2004). Much more privileged were incumbents in Brazil, where until 2002 they were protected by a national law that determined that the party must reselect them (Samuels 2008).

There are, however, cases where parties do not allow incumbents to be reselected after they have served a specific number of years or terms. High levels of turnover in the Italian Communist Party in 1976 resulted from the rule that legislators could serve only two terms, unless it was decided that they should continue (Wertman 1977). Other parties ask incumbents who have served for a certain period to face additional barriers, like being reapproved by special majorities, as was the case in the Labor Party in Israel between 1977 and 1984.

It appears that most parties do not have formal rules regarding incumbency, yet convention seems to allow for automatic readoption, without challengers, in many cases. Parties that have specific rules concerning the term limits of incumbents can significantly influence turnover, but even in these cases they might find that they have to ease them – as did the idealists of the Green Party in Germany (Poguntke 1993).

### *Inclusiveness: A nonlinear relationship with competition*

Is there variance in the levels of competition that results from the degree of inclusiveness of the candidate selection method? An assessment of the influence of differences in inclusiveness on competition – measured according to the number of candidates and the success rate of nonincumbents – reveals that the most exclusive selectorates (party elites) lead to low competition; inclusive selectorates (party members) lead to medium-level competition; and selectorates with a medium level of inclusiveness (party delegates) lead to the highest level of competition (Rahat, Hazan, and Katz 2008). This study was conducted within the same party system (Israel), and thus controlled for the possible influences of different national political cultures and government institutions. Additional studies are needed, however, to challenge or support these findings.

A recent cross-national comparative study of party leader selection found that "larger selectorates tend to attract more candidates, but also tend to produce less competitive contests" (Kenig 2009*b*: 246). This study found that the most competitive selectorate for party leaders is the parliamentary party group (a selectorate that does not exist when dealing with candidate selection for parliament). Party agencies where delegates are the selectors have a lower level of competition, and the lowest competition level is found in party primaries, when party members are the selectors.

Studies conducted in the United States found that blanket primaries benefit incumbents because voters tend to cross party lines when the incumbent is from the other party and stay with their own party candidate when the incumbent belongs to it (Persily 2001). In other words, and in line with the conclusions of the study mentioned above, there is less competition in the most inclusive type of primaries than in less inclusive types. A more general study of primaries to the US House of Representatives in 1994–8 came to the conclusion that, "It is clear that primary elections do not serve to stimulate more competition, and, to the extent that competition is an essential ingredient of democracy, it is not clear that they accomplished their intended purpose of enhancing U.S. democracy" (Maisel and Stone 2001: 43).

Obler (1970) actually found that incumbents in Belgium were more secure when they needed the support of the party members than when competing in other, less inclusive selectorates. While scholars sometimes claim that primaries are more competitive, they do not back this claim with data. Kristjánsson (1998), for example, argues that the adoption of primaries in Iceland made incumbents less safe than before. This may reflect the fact that competition is now more overt and public. The more inclusive candidate selection is, the more public the competition – that is, the more it is covered by the mass media. When a small group selects the candidates, personal communication is crucial; when hundreds, or even thousands of delegates are involved, there is some role for the media in communicating with the selectors, yet personal communication is still possible and crucial; when party members or voters are involved, the role of the mass media is central. While the media "image" of competition grows with an increase in inclusiveness, this is not necessarily the case for competition itself. The media image is possibly also due to the fact that those few candidates who succeed in defeating incumbents in the primaries capture higher positions than the larger group of newcomers who succeed in winning positions through selection by party delegates (Rahat, Hazan, and Katz 2008).

A challenging case is that of Argentina, where the use of highly inclusive candidate selection methods – with selectorates of party members and sometimes even party supporters – plays an important part in the explanation of high legislative turnover (Field 2006; Jones 2008). Scholars explain that this is a result of the fact that the "real" selector is not the wide selectorate, but rather a local boss who replaces incumbents in order to assure that no alternative power base is created (Field 2006). This leads us to take a closer look at the most exclusive type of selectorates – single leaders – and their influence on turnover. Strong single leaders may encourage high levels of turnover, as in some cases of candidate selection in Israel prior to the 2009 elections (Rahat Forthcoming). This, however, is not a sign of more democratic competition, but rather of a personal power base that characterizes leader-based parties.

Incumbency is an advantage in all kinds of selectorates. The differences are in the extent of this advantage. The inclusiveness of the selectorate is likely to affect the success rate of incumbents in their efforts to be reselected, because smaller selectorates allow aspirants a chance to become known and to contact their selectors personally. When the selectorate is inclusive, that is, composed of party members or the entire electorate, support cannot be based on personal affiliations and incumbency is thus likely to have a bigger advantage. This is mainly because as public officials, incumbents enjoy media exposure and the ability to demonstrate responsiveness to both interest groups and financial donors. This is not only true in the case of competition for a single candidacy but also for multivote party primaries – in which lists of candidates are selected. In those cases, incumbents are known and recognized, and they are thus more likely to be included in the teams that party members select (Obler 1970; Rahat and Sher-Hadar 1999*a*). When the selectorate is less inclusive and is composed of delegates, aspirants have a better chance of being recognized and can even try to contact many of their selectors. Incumbency is still an asset, but not as much as it is when more exposure, money, and votes are needed.

A different and separate explanation is needed to explain why selection by party elites is less competitive than selection by delegates, members, and even the entire electorate. That is, if we accept the logic that party agencies are more competitive than primaries because of the shorter "distance" between the candidates and the selectors, then we should expect party elite selectorates to be more competitive than the other two kinds of selectorates. It is easier for each candidate to make himself or herself known to each member of a small committee than to do the same in the broader party agency. However, highly exclusive selectorates – such as nominating committees – because of their small size and informal, nontransparent working procedures, suffer from a lack of popular democratic legitimacy. As Matthews and Valen (1999) explain in the Norwegian case, a nominating committee will design a list that it expects will satisfy both party delegates and members. Thus, the best strategy for the nominating committee to legitimize its decisions in the eyes of party agencies, party members, and even the general public is to present a list of candidates that will largely be composed of incumbents, that is, a list that reflects the existing balance of power, and will thus not raise much antagonism. Changes will be minimal, only to demonstrate that something was changed, that the nomination committee is not a rubber stamp.

### *Decentralization: Territorial decentralization breeds low competition*

As we saw in Chapter 4, even in those countries where the national level has a say in candidate selection, the selectorate at the district level is usually the dominant one. Therefore, parties in countries with single-member districts, because they require single candidacies, and also contests in small districts in personalized electoral systems (single transferable vote, STV, and single non-transferable vote, SNTV) usually use decentralized candidate selection methods. Parties in countries that use proportional representation list electoral systems in multimember districts usually use more centralized candidate selection methods – often with a dominant role for the party organization at the level of the multimember district, and sometimes even at the national level.

The available evidence demonstrates that in all cases where methods are decentralized to the level of the individual candidate – regardless of the different levels of inclusiveness of the selectorate – competition is low. In countries where parties place a single candidate in each district, the term "open seat" and "closed seat" are used to describe a district in which an incumbent does not compete and one in which there is an incumbent running. The mere fact that there is no parallel term when dealing with list systems points to the preferred status of incumbents under decentralized selection methods.

Candidate selection methods in the United States are highly decentralized at the single-member district level and highly inclusive (the selectorate is the electorate, with various conditions set by the different states). While scholars find some variations between the states in the level of competition, in general it is clear that we are dealing with rather low levels of competition. In the US House of Representatives in the 1946–98 period, turnover due to defeat in primaries was far lower than turnover due to retirement or defeat in general elections. On average, only 6.9 (1.6 percent) House members lost their seats in the primaries in each selection round, while 25.2 (5.8 percent) were defeated in general elections and 34.3 (7.9 percent) retired. This implies that the rest, 368.6 (84.7 percent) on average, kept their seats. From this we can conclude that even if we remove all of the incumbents who retired – although some might have done so fearing a loss in the primaries – out of the 400 incumbents that tried to be reselected, on average, only seven were defeated in primaries, which is 1.8 percent.[4] In a majority of the cases, candidacy for the House is decided without a contest (Herrnson 1997; Key 1967), and where there is competition, victory is usually decisive, with the winner getting more than double the votes of the second-placed candidate. The incumbents' advantage in primaries for the legislature at both the federal and the state levels was analyzed for the 1912–2005 period and was found to be high and increasing. For example, between 1996 and 2000, in less than 45 percent of cases was there even a contest for an open seat; and in closed seats, less than 30 percent of incumbents faced challengers. In less than 25 percent of cases of competition for an open seat, and in around 2–3 percent of cases where an incumbent was involved, the winner won less than 60 percent of the vote. Incumbents also faced fewer competitors in the primaries, which can be understood as the "scare off" effect – aspirants estimate that their chances to defeat an incumbent are low and prefer not to run (Ansolabehere et al. 2007).

Primaries for the Senate are somewhat more competitive. In 1946–92, total turnover for the Senate was 296, and only 41 of these resulted from a loss in a primary contest (Jackson 1994). This means that in only 5 percent of the cases did Senators lose their seat in primaries. In many states no contest takes place; Engstrom and Engstrom (2008) analyzed primaries for the US Senate in 1980–2002 and found that in only 61.7 percent of the cases did a contest take place.

Candidate selection in Canada is highly decentralized to the single-member district level and very inclusive (the selectorate is the party members) compared to other countries, but less so than the United States. The level of competition is also low and in most cases incumbents do not face challengers. Carty and Eagles (2003) reported that a contest between two candidates or more took place in about 40 percent of cases, mainly when there was an open seat. In 1988, there was a

---

[4] The analysis is based on data from Ornstein, Mann, and Malbin (2000), as cited in Goodliffe and Magleby (2000: 9).

contest for 57 percent of open safe seats, and in 1993, this figure rose to 83 percent. Where incumbents competed, they faced challengers in only 12 percent of cases in 1988, and in just 9 percent in 1993. Cases of deselection are rare, for example, only two incumbents were deselected in 1988, none in 1993, and four in 1997 (Carty, Cross, and Young 2000; Erickson and Carty 1991; Erickson 1997).

The United Kingdom presents a case in which candidate selection methods changed over time, incrementally becoming more inclusive – though still less so than in Canada – because of the involvement of party delegates and party elites in the multistage selection process. The power of the center has also increased over time, yet selection is still dominated by the local organization at the single-member district level, and in comparative terms it is still a decentralized system. Deselection of incumbents is rare, and its rate – about 1 percent – has not changed significantly over the years (Obler 1970; Ohman 2004). This was the case even after the Labour Party adopted rules for mandatory reselection at the beginning of the 1980s (Ball 1987; Criddle 1984, 1988, 1992). Norris and Lovenduski (1995: 68) reported that in the British Labour Party, 151 out of 217 (69.5 percent) incumbents did not face a challenger and only 8 out of 217 (3.7 percent) incumbents were deselected in 1980–3; 135 out of 177 (76.3 percent) did not face a challenger and only 6 out of 177 (3.4 percent) were deselected in 1983–7; and 146 out of 205 (71.2 percent) did not face a challenger and only 2 out of 205 (1 percent) were deselected in 1987–92.

When we look at data before the 1980s, when the selectorates were quite exclusive (elites and delegates), we see few attempts to deselect incumbents, and still fewer successful attempts. Butler (1978) reported that since 1922, there were between 32 and 43 cases of deselection in the Labour and Conservative parties, while Dickson (1975) noted 35 attempts to deselect incumbents in the Labour and Conservative parties in 1948–74.[5] More recent counts are as low as the earlier numbers – Cutts, Childs, and Fieldhouse (2008) reported that two incumbents were deselected in Labour before the 2005 election. As Benedetto and Hix (2007: 777) put it:

> Once an MP has been selected in a constituency, the MP is difficult to remove if he or she is supported by his or her local party elite. Contrast this with a national-based, party-list proportional representation system, which gives the national party leadership the power to move a candidate down the party list in the next election and so reduce his or her chances of being reelected.

These three cases, the United States, Canada, and the United Kingdom, tell us the same story of low competition in decentralized systems with various levels of inclusiveness. The reports on deselection by the National Party in New Zealand,

---

[5] Ranney (1965) identified 18 known attempts to challenge incumbents in the Conservative Party prior to the five elections between 1950 and 1964, 12 of which were successful. That is a rate of 0.84%. (12 out of 1,421). He also identified 16 known attempts to challenge incumbents in the Labour Party prior to the same five elections between 1950 and 1964, 12 of which were successful. That is a similar rate of 0.85% (12 out of 1,409).

which uses a decentralized method, tell the same story and exhibits only seven deselections in about fifty years (Jackson 1980; Stephens 2008). The accounts on deselection from the United States (Goodliffe and Magleby 2000), Canada (Cross 2006), and the United Kingdom (Butler and Kavanagh 1974; Criddle 1984, 1997; Rush 1988) also tell us that a significant part of the turnover can be attributed to redistricting. These low figures – which appear when using both inclusive and exclusive selection methods – and the influence of redistricting indicate that the territorial district becomes the source of solid and stable power for an incumbent within the party.

The case of the Indian National Congress Party is the exception that proves the rule. The Congress Party deselected many of its incumbents when it had the ability to do so – in the first decade after independence, when the party's national leadership was powerful. When the center lost its power as a result of struggles within the national elite, deselection declined (Graham 1986).

Ireland, where selection is territorially decentralized (sometimes to even lower levels than those of the small multimember district), demonstrates the same low levels of competition.[6] Gallagher (1980) reported that there were only three known cases of deselection in Ireland since 1937, and stated that, "Instances of incumbents failing to be reselected have been very rare in the past, numbering no more than about one every two elections" (Gallagher 1988*b*: 135). These low levels continue to the current decade, during which the system has become more inclusive – party members, rather than delegates, are now the selectorate in most parties. Galligan (2003) reported that there were only two cases of deselection prior to the 2003 elections, while Weeks (2007) pointed out that the eighteen incumbents who sought reselection in Irish Labour prior to the 2007 elections faced no challengers.

Reports on competition in candidate selection from Germany are especially interesting because there we have a more centralized candidate selection method, yet due to the use of single-members districts the role of the local district organization is central when it comes to the district seats. The overall rate of de-selection – Roberts (1988) estimated that no more than five to ten incumbents were deselected in each of the three largest parties in West Germany – was higher than in the United Kingdom, United States, and Canada. This could be expected in a system where the regional party organization plays a central role in candidate selection.[7] Moreover, when looking at single-member districts we see that in a majority of the cases incumbents do not face challengers, and when they do they usually win with high support (Borchert and Golsch 2003; Porter 1995; Schüttermeyer and Strum 2005; Szabo 1977). The more centralized Land level, on the other hand, seems to supply more than its share of newcomers (Loewenberg 1966).

---

[6] In Ireland, we witness a trend toward centralization of selection methods (Gallagher 1988*b*), yet the district level is still the dominant actor in candidate selection and in comparative terms it is still a highly decentralized system.

[7] In the 1950s and 1960s, though, West Germany's single-member districts produced relatively high levels of incumbent deselection of about 10% (Kitzinger 1960; Loewenberg 1966).

The difference in the status of incumbents in single-member districts and in lists designed for multimember districts is also evident in the United Kingdom. Mitchell and Bradbury (2004: 289) compared candidate selection in single-member districts to the lists for the mixed-member proportional electoral system that are used in the election of the Scottish Parliament and the Welsh Assembly, and claimed:

> In particular, in selection of regional list candidates incumbency counted for much less than has traditionally been expected for constituency reselection. Here, de-selection could effectively be achieved not just by non-selection, but by ranking candidates so low on the list that it was impossible for them to win a seat.

Indeed, "in single-member districts or smaller, multimember districts, incumbents are often protected by local party elites" (Benedetto and Hix 2007: 762). Where more centralized systems are found the picture is less clear. We find reports on various levels of competition and not only, as is the case for the decentralized systems, on low levels of competition. In Japan, there is a centralized candidate selection method with very low competition. Masahiko (2004) reported that incumbents were reselected in the Japanese Liberal Democratic Party during the 1960–90 period in 99.8 percent (2,761 out of 2,788) of cases. What might explain this is the electoral system that was in use until 1996, which encouraged incumbents to cultivate their personal machines in the small multi-member districts (Youn 1977). The center, it seems, reselected incumbents because it knew that they were likely to win.[8] Stirnemann (1989) reported high levels of incumbent reselection in Austria – 120 out of 124 (96.8 percent) in 1970, and 148 out of 151 (98 percent) in 1971 – where candidate selection clearly involves significant regional and national influences.

Accounts from other countries, where regional and sometimes national level selectorates play a significant role, point to higher levels of competition. Obler (1970) reported that 8.6 percent of incumbents (52 out of 607) were deselected in Belgium in the 1960s – that is, they were pushed off, or down, the candidate list. The rate of deselection for the Italian Communist and Christian Democratic parties in the 1976 elections, according to Wertman (1977), is estimated to be at least at the Belgian level. While this was not necessarily the norm – as the higher rate of reselection for the 1979 elections demonstrates (Wertman 1981) – it does point out that the parties' use of more centralized candidate selection methods enabled them to enhance turnover.

---

[8] Masahiko (2004) noted that since 1996, with the adoption of the new electoral system, incumbents were reselected in 97.5% of cases (588 out of 603). Whether this slight decrease is due to the reform that added an element of list selection is impossible to know on the basis of the data supplied. The German, Scottish, and Welsh experiences lead us to speculate that this is indeed the reason for the increase in deselection.

High levels of turnover in Spain and Portugal result from the power of the national organization. The replacement of incumbents allows the national organization to preserve its power and prevent the consolidation of a local and/or parliamentary power base (Montabes and Ortega 2005). Ohman (2002) reported that in Ghana, incumbent turnover was higher in the party with the more centralized candidate selection method (29 percent) than in the one with the more decentralized method (10 percent). Finally, an analysis of the Israeli case points to relatively high levels of competition in a highly centralized system. Rahat, Hazan, and Katz (2008) estimated that between 18.1 percent (in the case of nominating committees) and 24–5 percent (in the case of delegate and member selection) of incumbents lost in intraparty selection; that is, newcomers captured "their" positions.[9]

To summarize this section, we claim that highly decentralized systems in the territorial sense breed low competition, no matter how inclusive or exclusive the selectorate is. In parties that operate in countries with single-member districts, and also in countries where the electoral system has a strong personal element (e.g. STV in Ireland and SNTV in Japan before 1996), incumbents have an edge because they have a personal campaign machine that helps them get reelected (Ware 1996). This machine seems to work on their behalf also when it comes to intraparty selection (Matland and Studlar 2004). It can directly mobilize the hundreds or thousands of supporters or members needed in the inclusive selection methods, or indirectly convince members of more exclusive local selectorates (delegates or members of a small party elite) that they have the best chance to be reelected. When it comes to the more centralized methods, there is a variance in the levels of competition that can be partly explained by looking at the inclusiveness dimension, as previously elaborated.

### Social decentralization and competition

The adoption of representation correction mechanisms can influence competition, especially in terms of turnover. If a party adopts a quota that will significantly increase the number of women, then incumbent men might be in real danger of losing their seats or positions. However, politics usually does not work this way, and quotas are largely adopted after women have already succeeded in capturing a significant number of parliamentary seats (Matland 2004). In such cases, the influence of the representation correction mechanisms on competition

---

[9] However, Argentina's large parties, with a less centralized system than that of Spain, produced higher turnover (Field 2006; Jones 2008). This account does not weaken the main claim that the more decentralized systems exhibit low competition, because in Argentina we are dealing with middle-level decentralization, at the regional, multimember district level. Yet, what we do learn from this is that either the relationship between decentralization and competition is not linear, or that additional country-specific factors can influence intraparty competition.

is dependent on the gap between the existing level of representation and the aspired level.

Correction mechanisms can also have no impact on incumbents, as was the case with the adoption of all-women shortlists in the United Kingdom, a mechanism that was activated only in contests for "open" seats. In some cases, correction mechanisms can actually block turnover when they allow specific incumbents – "guarded" from the general competition – to be reselected again and again. Parties at times recognize this problem and do not allow incumbents to continuously benefit from such representation correction mechanisms.

### *Appointment/voting systems and competition*

When we think about democratic competition, we think about competition for the secret votes of individuals. Yet, even under appointment systems – in which a few leaders select the candidates – there is some competition. Competition in appointment systems is less formal, less explicit, and more restrained, but it exists. Some of the measures elaborated previously in this chapter can help determine the levels of competition under such systems.

The use of specific voting methods may influence the intensity of internal competition. The use of majoritarian voting systems (especially of the multivote kind) may encourage the consolidation of blocs of candidates within parties. This might lead to the ousting of the candidates of a minority (or minorities) within the party, and can even lead to defections from the party. Semi-proportional and proportional voting systems do not lead to such a zero-sum game, and by enabling representation for an intraparty minority can help contain competition within the party. The selection of candidates in several rounds could also quell internal conflicts, as corrections can be made along the selection process. The use of voting methods that require ranking and the counting of votes in a manner that supplies incentives for cooperation can also help contain competition within the party.

### *Multistage methods and competition*

When there is screening by party agencies, criticism might be heard about the party elite's (or elites') involvement harming free competition or blocking candidates that would otherwise have had a chance of being selected (Bradbury et al. 2000). Indeed, screening may limit competition at the last stage of selection: in the Labour Party in Scotland, 167 candidates (out of 534 applicants) contested 129 candidacies for the Scottish Parliament (Shaw 2001); at the same time, screening of Labour candidates for the Welsh Assembly left 164 candidates to contest 60 candidacies (Laffin, Shaw, and Taylor 2007). Yet once again, we should keep in mind that a lower number of candidates might allow for more fierce competition between incumbents and aspirants. If a multistage method leads to a final round in which each incumbent faces a single, impressive aspirant (in single-member districts), or each group of incumbents faces an equally large group of notable aspirants (likely under a list system), the chances for turnover could be somewhat higher.

## CHANGING THE METHOD, RATHER THAN ITS ATTRIBUTES?

From the point of view of adaptability, we can expect that competition will increase when a new candidate selection method is first implemented, and that over time candidates will adapt to it and competition will then decline.[10] Those who do not "fit" the new method, who find it hard to compete and win, will cease to participate, and over time it will draw largely upon those who do fit. For example, if primaries are adopted and if they require large resources, then those who are poor or do not have the ability to raise money will be ousted, while those who have money or are able to recruit it will be drawn into the system. After a while, all "open" seats or positions will be filled and a new "closed" club of incumbents will be in place.

Indeed, in their analysis of primary elections in the United States from 1912 to 2005 for federal and state houses, Ansolabehere et al. (2007) found that the "sophomore surge" – the gap between the percentage of votes candidates get when first elected and their subsequent bid as incumbents – increased over the years. The sophomore surge stood at an average of 4.7 percent in the 1920s and 1930s, 11 percent in the 1950s, and 14 percent in the 1990s.

The question that begs here is: What is the weight of the impact of the specific properties of the candidate selection method compared to simply the weight of a change of the method itself? Maybe a constant change of the candidate selection method will result in more competition – because competition increases when a new method is implemented – rather than adopting and preserving a theoretically more competitive method.

## INTERNAL COMPETITION AND EXTERNAL SUCCESS

One can argue that candidate selection is an intraparty matter, but can an intraparty battle help or hurt the party's fortunes in the interparty battlefield in general elections? On the one hand, competition might hurt the parties' electoral performance because it can lead to a focus on the intraparty conflict rather than on the

---

[10] We are in debt to our friend and colleague, Menachem Hofnung, who pointed us in this direction.

external interparty race. This may lead to a waste of energy and resources by the candidates and their supporters on the internal campaign. A fierce struggle might also create a dynamic that could alienate losing candidates and their supporters – and it could even push them to split from their party or to support other parties. On the other hand, competition might help because it creates media exposure, gives the party credit for being internally democratic, and often encourages the recruitment of new members and resources that could then be used in the general campaign (Carty and Eagles 2003; Galderisi, Ezra, and Lyons 2001).

In their study of candidate selection in Canada, Carty and Eagles (2003) found that in most cases internal competition did not influence the party's performance in the campaign or its electoral fortunes in general elections. Yet, they did find one party where competition helped the campaign, and another where it helped gain electoral support. In the case of US primaries, some argue that competitive primaries can be beneficial for new candidates – because they expose them to the public and enable them to activate and improve their machines before a general election – while they might harm the already known incumbents. Others claim that primaries have no influence on candidates' fortunes in general elections (Galderisi, Ezra, and Lyons 2001).

## WHAT WE KNOW ABOUT INTRAPARTY COMPETITION

In order to further assess intraparty competition, we are in need of additional comparative studies of candidate selection, especially of parties with centralized methods. Meanwhile, on the basis of the available country-specific data, we can suggest, first, that in all decentralized candidate selection methods we can expect low intraparty competition. Second, in cases of more centralized methods, we expect the highest competition when the selectorate is made up of party delegates, medium-level competition when party members are the selectors, and the lowest level when the party elite is the selectorate. While we lack comparisons that include the extremes – the most inclusive selectorate that encompasses the whole electorate and the most exclusive one that is composed of a single leader – we can suggest that in the case of the entire electorate, competition would be expected to be quite low, lower than selection by party members, because it increases those advantages that incumbents enjoy when facing large crowds. As for single party leaders, if they are strong enough they can oust incumbents, but this would be an indication of their power as leaders, not of democratic competition.

We also suggest that other factors can influence competition. Candidacy requirements and screening in the first stages of a multistage selection process, which lead to a reduction of the pool of candidates, can be seen as limiting competition but might actually lead to a more intensive struggle between incumbents and surviving newcomers. Special requirements for incumbents, and especially term limits, may open the way to newcomers. Mechanisms of social decentralization can also let newcomers in, if they are intended to change significantly the existing allocation of representation or if they are activated only for newcomers. In short, if we see turnover as a sign of competition, it seems that as in the case of representation, there is a need to interfere somewhat with the way that the political market works because it is clearly biased toward incumbents. To this we add the sound speculation that simply a change in selection method could have more influence on competition than any specific qualities of the adopted method.

Appointing candidates may keep competition an intraparty matter, but does not satisfy the most basic of democratic criteria. The struggle for the votes of the selectorate can become highly intense, to the point that the cohesion of the party might be under threat. The adoption of those voting systems that allow a minority to gain representation, and allow for correction, produce balanced incentives for cooperation and competition among the contesters that might help the party contain competition. The challenge for parties is to allow for some intraparty competition, while restraining competition so it will not affect parties' ability to compete in general elections.

# 9

# Responsiveness

Any discussion of responsiveness is inexorably linked to the concept of representation. When one mentions responsiveness, one is more often than not referring to the representatives elected by the people. In other words, the representatives are supposed to be responsive, and accountable, to their electorate. Representative responsiveness, therefore, posits that the representatives must be attentive to the interests, needs, and demands of their voters. This link is evident, for example, in the mandate–independence controversy, over which scholars have been divided for centuries. Both mandate and independence approaches expect the representative to be accountable. The essence of the controversy points to the nature of responsiveness the representatives must exhibit.

Mandate theorists, who perceive the representative as a delegate, identify with the concept of representation as simple and direct responsiveness. The representatives are supposed to pay continuous attention to their voters' positions and to act according to their will. They should be rewarded or punished according to the extent of their responsiveness. Independence theorists perceive the representatives as trustees, acting according to what they themselves consider the public interest. This "public interest" may differ from the specific interests of their voters.

Regardless, the essence of the discussion concerning the mandate–independence dilemma has failed to incorporate important actors beyond the voters into the bigger picture of responsiveness. That is, representative theorists have fallen short of confronting the mandate–independence dilemma with many factors representatives must face in reality while serving in the legislature, beyond their relationship with voters. The element most prominent in its absence is the political party of the representatives. For example, Fiorina (1974: 122) wrote, "The representative responds to someone. In other words, he is not a free agent. He has a 'constituency' that he represents . . . " Fiorina claimed that the representatives will most likely react to those who have the greatest influence on getting them reelected (see also Putnam 1976), but the party is completely missing from this discussion. Interestingly, Fiorina focused his analysis on the United States, and therefore we should not be surprised that party is not considered a highly influential factor. However, the selection process within parties that produces the candidates prior to the election is also absent, and this oversight cannot be explained by a focus on the United States.

Eulau and Karps (1977) decomposed the concept of "responsiveness" into four components, which they claimed correspond to the four targets of representation: policy responsiveness, how the represented and the representative interact with respect to the making of public policy; service responsiveness, referring to the nonlegislative services that the representatives perform for individuals or groups in their constituency; allocation responsiveness, addressing the benefits provided by the representative for the constituency as a whole; and symbolic responsiveness, which includes different symbolic actions the representatives undertake in order to sustain a sense of responsiveness among their constituents. Responsiveness, according to Eulau and Karps, is solely vis-à-vis the constituents or voters of the representative. Here, too, there is no mention of the party and its role or influence on representative behavior.

What does the theoretical literature on representative responsiveness teach the representatives in terms of their relations with their party? If adhering to party lines and obeying party discipline is considered subordinate to following the voters' interests and preferences, representatives will find themselves in a bind. If the representatives exhibit high levels of party unity, are they still responsive to the interests of their voters?

It would be safe to claim that according to many representation theorists, the answer to the question "whom is the representative responsive to?" is: the voters. Other factors such as the party leadership or – as is our focus – the candidate selection process are rarely taken into account. However, the fact of the matter is that there are many actors toward whom the representative can, or should, demonstrate responsiveness. When approaching such questions as "whom is the representative responsive to?" we must first assess to whom the representative is accountable.

The perception of representation as accountability is probably the most common one nowadays. A system of accountability presumes a system of representation (Fenno 1996). This accountability model follows the basic principle–agent format, in which the power relations from voter to representative follow a chain of delegation (Mitchell 2000). The normative understanding of accountability here is "that the representative is 'responsible to,' 'answerable to,' 'bound to,' and even 'bound by' his voters" (Mansbridge 2003: 516). While theorists have criticized the basic accountability model – for example, there is a limited capacity of those represented to formulate policy and a resulting asymmetry in the representational relationship – even when it comes to accountability, scholars of representation theory rarely mention the party and its role. The notion of accountability is, indeed, based on a set of relationships between the voters and their representatives, but one must take into account the fact that such relationships do not exist in isolation. There are additional important actors who must be considered. The main one is the political party of the representatives, which we argue not only has a significant effect on their behavior, but can also open or close the door to nonparty actors who wish to play a role in the political game. The main distinction here is between personal, candidate-centered responsiveness, and a more collective, party-centered type of responsiveness. We will show which features of the candidate selection method encourage candidate-centered responsiveness and which lead to a more party-centered type of responsiveness.

Responsiveness implies a binding demand for relative congruence between the representative and the represented. Party discipline implies a very different type of congruence between party representatives and the dictates of the party leadership. In this chapter we argue that candidate selection methods affect the balance of influence between party and nonparty actors on the selection process, and also within the party between the party leadership and other actors, and that they have an impact on the relationship between the representatives and each of these. Different candidate selection methods will produce different groups of selectors to whom the representative will be responsive, and will either enhance or hamper the ability of the party leadership to impose disciplinary measures on their representatives.

This chapter addresses each of the four main dimensions of candidate selection according to its impact on different aspects of responsiveness. We began by focusing on the mandate–independence controversy, particularly the gap between the theoretical literature on representative responsiveness and the role of political parties as intermediaries connecting the voters to their representatives. We now move to a discussion of party unity, seeing high levels of unity as a sign of party-centered responsiveness and low levels of it as a sign of candidate-centered responsiveness. We then assess the relationship between candidate selection and party unity, addressing each of the four dimensions and showing how the influence of candidate selection on responsiveness can vary significantly depending on which selection method is adopted. We also deal with an important associated aspect that is relevant for parties in general and for responsiveness in particular – party financing – and point to its relationship with candidate selection. Throughout the chapter we reflect on the influence of the democratization of candidate selection as we present our arguments and the empirical data for each of the issues under investigation. We conclude the chapter with a section that is dedicated to the influence of democratization on responsiveness.


## CANDIDACY AND RESPONSIVENESS: BETWEEN COHESION AND DISCIPLINE


At the inclusive pole of candidacy, every voter is allowed to run and there are no prerequisites to being a candidate. Here, the party has little to no influence as a gatekeeper and aspirants for office can practically impose themselves on the party, which must accept their candidacy, reluctantly or otherwise. Inclusivity may be the result of legal regulations, as is the case in the United States, but it can also be the trait of a party whose main interest is electoral success, and is therefore open to any candidate who could help increase the party's share of the vote. Inclusiveness increases the potential candidate pool, and as this number grows the personal qualifications of each of the candidates are emphasized. In other words, the more inclusive parties on the candidacy dimension are those that exhibit more personal, candidate-centered responsiveness, as opposed to the more collective, party-centered type of responsiveness.

At the other end, the exclusive pole, we encounter parties that impose a series of limitations upon aspirants. This may be due to an attempt by the party to control the supply side of potential candidates, so that those who fulfill the enhanced eligibility requirements, and are subsequently both selected and elected, will behave according to the party line. A party with strict candidacy requirements can arrive in office as a cohesive unit, manifesting a patent party culture of loyalty and unity; and by doing so it removes the need to utilize the available disciplinary measures – perks, career advancement, party whip, votes of confidence – in order to keep its elected representatives in line.[1] Moreover, the party leadership can use more exclusive candidacy requirements – such as long-term party membership and proof of party activity – to reward loyalists and long-time activists, thereby creating a structure of selective, party-focused incentives that will shape the focus of responsiveness for its candidates. In other words, specific candidacy restrictions may help not only to reduce the number of competitors, but also to assure certain behavioral patterns once in office and thus promote party-centered responsiveness.

## THE SELECTORATE AND RESPONSIVENESS: TWO APPROACHES

When it comes to the second dimension of candidate selection, the selectorate, there are two developing yet contradictory approaches concerning the influence of this dimension on responsiveness in general and the cohesiveness of political parties in particular. The first argues that there is a negative relationship between a more inclusive selectorate and the ability to maintain party unity, resulting in a decline in party-centered responsiveness and an increase in individual or candidate-centered responsiveness. The second approach posits that democracy within parties does not necessarily lead to a decline in party unity, nor to any decline in

---

[1] Party cohesion can be seen as the sociological aspect of party unity, based on factors influencing legislators prior to their election, such as cultural norms and ideological solidarity. The result is a unified party entering the legislature. Legislative discipline, on the other hand, can be perceived as the institutional aspect because it is based on party mechanisms that can impose unity, such as career advancement and the whip. The result is that a somewhat noncohesive party can still be expected to vote in a unified manner due to legislative discipline (Hazan 2003).

party-centered responsiveness. We begin by delineating the first of these two approaches, and then turn to the second one.

### *Selectorate I: A negative linear relationship*

How do different selectorates affect the responsiveness of members of parliament (MPs)? While modern democracy is largely about representatives who are responsive to the people, this responsiveness is mediated by either party or nonparty actors. Legislative performance is likely to be influenced by the way legislators respond to different selectorates. Party unity is likely to be higher when legislators respond to party actors and lower when nonparty mediators are involved.

Bowler (2000) argued that the best explanation of the collective action of legislators lies in the nomination procedures in general, and who does the nominating in particular. Since a basic motivation in the behavior of legislators is their desire to be reselected, they will be responsive to the demands of their selectorates. Following this logic, when legislators are selected by small selectorates – the party leader, a few local leaders, or a small party agency – they will display a rather high level of party cohesion. The aim will be to satisfy the small oligarchies who have the power to reselect them, or at least play a dominant role in their reselection. When selected by a very inclusive selectorate – such as the entire electorate or all party members – legislators will be exposed to various, and sometimes conflicting, pressures. Seeking to respond to the range of such cross-pressures could lead legislators to deviate from the party program or act in a way that reduces party cohesion. This conviction concerning candidate selection and parliamentary cohesion was expressed by Epstein (1964: 55) when he argued, "It appears illogical to combine primaries, intended to make legislators independent of party, with a parliamentary system that requires cohesive legislative parties in order to provide stable government." As Figure 9.1 suggests, the inclusiveness of the selectorate is thus an explanatory variable in differentiating between candidate-centered and party-centered responsiveness.

The more inclusive the candidate selection method is, the less cohesive the party will be, because legislators will face effective – and even nonparty – cross-

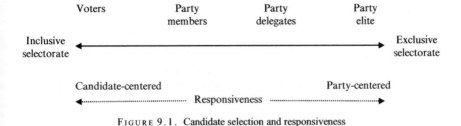

FIGURE 9.1. Candidate selection and responsiveness

pressures. Facing a large and fluid selectorate, legislators will be responsive to those who can supply the resources, votes, and access to such a selectorate. Responsiveness cannot be to the individual party members per se (e.g. in the case of party primaries) because it is too costly to invest in direct contact with members of a large, unstable, and amorphous selectorate. Legislators will, therefore, be responsive to at least three kinds of nonparty moderators that can facilitate their link with such a wide selectorate (Rahat 2008*b*). First there are the capital holders, who supply the finances necessary to enable a candidate to identify himself or herself to the selectorate through a personalized campaign. Then there are leaders of groups of various kinds (unions, clans), who can supply the candidate with campaign activists and selectors.[2] Finally, there is the mass media that boasts an immediate and wide audience, with its special requirements for newsworthiness. These moderators could promote different interests, or even interests that are at odds with those of the party, its ideology, or its leaders. As Narud, Pedersen, and Valen (2002*b*: 227) argued, "The opening up of the nomination process gives other actors . . . potential influence on the question of candidate selection." Ranney (1965: 781) was quite clear when he wrote that US primaries "empower mass communications media and various non-party organizations . . . to perform tasks that elsewhere belong to parties." Sheafer and Tzionit (2006) showed that media-political skills are indeed most important to the success of candidates selected by party members, less so when party delegates are the selectors, and not important when selection is highly exclusive.

The more exclusive the candidate selection method, the more central is the role of the party vis-à-vis other possible actors, as shown in Table 9.1. The role of nonparty actors in candidate selection increases with the expansion of an exclusive selectorate, as does their importance as objects for responsiveness. When the party elite selects the legislators, they are likely to be first and foremost party players. Legislators who are selected by party delegates are likely to be party

TABLE 9.1. *The selectorate, responsiveness, and party unity*

| Selectorate | Responsiveness | Party unity |
| --- | --- | --- |
| Party elite | Party | Very high (party-centered) |
| Party delegates | More party than nonparty | High (mainly party-centered) |
| Party members | Party and nonparty | Moderate–high (conflicting pressures) |
| Voters | More nonparty than party | Low (candidate-centered) |

[2] We do not include in our category of nonparty actors those interest groups that are an integral element of parties, such as the trade unions in many European social democratic parties. When (and if) these historical relationships come to an end, we will then be able to consider them nonparty actors. Indeed, in Israel, several trade unions cut their historical links with Labor and were active in candidate selection within both center and right-wing parties (Rahat 2008*b*).

players at most times, but may nevertheless be predisposed to promoting the demands and interests of certain groups within the party – that is, the groups that serve as their power base. Legislators who are selected in primaries need the help of nonparty actors in order to be reselected. Therefore, they are more likely to be exposed to the pressures of these groups and to be responsive to them. When legislators face a plethora of potentially conflicting pressures, party unity is likely to decrease. When it comes to the most inclusive selectorate, the voters, party unity will be at its lowest because the party will become just another actor that the legislators have to be responsive to, and not necessarily the main one.

As Key (1967: 452) put it in terms of the United States, "The nomination stage is the point at which party discipline can be applied most effectively. Yet, the direct primary is a procedure not easily usable, either by the national leadership or by the voters of a district, for that purpose." The adoption of primaries thus led to a decline in party cohesion in the United States (Crotty 2006). Ansolabehere, Hirano, and Snyder (2007) showed this to be true not only over time in general, but concerning the same legislators in particular, as new and more inclusive candidate selection methods were adopted. Moreover, while the effect was moderate at most times, it was apparent not only when legislators dealt with minor issues, but when they dealt with highly controversial and symbolic matters as well. In the case of the United States, we have reached a point where the role of the party in candidate recruitment is no longer taken as a given (Kazee and Thornberry 1990).

Responsiveness, the opening up of the selectorate, and party cohesion are therefore related. Put another way, democratizing the selectorate promotes personalized politics over and above party politics (Rahat and Sheafer 2007). Key (1967: 371) argued long ago that "the necessity for popular appeal to win nominations tends to splinter the leadership into cliques, factions, and even lone-wolf, individual aspirants for party power." Later, based on comparative evidence, Gallagher (1988c: 271, emphasis in original) declared that in order to maintain cohesion and party-centered responsiveness, "it may not matter much, in this sense *which* party agency selects candidates, but it does matter that *some* party agency selects them."

In their studies of the voting behavior of members of the European Parliament, both Faas (2003) and Hix (2004) found that candidate selection method influences party unity, and that more exclusive methods give national parties more influence over the behavior of their representatives. Data from Israel support this claim. The overall tendency to open up candidate selection methods has gone hand in hand with an increase in both the proposing and the passage of private member bills (Hazan 1997b, 1999b; Rahat and Sheafer 2007), along with other types of personalized behavior (Dotan and Hofnung 2005).[3] Moreover, as Kenig and Barnea (2009: 269) demonstrated in their study of the selection of ministers,

---

[3] For two differing analyses of the Israeli case, see Shomer (2009) and Akirav (2010).

"The decisive set of criteria changes throughout the years in Israel from seniority and loyalty to intra-party political power ... this shift was facilitated by the democratization of the candidate selection methods."

Kristjánsson (1998) claimed that widening participation in the selection process proved to be a successful strategy for the electoral survival of the Icelandic parties. This fits the party evolution model's claim of adaptability. At the same time, though, he explained that the unintended price was a decrease in party cohesion "The primary election period in Iceland, since the early 1970s, coincides with decreasing party cohesion. Increasingly, Icelandic political parties resemble umbrella organizations for individual politicians rather than highly disciplined organizations" (Kristjánsson 1998: 177). This led him to conclude that decreased cohesion will make it more difficult for parties to be responsive to the people.

Taiwan's experience with primaries points to a similar conclusion. The primaries adopted during democratization led to more independent behavior by the representatives, thus eroding party cohesion even in the once-Leninist and disciplined Kuomintang Party, and as a result the party tried to move away from them (Baum and Robinson 1999; Wu 2001; Wu and Fell 2001). In Mexico, the adoption of primaries not only damaged party cohesion, it also brought about the phenomenon of deserters who crossed from one party to another, along with their supporters, if they did not win the selection process in their original party (Combes 2003).

### Selectorate II: A nonlinear relationship, or maybe even no relationship

An alternative approach to the consequences of democratizing candidate selection is based on two developing and associated models of political parties. The first is that of the cartel party (Mair 1994, 1997; Katz and Mair 1995; Katz 2001), and the second is that of the stratarchically organized party (Carty 2004, 2008; Carty and Cross 2006). The latter builds on the former, particularly when it comes to the expanding role of party members, and as such both models can be considered quite similar in their approaches to the ramifications of intraparty democracy.

Cartel party leaders see the problems of government in managerial rather than in ideological terms. They desire autonomy – particularly from those who are motivated ideologically. In short, the cartel model requires that the party leadership be able to compromise across party lines. This, in turn, necessitates a leadership that is not limited by constraints imposed on them from a group of ideological activists. Logically, then, the leaders of the cartel party have to neutralize party activists. This strategy is aimed at denying to ideologically motivated activists the opportunity to organize and speak for party members.

A prime example of this strategy is to have party decisions, such as candidate selection, opened up to the full membership.

Thus, according to the cartel party model, the pattern of interparty relationships postulated to exist among the parties forming the cartel assumes and requires a considerable degree of elite autonomy in order to participate effectively in the cross-party cartel. The model suggests that one possible strategy used by party leaders in order to achieve this necessary autonomy is to empower the ordinary party member. An increase in the nominal power of the base of the party will come at the expense of the power of middle-level activists, who are more likely to be motivated by ideology and also most likely to be able to coordinate an effective challenge to the autonomy of the party leaders.

Thus, the cartel party model guides party leaders to adopt a democratization strategy that will give them greater leverage and will dilute the influence of ideologically motivated and organizationally entrenched activists. The rationale behind this option is that the less intensely involved rank-and-file party members are more likely to be swayed by such factors as name recognition, and hence more likely to take cues from the highly visible party leadership. Mair (1997: 148–50) explained this strategy:

> The somewhat curious pattern that is developing therefore seems to be one in which the party in public office is afforded more power or autonomy... and in which, at the same time, through enhanced democratization, the ordinary members themselves, albeit sometimes fewer in number, are being afforded a greater role ... the process of intra-party democratization is being extended to the members as individuals rather than to what might be called the organized party on the ground. In other words, it is not the party congress, or the middle-level elite, or the activists who are being empowered, but rather the "ordinary" members, who are at once more docile and more likely to endorse the policies (and candidates) proposed by the party leadership and by the party in public office. This is, in fact, one of the most commonly distinct trends we see today ... it may well be the case that a fully democratized party is more susceptible to control by the party in public office.

This strategy will maintain, or even increase, the power of the party leaders, rather than diminish it and bring about the associated decline in party unity previously outlined. According to this approach, the expansion of the selectorate did not result in the shifting of power in a single direction, but rather it has simultaneously shifted both up (to the leaders) and down (to the members), at the expense of the middle (the activists).

The most significant aspect of this strategy is that despite embracing a more inclusive selectorate, this democratization of the candidate selection process is only an elusive empowerment of the party's base. The goal of this particular democratization strategy is to reorient MPs away from the local party activists and toward the national party in public office. If successful, this strategy might avoid the consequences elaborated earlier – no weakening of party cohesiveness in the parliamentary arena. A successful example of this strategy was that of New Labour in Britain under Tony Blair.

To sum up, the cartel party approach expects party unity to be lower when candidates are selected by delegates and higher when atomistic crowds of members or voters perform this task. While not explicit about it, cartel theorists – similar to those scholars who espouse the competing approach presented above (Selectorate I) – seem to think that selection by the party elite will result in the greatest degree of unity.

The stratarchically organized party model takes these internal party developments one step further. It points out some of the current characteristics of modern party organization and suggests that they define a new pattern of internal relationships. This model declares that individual party members are gaining increased decision-making power, especially over crucial personnel choices, and that simultaneously party identification is in decline, forcing parties to resort increasingly to opportunistic electoral appeals. The result is that political parties are more leader-driven yet at the same time internally democratic, and have to compete in a more open electoral market with a less solid support base. If in the past parties were essentially hierarchical organizations within which individuals competed for power, and this contest was a zero-sum game where power held by one came at the expense of the others, they have now become multilevel organizations in which the separate levels enjoy significant autonomy. In other words, parties have become something akin to federal systems, or a network of affiliated organizations.

Carty (2004) argued that parties have become a franchise system which couples efficiencies of scale and standardization with the advantages of local participation in the delivery of the organization's product. There is no longer a zero-sum contest for power – power is broadly shared, and the autonomy of the different units is constrained by the interdependence of its parts. The economic analogy of a franchise to the political world and the multilevel stratarchical organization of political parties are explained by Carty (2004: 11–12), as follows:

> As a whole, the party embodies and sustains a brand that defines its place in the political spectrum and is the focus for supporters' generalized loyalties. Typically, parties' central organizations are responsible for providing the basic product line (policy and leadership), for devising and directing the major communication line (the national campaign) and for establishing standard organizational management, training and financing functions. In office, the central party is likely to play the principal part in any governance responsibilities the party assumes. Local units, however they are defined (geographically or otherwise), more often provide the basic organizational home of most party members, and are typically charged with delivering the product, i.e., creating organizations that can find and support candidates as well as mobilizing campaigns to deliver the vote on the ground. Intermediary and specialized units can support these activities, but, once institutionalized, all elements must

recognize their part and accept the power and role trade-offs as a necessary part
of the bargain for making the party, as a whole, successful.

The functional autonomy of the party's organizational elements does not proscribe
any particular pattern of influence, and quite different solutions to the problems of
policy development or candidate selection can be found. At the heart of the
stratarchical party is a franchise contract, argued Carty (2004), which defines the
internal organization of the party. It delineates the party units in terms of their
autonomous powers and responsibilities. In other words, it is a bargain between
the various levels over rights and duties. This allows the stratarchical party to
avoid the loss of unity associated with giving party members more power within
their organizations, especially with regard to candidate selection. Members select
and representatives follow the party line; the two do not have much to do with each
other.

Both the cartel and the stratarchical party models thus argue that increasing
inclusiveness need not result in organizational consequences that will impair the
party's ability to remain cohesive (see also Scarrow 1999*a*, 1999*b*). However,
both models are based on the underlying fact that the power of the members
is considerable, but clearly constrained. Control over candidate selection is
predicated by members' willingness either to follow the cues offered by the
party leaders or to avoid any attempt to influence the position taken by the parties
on the policies over which national elections are fought. As Carty (2004: 19)
explained:

> Party selectors enjoy their powers only by virtue of the stratarchical distribu-
> tion of authority within the wider party organization. Thus, in Canada, Ireland
> and New Zealand, local party members know that the right to name their
> candidates is part of a more complex and encompassing franchise bargain in
> which the various organizational units embrace the opportunities but accept
> the limitations that the structure provides.

### The two approaches in light of empirical evidence

Indeed, while in Iceland, Israel, Mexico, and Taiwan we have clear evidence that
democracy within parties brought about a reduction in party unity, in several
countries we have witnessed the expansion of intraparty democracy without
many of the associated consequences. We turn now to these cases in order to
understand why. What were the factors that enabled parties in these countries to
avoid the ramifications of the expansion of the selectorate evident in some of the
other cases?

In Canada – upon which much of the stratarchical model literature is based – the
parties have exchanged local autonomy for strict national cohesion (Carty, Cross,
and Young 2000; Carty and Eagles 2003; Cross 2004). That is, inclusiveness has not
led to a decrease in party cohesion because the local selectorates choose candidates

who will stick to the party line in the national legislature. Malloy (2003) added that the volatile membership patterns associated with a more inclusive selectorate can actually work in favor of keeping MPs loyal, since the unstable membership in the constituency means that dissenting MPs cannot count on retaining the support of the constituency organization if a challenger signs up more members. In other words, while the Canadian case shows a more democratized candidate selection process, this process is constrained by the particularly Canadian constellation of a parliamentary system with strong legislative incentives for discipline, despite a lack of party cohesion. This constellation, coupled with the distinct geographically based distribution of party support in Canada and a complicated dissonant relationship between the national and the provincial parties, results in multilevel, autonomous, stratarchically organized parties.

Other countries, with geographically based sociopolitical cleavages, do not necessarily reproduce the Canadian example of local support for national party unity. Obler (1970), who studied the Belgian parties, claimed that MPs who consistently toed the party line, and refused to deviate even when it ran counter to the demands of the local organization, were sometimes denied reselection. Obler explained this based on the complicated social cleavages in Belgium, which can pit the local and regional levels against the national level.

Bolleyer (2009) argued that opening membership and keeping candidate selection at the local level are two dynamics ascribed to the cartel model, but that these two are difficult to reconcile with maintaining party unity. The organizational vulnerability of cartel parties can be overcome by the use of selective benefits, such as political appointments and patronage. One example is Fianna Fail in Ireland, which uses patronage when in power and internal reforms when in opposition to generate party unity.

In short, while the first approach outlined in this section on the selectorate focuses on the responsiveness of legislators and the systemic consequences of democracy within parties, the second is based on the cartel model and on the distribution of power inside parties. The first approach argues that real intraparty democracy makes it difficult for parties to be responsive to their voters. The cartel approach interprets some forms of democratization as instruments used by the party elite in an attempt to control the base. While these two approaches have contradicting implications for party unity, when it comes to responsiveness they both lead essentially to the same conclusion – there is a tradeoff between democracy within parties and responsiveness to a party's voters.

Moreover, we need not exaggerate claims concerning the decline in cohesion when dealing with parliamentary systems, because such systems are designed to maintain a relatively high level of cohesion if the government is to survive in power. After all, as Ranney (1968) argued, cohesion is influenced by a group of factors, based first and foremost on the parliamentary regime, which supplies strong positive incentives to maintain party unity. We can thus talk about a decline in cohesion, not about a wholesale change.

It might be that while candidate selection reforms immediately influenced, for example, Israel's still developing and fluid political system, Iceland's small and intimate polity, and Taiwan's and Mexico's young democracies, in Europe the consequences are simply delayed. That is, Europe's larger polities, which are based on older political traditions, have yet to exhibit the expected influence of adopting more inclusive candidate selection methods as outlined by the first approach. Thus, while we may find only preliminary signs of increasingly independent behavior on the part of parliamentarians, as indicated by Whiteley and Seyd (1999) in their study of the British Conservative Party, the potential is there. If democracy within parties is fully adopted – without the screening done by exclusive selectorates – the structures of reward and punishment will likely reduce cohesion in the future.

Furthermore, the relationship between the inclusiveness of the candidate selection method and party cohesion might not be linear. It may be that party cohesion declines significantly only when the level of inclusiveness passes a certain threshold, rather than running parallel to the degree of inclusiveness. That is, cohesion declines significantly when selection is completely in the hands of party members or the voters. But if other, less inclusive selectorates are involved – as is the case with multistage and weighted candidate selection methods – then party cohesion, or at least legislative discipline, can be sustained. Candidates who know that in order to be reselected they have to satisfy party-oriented selectorates – such as party elites or party delegates – are less likely to deviate from the party line than those who have to face only members or supporters. As Hopkin (2001: 358) concluded in his study of the impact of involving party members in candidate selection in Britain and Spain, "The powers that party leaders *retain* ensure organizational cohesion" [emphasis added].

## DECENTRALIZATION AND RESPONSIVENESS: SOME SPECULATIONS

Hix (2004) and Benedetto and Hix (2007) claimed that more centralized candidate selection systems lead to more party control over its representatives. Sieberer (2006) studied eleven parliamentary democracies, and found that central party control over nominations indeed affects party unity. Decentralization is dichotomized in Sieberer's study, and the Rice Index of party cohesion (Rice 1925) in countries with centralized candidate selection methods stands at 98.19, slightly higher than 96.65 in countries with decentralized methods.[4]

---

[4] It should be noted, however, that like many other scholars, Sieberer (2006) combined decentralization and the inclusiveness of the selectorate in his measure.

Party unity in a decentralized system is based on the desire of party activists to produce candidates who are responsive to both local interests and the national party line. Or to put it another way, it is the local party activists who guarantee party unity at the national level due to their national orientation. Ranney (1965, 1968) described local control over candidate selection in Britain as a handful of local activists doing the work for the national party leadership. Denver (1988) also concluded that a combination of decentralized selection and a still somewhat exclusive party selectorate makes candidates dependent directly on the satisfaction of the party activists in the constituency (see also Epstein 1960). As Epstein (1977*a*: 17) put it when referring to the similar case of the Australian parties:

> Local activists ... tend to reinforce their national party cause by selecting
> candidates known to be as loyal to that cause as are the activists themselves.
> Usually no central party authority need direct these activists to choose a loyal
> party candidate or to drop a disloyal one. The active party members them-
> selves want to help their national cause, and the way to do so is to select not
> just winning candidates but also faithful ones ... Control of this kind appears
> to be an ingredient of a system dependent on regularly cohesive parliamentary
> voting. To allow a rebel MP to appeal to all of his party's voters, in an
> American-style direct primary, would be manifestly dangerous to the accepted
> dictates of the system.

Roberts (1988: 113) made a similar case for Germany, arguing that "the influence of the local and regional elites over candidate selection, especially of list candidates, does reinforce party discipline." Once again, the emphasis in all of these cases is on local *elites*; so while decentralization can be extensive, the selectorate is still not at the inclusive end of its dimension.

In their study of six presidential democracies, Crisp et al. (2004) found that the influence of the national leadership over candidate selection enabled them to control legislators, regardless of the size of the district. In other words, no relationship between decentralization and party control over candidate selection was found. Party unity, and its resulting influence on responsiveness, is not affected by decentralization as long as the party can maintain control – which we argue can be done either by imposing candidacy requirements, limiting the inclusiveness of the selectorate, or increasing the extent of nominations.

However, if national party leaders do not maintain control over candidate selection, then Crisp et al. (2004) did see a relationship between decentralization and party unity. More centralized *and* exclusive candidate selection methods produced legislators who focused on national legislation, as opposed to more decentralized and inclusive selection methods which resulted in representatives' focusing on private legislation. That is, if candidate selection moves along the other dimensions as well, then a shift from more centralized to decentralized methods will result in a decline in party unity and the ability to be responsive to the overall party voters. Epstein (1980) pointed out that the lack of unity and the focus on local responsiveness of American parties is due not only to decentralization but also to the general weakness of party organization.

In short, the ambition to be reselected breeds responsiveness because it leads representatives to try to satisfy their selectorates – to be responsive to them. Decentralizing candidate selection could lead to conflicts between the pressures emanating from the district and those coming from the national party leadership.[5] The party can control this by utilizing the other dimensions of candidate selection. However, if the party is "weak" on several dimensions, both party unity and party responsiveness are in jeopardy.

In Argentina, we see an interesting case of a candidate selection method with a rather decentralized and inclusive selectorate that still results in party unity. Both Jones (2008) and Scherlis (2008) explain this based on patronage. Party deputies are loyalists because they either seek some future support in their bid for the next political position from the party's regional and national machines, or because they want to gain resources for their constituency from either the governor or the president, and in exchange deliver support in parliament. This case demonstrates that a patron–client relationship (and possibly personal corruption) may enable parties (or rather their leader) to maintain discipline even when using a highly inclusive and fairly decentralized selection method.

Gabel and Scheve (2007) pointed out an interesting distinction. A more centralized and exclusive selection method results in a division of opinions within the party – between leaders and activists – thereby impacting negatively on party cohesion. A more decentralized and inclusive selection process, on the other hand, could produce a party with more shared preferences – and hence more ideological cohesion – because here the leaders have to recruit the support of both the activists and the rank-and-file party members. However, these findings relate to opinions, and the differences in cohesion do not have to translate into actual legislative behavior. In the first, centralized and exclusive case, the party can overcome lower cohesion by imposing legislative discipline. In the second, decentralized and inclusive case – when local and national interests clash – the party will be unable to impose legislative discipline in an effective manner. This is in line with our argument that decentralization is important for responsiveness, but that its impact can be either offset or exacerbated by the other dimensions of candidate selection.

---

[5] Another possibility is a threefold division between local, regional, and national interests. In Argentina, for example, representatives are mainly responsive to the regional level – not the local or the national levels – who work directly with the president, providing legislative votes in exchange for regional favors (Jones 2002, 2008).

## THE IMPACT OF APPOINTMENT AND VOTING
## ON RESPONSIVENESS

As previously stated, this dimension is largely ignored in the research literature, so our discussion here is based on a reasonable theoretical premise. It should also be noted that it is difficult to isolate the impact of the appointment and voting systems from those at the level of inclusiveness of the selectorate. That is, appointment will necessarily take place in smaller and more exclusive selectorates, while voting will be found in more inclusive ones, becoming a necessity when the selectorate includes more than a few dozen selectors.

An appointment procedure means that the power of selection is concentrated in the hands of a small group. This group deliberates and selects a team of candidates, which means that being a team player can help a candidate ensure reselection. In an appointment system the party has a better chance of controlling selection – and enhancing cohesion – and can also use selection as a disciplinary tool. In this case, personal responsiveness takes a back seat, and party responsiveness is best served. The exact nature of this responsiveness is dependent upon the nature of the party. If it is an aggregative pluralistic party, then a unified and cohesive team will be the end product of deliberation and compromises. If it is a leadership party, then cohesion will be a sign of the leader's organizational control.

When voting exists, it is much harder to coordinate and control the results. The connection between voting and personal responsiveness is apparent – only voting procedures allow explicit competition among contestants; and where candidates compete with one another in intraparty elections for the party nomination, it is not surprising that they will emphasize personal responsiveness over party responsiveness. To paraphrase Carey and Shugart (1995), voting procedures that differentiate candidates both from each other and from their parties may induce politicians to cultivate a "personal intraparty vote," thus emphasizing personal over party responsiveness.

Different voting systems can also mean different results in terms of responsiveness. Multi-round systems supply more opportunity for the party organization to navigate selection than a single-round selection. When candidates are selected one by one, or even in small groups, it is easier to ensure that no mavericks reach realistic positions. When all are selected in a single-round, it is more likely that mavericks will get in.

The specific impact of the different voting formulas on responsiveness, however, is more difficult to pinpoint. On the one hand, majoritarianism might be the ideal tool to guarantee cohesion and discipline, because it ensures that selected candidates will need majority support in order to be reselected. Other, more proportional formulas allow minority candidates to win realistic positions and thus might allow more intraparty pluralism, which could be translated into a decrease in party cohesion. On the other hand, majoritarianism creates a winner-take-all competition that might lead to a majoritarian takeover of all realistic positions and could result in a party split, while proportionality could enable the regulation of differences within the party.

All selections are competitive by their very nature. However, some preference voting systems might supply incentives that would somewhat check the intensity of competition. For example, the "sophisticated" points system that we presented in Chapter 5 gives incentives for candidates to cooperate – or at least avoid alienating the supporters of other candidates – because they are interested in securing the lower preferences of the other candidates' supporters. In short, some voting systems can do a better job of checking intraparty competition, and are thus less likely to encourage intraparty tensions that can damage party cohesion.

To summarize, we argue that there is a largely dichotomous relationship between appointment and voting. The first is likely to breed party responsiveness, and the second personal responsiveness. The extent of one kind of responsiveness vis-à-vis the other can be affected, however, by the specific properties of the voting system or by the scope of appointments.

## PARTY FINANCING

We must remember that it was the aim of some of the main proponents of more inclusive primaries to break the power of the party leadership and its organization over the selection of candidates (Duverger 1954; Ware 2002). What they might not have taken into consideration was that the more inclusive the candidate selection method is, the more legislators will face nonparty pressures. Facing a massive and amorphous selectorate, legislators will be responsive to those who can supply the resources needed to access such a selectorate. Responsiveness cannot be to the individual party members because there are too many in an inclusive selectorate, and they constantly come and go. Direct contact with the members of a large and unstable selectorate is either impractical or impossible. Candidates need money to buy access to the selectorate, to address it either directly through the "paid" media or indirectly as instructed by their paid campaign professionals. Money becomes more and more important as the inclusiveness of the selectorates increases. As Breaux and Gierzynski (1991: 439) argued in their study of the highly inclusive candidate selection methods that are in use in the United States:

> Campaign expenditures are an important determinant of state legislative primary outcomes. Candidates hopeful of winning state legislative primaries are able to increase their share of the vote by spending large sums of money. Candidates are also able to decrease their opponents' share of the primary vote by increasing their own level of campaign spending.

After incumbency, which affords a dramatic advantage in the primaries, money is probably the next most significant factor – particularly when an opponent is challenging an incumbent. Indeed, incumbents often find it easier to raise funds, making incumbency and finances an almost unbeatable combination in a more inclusive selectorate (Goodliffe and Magleby 2001). This phenomenon is not strictly an American one. For example, Jones (2008) and Scherlis (2008) point out that success in Argentine primaries was connected to candidates' success in recruiting financial and material resources.

The influence of finances in candidate selection is not a new issue; parties have been dealing with it for decades. The old practice in the British Conservative Party of "buying" a constituency candidacy in return for financing the local organization and the election campaign was ended by the Maxwell Fyfe Report on party finance in 1948–9. These findings were echoed by the Labour Party in the Wilson Report of 1957, which curbed the personal financing of candidate expenses (Norris and Lovenduski 1995; Ranney 1965). In Germany, legal provisions in the 1967 Law on Political Parties prevented interest groups from buying, through donations, safe seats for their representatives (Roberts 1988). In Canada, it took until 2000 for the Liberal Party to address intraparty campaign funding, when it passed rules limiting the amount of money that could be spent and required a report on those funds that were spent (Carty and Eagles 2003). In Israel, the financial regulation of internal party races was implemented in 1992, with the adoption of party primaries (Hofnung 1996a, 1996b). However, significant regulation of the financing of intraparty races is still largely absent in most countries, despite the increase in both the financing and the regulation of interparty competition (Hofnung 2008).

Hofnung (2006, 2008) has studied campaign financing and argues that while state subsidies are granted to parties in a majority of cases, and regulation of finance is the norm in the interparty realm, intraparty public financing hardly exists and most times is not regulated or is underregulated. The lack of public financing forces candidates to seek private financial backers in order to improve their chances, and the lack of regulation allows them to do so in a manner that can influence their responsiveness to a greater extent than the search for funds in the general election – what Hofnung calls seeking financial support from dubious sources regardless of possible future consequences.

While there is a dearth of literature on intraparty financing, and it is somewhat distant from the focus of this book, it is nonetheless important to mention it. The financing of political parties, particularly the intraparty selection process, is extremely important when it comes to responsiveness. Loopholes in existing finance laws, or the lack of such laws, can lead to representatives being beholden to financial backers whose interests can be quite distinct from those of the parties or their voters. Moreover, the extreme case of the negative influence of intraparty finance is the complete overturning of responsiveness on its head: political corruption. The relationship between democracy within parties and responsiveness thus underlines the need to pay special attention to the influence of party finance on candidate selection, especially when the latter becomes more inclusive.

## DEMOCRATIZATION, DELIBERATION, AND RESPONSIVENESS

If the aim is an increase in intraparty democracy without a negative impact on responsiveness, one must hope that a larger selectorate can still be deliberative. If a massive and fluid party membership cannot deliberate with the candidates, assess their attitudes, and ascertain their positions on most of the major issues, how can those selected then know how to be responsive? In other words, if a vast and inchoate group of selectors make their decisions in a rather superficial manner, then we not only face yet another problem associated with intraparty democracy, but also make it increasingly difficult for the representatives to be responsive to the members of the selectorate. Regretfully, such is the case.

Criddle (1984: 229) stated that the more inclusive one-member–one-vote with postal ballots candidate selection method adopted by the Social Democrats in Britain was initially idealistic, but was soon tempered by experience. He concluded that:

> ... many members who had not attended the selection meeting and had not
> therefore seen or heard the candidates, were inclined to vote either on the
> basis of the names they recognized (that is, usually, local people, instead of
> perhaps more suitable outsiders), or simply on the basis of the candidates'
> paper qualifications and statements, without having any idea of their political
> competence.

Britain is one of the main examples of cartel parties. Canada, on the other hand, is the source for the stratarchical model; but here, too, Cross (2004) states that primaries are not deliberative, that many of those who participate are either family members or friends who turn out simply to vote for their candidate and not to listen to the different opinions of the candidates. In other words, they come to vote, not to choose.

In large selectorates, the selected have strong incentives to be responsive to nonparty mediators. Democracies cope with a similar problem of the nonproportional influence of powerful interests in the realm of general elections, but there they have the parties to aggregate the interests of their voters. Moreover, at the interparty level, public subsidies and regulations are used to cope with the challenge of the influence of economic interests in politics. Parties do not have the ability that the state has to manage such challenges. Moreover, state regulation of the interparty arena can result – as exhibited by the American experience with the individual states' regulating candidate selection – in a weakening of party organizations. This, in turn, exposes parties even more to external influences, and thereby strengthens the role of nonparty mediators.

In short – and regardless of the differences between the two alternative models delineated in the section on the selectorate – democracy within parties leads to a loss of control or to a shift of control. There is, therefore, an apparent connection between intraparty democracy and responsiveness. If more democracy within parties leads to a loss of control, then parties and their representatives will find it increasingly difficult to be responsive either to their party selectorate or to their party voters. By the same token, even if intraparty democracy leads only to a shift in control, but the extensive and empowered members are incapable of being deliberative, then this shift in control will still extract a price when it comes to responsiveness. Democracy within parties is unlike democracy between parties – and it requires different arrangements, as our final chapter points out.

# 10

# Candidate Selection, Political Parties, and Democracy

Democratic theory places great importance upon the conduct of elections, but it is not often recognized by theorists and empirical scholars that the (s)electoral game takes place in two arenas: not only between parties, but also within them. Democratic elements such as participation, representation, competition, and responsiveness should be understood and achieved in terms of both intraparty selection and interparty election. The fundamental question concerns the relationship between the system level and the intraparty level. Should both levels use similar mechanisms and rules in order to achieve similar democratic norms? Or, should the intraparty level compensate for the deficiencies of the system level, using different mechanisms and rules in order to serve similar democratic norms?

A number of nongovernmental organizations (NGOs) that are interested in helping establish and sustain democracy – especially in new democracies – are concerned with political parties in general, and with the question of candidate selection in particular. Many of these organizations believe that system-level democracy requires the associations that institutionalize democracy to be internally democratic as well. This concern has been especially prominent with respect to political parties, as exhibited by the commitment of many NGOs to internal party democracy. However, their views on the matter are far from naïve; they do not see participation as the only aspect through which the extent of democracy in candidate selection should be evaluated. Several reports produced by such NGOs over the past decade indicate clearly that they seek intraparty democracy yet recognize the dilemmas, tradeoffs, and risks involved with democracy within parties (Ashiagbor 2008; Norris 2004; Scarrow 2005). For example, the protocol of a meeting between academics and practitioners who work for democracy-promoting NGOs reflects this, stating, "Internal party democratization is not a goal as such but should have positive effects on the state and development of democracy in society. Intra-party democracy may also entail some risks" (Netherlands Institute for Multiparty Democracy 2007: 6).

We share the same intuition of aspiring for intraparty democracy, but also recognize the dilemmas and dangers that it evokes. We, therefore, suggest a broader perspective for evaluating the contribution of candidate selection methods to democracy. Following the proposed framework for analyzing candidate selection methods and their political consequences that was presented in the previous chapters, we can now reexamine the question: Which candidate selection method better serves democracy? Yet, before starting to answer this question, we should first clarify exactly what we mean by the phrase "serving democracy."

## HOW CAN CANDIDATE SELECTION SERVE DEMOCRACY?

In order to assess whether a particular candidate selection method serves democracy we should ask three questions:

1. Does the candidate selection method enable the expression of democratic norms (participation and competition), and does it produce democratic outputs (representation and responsiveness)?
2. Does the candidate selection method serve the liberal norm of power diffusion?
3. Does the candidate selection method enhance the general health of the party as a crucial organization for the functioning of democracy?

The first two questions concern two current, commonly shared general perceptions of (liberal) democracy in general, while the third focuses on the well-being and functioning of the party organization in particular. We now turn to look closely at each of these aspects.

### *Democratic norms and outputs*

If democracy is a system that should work according to specific norms, and produce specific outputs, then we should see candidate selection methods as serving democracy if they promote the four basic democratic elements on which Part II was based: participation, representation, competition, and responsiveness. These four elements appear in the most basic notions of democracy. That is, democracy is a system that allows all citizens to participate in choosing between candidates and groups that claim to better represent their interests and values. These candidates compete amongst themselves for the citizens' support, and after being elected, governing officials are expected to remain responsive to the demands and grievances of their voters.

Participation and competition are two basic norms that are part of even the most minimal definition of democracy (Schumpeter 1943).[1] Representation and responsiveness are two related outputs of a democratic system. Representation – as presence and of ideas – is a central element in modern representative democracy.

---

[1] See also the review of the definitions of democracy in Vanhanen (1990: 7–11).

The theory of representative democracy also expects that the elected representatives will be responsive to their respective (s)electorates.

From this viewpoint, the more democratic candidate selection method would be the one that contributes to the fulfillment of *all four* dimensions of democracy: a high rate of meaningful political participation; representation of relevant social forces and various opinions; true competition for realistic seats or realistic positions on the party's candidate list; and a viable electoral connection that would pressure the (s)elected to be responsive to the needs and grievances of the public (Rahat 2009).

However, as Part II of the book has demonstrated, fulfilling the norm of inclusive participation could result in a decline in the ability to balance representation, might not produce a highly competitive race, and can also create distortions in patterns of responsiveness. This means that we cannot hope to find an ideal system that will at one and the same time both adhere to the basic norms and also produce the necessary outputs; but we can realistically seek one that will optimally balance them.

### Diffusion of power

Another way to look at democracy is as a system that is very suspicious of political power, and thus instead of attempting to stand by specific norms and produce specific products, it aims first and foremost to constrain power. In the intraparty context, the main aim is to prevent the fulfillment of Michels' (1915) "iron law of the oligarchy." From this perspective, power diffusion is the key for democracy. Selection by a single leader, or even a small elite, is obviously bad. We want to clarify, however, that Michels' logic also leads us to refrain from using *any* single selectorate – whether it be local or national, highly inclusive or strictly exclusive. We need to create checks and balances among several selectorates, rather than trust a single selectorate to refrain from developing nondemocratic pathologies. In short, a candidate selection method will better serve democracy if it spreads power among several political actors, rather than concentrating it in the hands of a single selectorate.

### The health of the party

Political parties are an inseparable part of a viable democratic system. Candidate selection poses an opportunity and a challenge for parties. It is an opportunity for payback to the loyal and active members, enabling them to have an influence on who is selected and even to be selected as the party representatives. In order to encourage higher, genuine levels of activism by their members beyond just the selection of candidates, parties must have the ability to distribute special privileges. In other words, candidate selection is an opportunity for the party to provide selective incentives to its members, and thus preserve and even enhance its voluntary component. When the privileges of long-time loyal activists become equivalent to those of new, temporary, and unfaithful members, the differential structure of rewards in parties becomes faulty. Candidate selection is also a challenge for the party because it involves an internal conflict that might – if it is not regulated and constrained – harm the party's ability to mobilize all of its resources for the interparty contest, and may even cause defections and splits.

If political parties are crucial organizations for democracy, and if their well-being is vital for the health of democracy in general, then this implies that it is essential that candidate selection will not harm the party and, as a result, the well-being of the democratic system as a whole. For example, if a party attempts to neutralize its activists by adopting a more democratic candidate selection method – that is, inclusive primaries – it may itself be hurt when it finds out that it has no one to count on when the election nears and it needs campaign volunteers. The party could also discover that selection is no longer an intraparty matter, and that candidate selection is being unduly influenced by nonparty actors. Alternatively, a party in which one group clearly dominates and as a result captures all of the realistic candidacies, could compel the minority to split from the party, and thus hurt the party in any approaching electoral contest with other parties. In short, parties require the ability to reward their members and always need to face the fact that "exit" is an option, which could be chosen due to an inability to supply selective incentives or the failure to contain the contest between candidates within the party.


## HOW INCLUSIVE SHOULD CANDIDACY BE?


Contemporary democracy means that, in principle, every citizen has the right to be elected. But this does not imply that each party must allow every citizen who wishes to compete for votes to do so. First, it is the role of the state to guarantee this universal right, not a specific party. Second, if everyone were eligible to compete for candidacy in all parties, parties would lose their ability to represent coherent interests, values, and policy programs. However, while it is possible for motivated citizens to establish a new party, one must acknowledge that the existing parties are still the main platforms for implementing the basic democratic right of being elected. We thus argue that candidacy should be moderately restricted, but only in such a way that a citizen with serious political aspirations would still be able to compete.

Moderate limitations can help reduce the number of competitors so that a small number of serious aspirants can effectively challenge incumbents. Such limitations can also be constructive in terms of responsiveness, since they are likely to produce a group of candidates who share interests and values, and can thus be expected to function in a relatively cohesive manner. At the same time it still allows, within certain boundaries, for a variety of candidates with somewhat different perceptions of the party's interests and values. Moderate candidacy rules also serve the health of the party organization. They do not permit the party to become an empty vessel, a mere platform for promoting personal aspirations, but still allow for candidacies that are beyond the standard, typical, conformist type.

## WHICH SELECTORATE? OR RATHER, WHICH SELECTORATES?

Based on the analyses in the previous chapters, we can present a schematic picture of the relationships among four general kinds of selectorates in Table 10.1 – derived from their levels of inclusiveness: low, medium, high, and very high (only the very low selectorate of a single leader is excluded).

If we have a clear preference regarding the four proposed democratic dimensions, then Table 10.1 can help us decide which type of selectorate to adopt, and it will also let us know the price that we will pay for this choice. For example, if wide participation is the highest priority, we will stick to the most inclusive selectorate, knowing that we might pay dearly in terms of representation, that competition will not be the greatest possible, and that party actors will lose control to nonparty actors.

But we suggest another path, one that will not produce the highest reward in terms of one dimension, and thus will not require significant payment in terms of the other three dimensions. We do this by striving to achieve, simultaneously, as much as possible on *all four* dimensions.

If we are looking for wide participation, then our choice will be the most inclusive selectorate. However, we saw that we will likely pay a price – *even in terms of participation* – when an increase in the quantity of participation leads to a decrease in its quality (Chapter 6). The solution might be to pose some reasonable obstacles to participation in candidate selection, such as demanding a minimally

TABLE 10.1. *The relationships within parties between participation, representation, competition, and responsiveness in four kinds of party selectorates*

| Selectorate | Participation | Representation | Competition | Responsiveness |
|---|---|---|---|---|
| Party elite | Low | High | Low | Party |
| Party delegates | Medium | Medium | High | Mainly party |
| Party members | High | Low | Medium | Party and nonparty |
| Voters | Highest | Lowest | Medium–low | More nonparty than party |

*Source*: updated from Rahat, Hazan, and Katz (2008).

meaningful term of party membership – one that requires at least two years of paying membership dues, for example – before acquiring the right to participate. This would not be an easy step to adopt, because parties seem to like the demonstration of power that is linked to the mass recruitment of members by competing candidates. Successful candidates might also be reluctant, as their source of success might be their ability to instantly register personal supporters as party members. Yet the health of the party organization, in the long run, will be much better off with a higher quality membership rather than just a larger number of members.

Smaller, more exclusive selectorates can do a better job when it comes to representation (Chapter 7). Yet, it is possible both to involve wider selectorates and to ensure representation by somewhat constraining the selectors' choices, using mechanisms such as quotas. However, these mechanisms should be used wisely, otherwise they may damage representation rather than enhance it. As elaborated in Chapter 7, the wise use of such mechanisms requires parties to be generous, rather than to ensure only a minimum level of representation equal to the existing level of (under)representation. In other words, quotas should not become a rationale for the preservation of underrepresentation. Parties must also gently confront the problem of incumbency. On the one hand, parties should make room for new and more representative candidates, but on the other hand they must not push too hard because this could turn the powerful group of incumbents into the enemies of representation. Parties should, therefore, adopt quotas that will progressively increase with each election in list systems, and concentrate their efforts on "open" seats in single-member district systems.

As for competition, the choice does not have to be – from a democratic point of view – the most competitive candidate selection method (Chapter 8). Other factors, such as the electoral system and voter behavior, also affect competition. If the overall level of competition at the system level is sufficient, then there is no need to reproduce a similar amount also at the intraparty level. Yet, the parties themselves should be interested in at least a minimal amount of competition and turnover in order to sustain the responsiveness and accountability of incumbents, and to give hope to those candidates who see themselves as next in line. When system-level competition and turnover are extremely low, then producing a high level of intraparty competition could serve the general cause of democracy.

Responsiveness to any of the four types of selectorates can be justified by certain democratic notions. The more party-centered notions might lead to a preference for a more exclusive selectorate, while the more popular notions might lead toward a more inclusive one. Our argument is that any continuous use of a single selectorate to choose candidates will result in specific pathologies that we should try to avoid from both democratic and organizational points of view (Chapter 9). These pathologies could include corrupt practices, patron–client relations, dwindling cohesion, or lack of any pluralism under the rule of a singleminded elite.

Since no single selectorate can provide us with what we strive to achieve, it is necessary to involve more than just one selectorate in the candidate selection process. Using several selectorates with different levels of inclusiveness can enable the party to overcome the specific pathologies of a particular selectorate, because power will be spread out and no single selectorate will have full control. It will also mean that selected candidates must balance between party-centered and personal patterns of responsiveness. Moreover, involving several selectorates contributes to the notion that power should be diffused rather than concentrated. Furthermore, parties will be able to involve wide selectorates and at the same time grant their activists selective incentives, giving them a greater role than that of the mostly passive members.

## WHICH, AND HOW MUCH, DECENTRALIZATION?

Territorial decentralization allows parties to reflect regional and local identities that are sometimes entrenched in history, it enables the representation of regional or local interests and values, and it also has an organizational logic related to the level of decentralization of the electoral system in use. But territorial decentralization, while enabling regional and local representation, may impair attempts to secure other kinds of representation (Chapter 6). Competition, we demonstrated (Chapter 8), is at its lowest when using decentralized methods. Decentralization could enhance the power of local selectorates to the point that it weakens the ability of the party to promote national party programs and policies – and it could lead to an overabundance of pork-barrel politics. Responsiveness needs to be balanced between the different levels, the national and the local (and possibly, if relevant, also the regional). In short, it seems that the involvement of both regional and national selectorates might be necessary to allow the balancing of different, and sometimes even conflicting democratic ideals, local versus national values and interests, and organizational needs. Yet this should be done with much caution, because the party as a national entity cannot – and should not – lose its foot soldiers. Finally, territorial decentralization means the distribution of power among many subunits of the party, and in terms of power dispersion surely serves democracy.

From the perspective of power distribution, decentralization aimed at territorial representation is not unlike decentralization that targets social representation. There could be variations, however, because of the different ways that these kinds of representation are usually assured. Mechanisms that guarantee territorial representation are typically more decentralized because they imply that a selectorate in a specific district selects that district's representative. By contrast, the most common representation correction mechanism used is the quota (for women), and it is less decentralized. That is, while candidacy is decentralized when using quotas for women, the selectorate is not, as it is composed of both men and women.[2]

Mechanisms such as quotas help fulfill the democratic goal of social representation. At the same time, they limit competition when they distinguish between certain kinds of candidates (women, minorities) and the rest. However, such mechanisms can be democratically justified as long as they are perceived as temporary, intended to guarantee that all contestants stand on the same starting line without giving anyone an advantage. Responsiveness can also be influenced by the use of certain representation correction mechanisms. If quotas are in use, then the candidates selected by quotas owe their selection to the same selectorate as their fellow candidates. But if certain candidates are selected by selectors of their own kind – a specific ethnic minority representative by party members or delegates who belong to the same minority group, a union representative by only party members or delegates who are affiliated with the specific union, etc. – then they will be more attentive to the demands of their specific groups, and may put the interests and views of these groups above those of their party. Such behavior could serve the cause of representation, but it could also impair the party's ability to aggregate interests and to work cohesively in the legislative arena. In short, here too we look for the optimal balance between the different levels (national, regional, and local) and types (territorial and social) of representation.

## WHAT KIND, OR COMBINATION, OF APPOINTMENT AND VOTING SYSTEMS?

Voting is clearly a more democratic procedure than appointment. Only a voting procedure allows for meaningful participation by more than a few people; only voting allows for meaningful democratic competition among contestants. At the same time, by its very nature, voting does not allow parties to balance representation. The use of representation correction mechanisms can help to a certain extent but, as already argued, their use is not without a price for those groups that they aim to empower.

From the perspective of the diffusion of power, voting is surely preferable because it implies dispersing power among the individual selectors, as opposed to concentrating it in the hands of a small appointing group. However, nomination committees are usually not closed, singleminded oligarchies; rather, they are frequently composed of representatives of the major rival groups within a party and thus allow for compromises rather than for a majoritarian takeover. It seems

---

[2] While it is also possible to guarantee territorial representation through the use of quotas, or the representation of women by designing districts for women, this is either far less frequent or nonexistent.

that democracy will be optimally served, once again, by the well-crafted use of both systems: appointment for creating a representative shortlist by an exclusive selectorate; and voting for amending and ranking by an inclusive selectorate.

The selection of candidates can be made via various types of voting system. These systems can be distinguished according to their levels of proportionality (Chapter 5). The question of which of these systems is more democratic can be analyzed through the prism of the age-old debate between the advocates of proportional representation and majoritarian electoral systems (Taagepera and Shugart 1989: 47–57). Proportional representation is considered more representative, while majoritarian systems claim to lead to more stable and effective governance. Indeed, more proportional voting systems are more democratic in their treatment of representation by giving the minority a chance to be represented, but on the other hand, they could lead the minority to be responsive to a specific group rather than to the party as a whole. Proportional representation voting systems do, however, have the upper hand when it comes to the goal of checking power through its diffusion (Riker 1984).

Another question regarding voting systems is whether to select all candidates at the same time or to fill realistic candidacies gradually. Selection at the same time means that each candidate is competing with all others simultaneously, which can be seen as the fairest form of competition among individuals. However, in terms of the needs of the party as an organization – such as the need to balance representation – gradual selection seems to work better.

It may be easier to maintain internal peace among different groups within the party when candidacy is decided by appointment, as a result of deliberation among the representatives of these groups. Internal peace can also be kept when using voting systems, if they allow for balancing representation through the use of proportional or semi-proportional representation and gradual selection. There are additional considerations that have to do with the kind of voting, such as whether it involves ranking and how the ranking would be tallied. As demonstrated in Chapter 5, certain counting methods can be useful in restraining competition and might thus be constructive for maintaining internal peace, while other methods can escalate competition and develop into a zero-sum game with its associated negative impact on the party at election time.

## A PROPOSED CANDIDATE SELECTION METHOD

A major conclusion that arises from our analyses and comparisons of the political ramifications of different candidate selection methods is that there is no single method that ideally serves our three goals: expressing democratic norms and producing democratic outputs, the diffusion of political power, and the health of the party organization. In short, each candidate selection method has its pros and cons, and the implementation of any one of them is not a mere mechanical choice, but rather implies an important political decision to accept a certain tradeoff regarding a set of democratic goals that cannot all be maximally pursued at once. Thus, what we are looking for is a system that optimally (rather than ideally) balances all of these goals concurrently.

This leads us to propose a three-stage candidate selection method based on three different selectorates. We also recommend using moderate requirements for candidacy and participation in the selectorate, and allowing the national center a say in candidate selection. The multistage process integrates three kinds of selectorates that make use of both appointment and voting systems. We thus follow the ancient political philosophers, who argued that the structure of the "good regime" should be a mixed balance of several forces, and posit that a candidate selection method that integrates several elements will better serve democracy than one that adheres to a particular value or to a single, specific principle.

The logic of the proposed method should be convincing, even to those who do not accept all of the claims that appear in Table 10.1 concerning the fulfillment of democratic norms and the production of democratic outputs by different selectorates. The very idea that there is a tradeoff – that certain selectorates can serve some goals better, while other selectorates can promote accompanying goals more efficiently – is sufficient for accepting the logic of the proposed method that suggests combining several selectorates in the candidate selection process.

The multistage system that we propose involves several selectorates, and is presented in Figure 10.1. Note that we start with a most exclusive selectorate and end the process with a most inclusive one, recognizing that this is the right sequence in terms of legitimacy. That is, people will agree to a preliminary screening by an exclusive selectorate before the final decision is made by an inclusive selectorate more easily than they will consent to the opposite – a final decision by an exclusive selectorate that could counter the earlier choice by the more inclusive one.

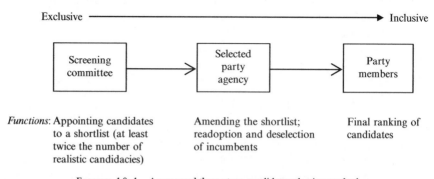

FIGURE 10.1. A proposed three-stage candidate selection method

*Source*: updated from Rahat (2009).

The process begins with an exclusive selectorate that filters candidates, a screening committee that deliberates and appoints a shortlist the size of which is at least twice the number of realistic party candidacies. That is, the committee's role is only to filter – to remove those potential candidates who are perceived as detrimental to the party – and not to decide which of those accepted should be selected. This screening committee should be composed mainly of people with a strong affiliation to the party but no immediate stake in the forthcoming contest, such as retired politicians, but it should also include rank-and-file party members who are selected randomly. It might also include representatives of the main currents, or camps, in the party in order to assure that these forces are satisfied with the screening. In terms of centralization and decentralization, the filtering process should be done in a coordinated manner so that both local and national levels can have a significant input.

At the second stage, a more inclusive selectorate – party delegates – comes in with two roles: First, it can amend the list of candidates that was proposed by the screening committee, but in a limited manner (up to a certain percentage, conditioned on the support of a majority, etc.). Second, it approves or denies the candidacy of incumbents. This selectorate can be a standing inclusive party agency such as a party central committee, convention, or congress that meets from time to time to deal with issues that have to do with the life of the party, or a special delegate convention selected by the members for the specific purpose of candidate selection. In terms of decentralization, the party agency should be at the level of the electoral district, with representation in the selection meeting of various social groups and ideological currents within the party.

The final stage is where a most inclusive selectorate, the party members, decide on the realistic candidacies from among those who passed the screening and survived the delegate selection. The selection can be at the level of the electoral district, or lower than this in the case of a large, multimember district. As mentioned earlier, we recommend somewhat limiting selection to those who have been dues-paying party members for a meaningful period of time. We also recommend a nonmajoritarian voting method in this final selection stage.

This combination allows for wide participation by party members, while at the same time it gives special privileges (but not all the power) to loyal party activists. It allows some practice of deliberative democracy in the first stage, especially if rank-and-file members are involved, and it fulfills the participatory ideal without extracting a high price in terms of quality. The screening committee can ensure that the shortlist is representative, but the use of correction mechanisms in the final stage might still be required. This method will allow for competition, first because of the trial for incumbents at the second stage, and then due to the fact that competition in the third stage is concentrated between incumbents and a limited number of serious newcomers – thus anti-incumbent or renewal voting is not spread across many newcomers. In terms of responsiveness, this method includes both party and candidate-centered pressures, with a balance of influence between different intraparty actors along with some influence from the outside.

Combining several selectorates forces the candidates to be agents of many principals and to try to be responsive to them, mainly because they have to be careful not to alienate too many selectors. This should create an optimal combination of pressures, or at least one that will not develop the pathologies that are the result of serving a single, powerful principal. This structure, of course, serves the notion that power should be diffused. While the spreading of power among several selectorates institutionalizes intraparty conflict, it might be better for democracy than an internal party peace that is the result of the concentration of power in the hands of a single selectorate.

The method suggested can (and should) be tailored to the culture and tradition of the specific party in a given state. The overarching principle that must be adhered to is the involvement of several selectorates in the process of candidate selection. Beyond that, the proposed model allows much flexibility regarding all of its elements: the exact requirements for candidacy; the characteristics of the three different selectorates (how to determine the composition of the nomination committee, the party agency that will take part in the process, and the specific requirements for party membership); the weight of the national center versus regional and local organizations; and the specific voting system that will be in use.

## DEMOCRACY WITHIN PARTIES

While the exact design of the candidate selection method adopted by a given party in a specific country must be sensitive to contextual factors, what we maintain here is that the three-stage method outlined above will contribute to democracy in all cases, due to its internal logic. The liberal dispersal of power among three separate selectorates, each with its specific advantages and potential pathologies, together produce an outcome that best serves democracy. The best candidate selection method for democracy is thus not the most democratic of selection methods in terms of its adherence to the participatory principle alone.

Or, to put it differently, the questions "which is the most democratic candidate selection method?" and "which is the best candidate selection method for democracy?" are not identical, and could be answered differently based on how one perceives democracy. If democracy is equivalent to inclusive participation, then the answer to the first question is clearly the most inclusive candidate selection method – but this is not necessarily the correct answer to the second question. However, if democracy is defined as more than just participation, as entailing several equally important elements such as competition, representation, and responsiveness alongside participation, then the most democratic candidate selection method will attempt to achieve as much as possible of all four elements, and as such it will also be the best candidate selection method for democracy. That is, additional democracy within parties – if, and only if, it is defined as more than participation alone – can be better for democracy.

If scholars of democracy address the system (interparty) and the candidate selection (intraparty) levels concurrently, and require similar elements – such as universal participation – at both levels, then we will have a myopic vision of party democracy. But if instead they choose to look at democracy as relating to more than one level of a given political system, then they can arrive at a more healthy conclusion – the many values of democracy cannot be merely reproduced as one moves from one level to another. Indeed, for a state to be a democracy it must guarantee its citizens the potential for universal participation. Parties, however, as associations contained within the system level of democracy, may set up their own rules. Instead of directing their energy toward expanding inclusiveness within, parties can help serve democracy by enhancing other democratic dimensions. That is, parties can, by adopting certain types of candidate selection methods, ameliorate system-level democracy.

Putnam's (2000) concern with social capital led him to claim that the health of democracy in general, and public institutions in particular, depends, at least in part, on "widespread participation" in private voluntary groups such as political parties. Our multidimensional perspective of democracy, which is the result of interactions and complementarity between the state and the party levels, shows us that this is not an "either–or" situation. Dahl (1970: 5, emphasis in original) captured the difference between the state and intraparty levels when he asked, "If the main reason we need political parties at all is in order for them to facilitate democracy in the *government of the country*, then might not parties that are internally oligarchic serve that purpose just as well, or maybe better than, parties that are internally more or less democratic?" Sartori (1965: 124) did the same when he wrote, "Democracy on a large scale is not the sum of many little democracies," as did Schattschneider (1942: 60, emphasis in original) when, after declaring that candidate selection was the most important activity of party, he stated, "Democracy is not found *in* the parties but *between* the parties." While we adopt and emphasize the distinction between intraparty and system-level democracy, we clearly do not give up on democracy within parties. We simply claim two things: First, democracy within parties does not equal inclusive participation alone – there is much more to democracy than just inclusiveness. Second, democracy within parties is somewhat different from democracy at the state level in its balance between what we see as no less important democratic and liberal values.

We argue that political parties should be inclusive, but not only inclusive. The three-stage candidate selection method we propose does include a selectorate that is very inclusive, but this is tempered by other selectorates who offset the negative impact of democratizing the selectorate within parties on the overall health of democracy. Moreover, if a three-stage candidate selection method is, for whatever reason, impossible for a particular party to adopt, then there are two important issues to consider: First, a two-stage method is still much better than a single-stage method, regardless of which single stage is chosen. Second, if only two stages are possible, one of them *must* be the third, inclusive stage based on party members.

Since we believe that the voluntary aspect of the organization of parties should be preserved, we think the parties should be free to decide which candidate selection method to use. Nevertheless, because we think candidate selection is indeed an important institution within democracies in general and political parties in particular, we think that the state should be allowed to adopt laws that reward those parties that implement methods that serve democracy better – that is, methods that supply the democratic system with the best possible mix of democratic qualities, rather than focusing on one element and creating systemic problems on the others. Since we found that the main values that serve democracy better are unlikely to be simultaneously maximized in a single institution, the state must guarantee what is its fundamental core value – participation – and encourage extragovernmental organizations, first and foremost the political parties, to pursue other goals. Party funding, for example, can be granted to those parties that implement particular candidate selection methods. Representation quotas can be implemented at the state level, via legislation, or incentives can be provided for those parties that implement quotas beyond a minimal level. In short, we call upon the state to supply incentives that will encourage democracy within parties. But at the same time, we ask that the state not take over, since that might lead to the unfortunate result that intraparty democracy will become all too similar to interparty democracy.

Political parties – like other important enclaves in modern democracies (courts are the most prominent example) – are not subject to the universal participatory prerequisite. Ware (2002) correctly saw that the relative weakness of American parties was due to their adherence to the participatory ideal, which led them to lose their capacity as intermediaries between state and society. Katz (1997: 6) recognized that democratization in certain aspects will lead to less democracy in others when he claimed that, "the problem is to determine the most desirable of the feasible combination of values." If, indeed, "there is more to democracy than suffrage" (Katz 2001: 293), then parties should be used to fine-tune other aspects of the democratic polity, beyond inclusive participation. As long as parties act within the framework of a democratic state that abides by the participatory prerequisite, they can serve democracy on other, not insignificant, dimensions which require compensation due to the necessary price extracted at the state level by the requirement for universal participation.

Our conclusions should, therefore, be interpreted optimistically. We do not point out the limitations of the potential for democracy within parties, but only wish to channel it properly in order to maximize its potential. A correct "division of labor" between parties and the state, on the one hand, and within parties, on the other, will allow both the system and subsystem levels to compensate for each other's deficiencies with regard to the main values of democracy, in order to maximize the democratic features of the system as a whole.

# References

Akirav, Osnat. 2010. 'Candidate Selection and a Crowded Parliament: The Israeli Knesset 1988–2006.' *Journal of Legislative Studies*, 16 (1), pp. 96–120.

Almond, Gabriel A. 1960. 'Introduction: A Functional Approach to Comparative Politics.' In: Gabriel A. Almond and James S. Coleman (eds.), *The Politics of the Developing Areas*. Princeton, NJ: Princeton University Press.

Alvarez, R. Michael and Jonathan Nagler. 2001. 'The Likely Consequences of Internet Voting for Political Representation.' *Loyola of Los Angeles Law Review*, 34 (3), pp. 1115–52.

Andeweg, Rudy B. and Galen A. Irwin. 2002. *Governance and Politics of the Netherlands*. Houndmills: Palgrave Macmillan.

Ansolabehere, Stephen, John Mark Hansen, Shigeo Hirano, and James M. Snyder, Jr. 2007. 'The Incumbency Advantage in U.S. Primary Elections.' *Electoral Studies*, 26 (3), pp. 660–8.

——— Shigeo Hirano, and James M. Snyder, Jr. 2007. 'What Did the Direct Primary Do to Party Loyalty in Congress?' In: David Brady and Matthew D. McCubbins (eds.), *Party, Process, and Political Change in Congress, Volume 2: Further New Perspectives on the History of Congress*. Stanford, CA: Stanford University Press.

Arian, Asher and Ruth Amir. 1997. *The Next Elections in Israel: How Should We Vote?* Jerusalem: Israel Democracy Institute [in Hebrew].

Ashiagbor, Sefakor. 2008. *Political Parties and Democracy in Theoretical and Practical Perspectives: Selecting Candidates for Legislative Office*. Washington, DC: National Democratic Institute. www.ndi.org/files/2406_polpart_report_engpdf_100708.pdf [accessed February 24, 2010].

Aylott, Nicholas. 2005. 'Europeanization and British Political Parties.' Paper presented at the Nordic Political Science Association conference, Reykjavik, Iceland.

Bacchi, Carol. 2006. 'Arguing For and Against Quotas: Theoretical Issues.' In: Drude Dahlerup (ed.), *Women, Quotas and Politics*. New York: Routledge.

Back, Les and John Solomos. 1994. 'Labour and Racism: Trade Unions and the Selection of Parliamentary Candidates.' *Sociological Review*, 42 (2), pp. 165–201.

Baldez, Lisa. 2007. 'Primaries vs. Quotas: Gender and Candidate Nominations in Mexico, 2003.' *Latin American Politics and Society*, 49 (3), pp. 69–96.

Ball, Alan R. 1987. *British Political Parties: The Emergence of a Modern Party System*. London: Macmillan.

Bardi, Luciano and Leonardo Morlino. 1992. 'Italy.' In: Richard S. Katz and Peter Mair (eds.), *Party Organizations: A Data Handbook on Party Organizations in Western Democracies, 1960–90*. London: Sage.

Barnea, Shlomit and Gideon Rahat. 2007. 'Reforming Candidate Selection Methods: A Three-Level Approach.' *Party Politics*, 13 (3), pp. 375–94.

Baum, Julian and James A. Robinson. 1995. 'Party Primaries in Taiwan: A Reappraisal.' *Asian Affairs: An American Review*, 22 (2), pp. 3–14.

Baum, Julian and James A. Robinson. 1999. 'Party Primaries in Taiwan: Trends, Conditions, and Projections in Candidate Selection.' *Occasional Paper/Reprints Series in Contemporary Asian Studies*, 6 (155).

Benedetto, Giacomo and Simon Hix. 2007. 'The Rejected, the Ejected, and the Dejected: Explaining Government Rebels in the 2001–2005 British House of Commons.' *Comparative Political Studies*, 40 (7), pp. 755–81.

Best, Heinrich and Maurizio Cotta. 2000a. 'Elite Transformation and Modes of Representation since the Mid-Nineteenth Century: Some Theoretical Considerations.' In: Heinrich Best and Maurizio Cotta (eds.), *Parliamentary Representatives in Europe 1848–2000: Legislative Recruitment and Careers in Eleven European Countries*. Oxford: Oxford University Press.

—— —— (eds.) 2000b. *Parliamentary Representatives in Europe 1848–2000: Legislative Recruitment and Careers in Eleven European Countries*. Oxford: Oxford University Press.

Bille, Lars. 1992. 'Internal Party Democracy: The Role of Party Members.' Paper presented at the European Consortium for Political Research Joint Sessions of Workshops, Limerick, Ireland.

—— 1994. 'Denmark: The Decline of the Membership Party.' In: Richard S. Katz and Peter Mair (eds.), *How Parties Organize: Change and Adaptation in Party Organizations in Western Democracies*. London: Sage.

—— 2001. 'Democratizing a Democratic Procedure: Myth or Reality? Candidate Selection in Western European Parties 1960–1990.' *Party Politics*, 7 (3), pp. 363–80.

Birch, Anthony H. 1971. *Representation*. New York: Praeger.

—— 1993. *The Concepts and Theories of Modern Democracy*. London: Routledge.

Bochel, John and David Denver. 1983. 'Candidate Selection in the Labour Party: What the Selectors Seek.' *British Journal of Political Science*, 13 (1), pp. 45–69.

Bolleyer, Nicole. 2009. 'Inside the Cartel Party: Party Organization in Government and Opposition.' *Political Studies*, 57 (3), pp. 559–79.

Borchert, Jens and Zeiss Golsch. 2003. 'Germany: From "Guilds of Notables" to Political Class.' In: Jens Borchert and Jürgen Zeiss (eds.), *The Political Class in Advanced Democracies: A Comparative Handbook*. Oxford: Oxford University Press.

Bowler, Shaun. 2000. 'Parties in Legislatures: Two Competing Explanations.' In: Russell J. Dalton and Martin P. Wattenberg (eds.), *Parties Without Partisans: Political Change in Advanced Industrial Democracies*. Oxford: Oxford University Press.

Bradbury, Jonathan, James Mitchell, Lynn Bennie, and David Denver. 2000. 'Candidate Selection, Devolution and Modernization.' *British Elections and Parties Review*, 10 (1), pp. 151–72.

Brams, Steven J. and Peter C. Fishburn. 2002. 'Voting Procedures.' In: Kenneth J. Arrow, Amartya K. Sen, and Kotaro Suzumura (eds.), *Handbook of Social Choice and Welfare, Volume 1*. Amsterdam: Elsevier Science.

Breaux, David A. and Anthony Gierzynski. 1991. '"It's Money that Matters": Campaign Expenditures and State Legislative Primaries.' *Legislative Studies Quarterly*, 16 (3), pp. 429–43.

Brichta, Avraham. 1977. *Democracy and Elections*. Tel Aviv: Am Oved [in Hebrew].

Bueno de Mesquita, Bruce, James D. Morrow, Randolph Siverson, and Alastair Smith. 2002. 'The Selectorate Model: A Theory of Political Institutions.' In: Joseph Berger and Morris Zelditch, Jr. (eds.), *New Directions in Contemporary Sociological Theory*. Lanham, MD: Rowman and Littlefield.

—— Alastair Smith, Randolph M. Siverson, and James D. Morrow. 2003. *The Logic of Political Survival*. Cambridge, MA: MIT Press.

Burrell, Barbara C. 1992. 'Women Candidates in Open-Seat Primaries for the U.S. House: 1968–1990.' *Legislative Studies Quarterly*, 17 (4), pp. 493–508.

Butler, David. 1978. 'The Renomination of M.P.s: A Note.' *Parliamentary Affairs*, 31 (2), pp. 210–12.

—— and Dennis Kavanagh. 1974. *The British General Election of February 1974*. London: Macmillan.

Carey, John M. and Matthew S. Shugart. 1995. 'Incentives to Cultivate a Personal Vote: A Rank Ordering of Electoral Formulas.' *Electoral Studies*, 14 (4), pp. 417–39.

Carty, R. Kenneth. 2004. 'Parties as Franchise Systems: The Stratarchical Organizational Imperative.' *Party Politics*, 10 (1), pp. 5–24.

—— 2008. 'Brokerage Politics, Stratarchical Organization and Party Members: The Liberal Party of Canada.' In: Karina Kosiara-Pedersen and Peter Kurrild-Klitgaard (eds.), *Partier og Partisystemer I Forandring: Festskrift til Lars Bille*. Odense: University of southern Denmark Press.

—— and William Cross. 2006. 'Can Stratarchically Organized Parties be Democratic? The Canadian Case.' *Journal of Elections, Public Opinion and Parties*, 16 (2), pp. 93–114.

—— and Munroe Eagles. 2003. 'Local Conflict Within National Parties: The Case of Canada.' Paper presented at the Annual Meeting of the American Political Science Association, Philadelphia.

—— William Cross, and Lisa Young. 2000. *Rebuilding Canadian Party Politics*. Vancouver: University of British Columbia Press.

Catt, Helena. 1997. 'New Zealand.' In: Pippa Norris (ed.), *Passages to Power: Legislative Recruitment in Advanced Democracies*. Cambridge: Cambridge University Press.

Caul, Miki. 2001. 'Political Parties and the Adoption of Candidate Gender Quotas: A Cross-National Analysis.' *Journal of Politics*, 63 (4), pp. 1214–29.

Citizens' Empowerment Center in Israel. 2007. *Parties in the Era of Electronic Communication*. Tel Aviv: Citizens' Empowerment Center in Israel [in Hebrew].

Combes, Hélène. 2003. 'Internal Elections and Democratic Transition: The Case of the Democratic Revolution Party in Mexico (1989–2001).' Paper presented at the European Consortium for Political Research Joint Sessions of Workshops, Edinburgh.

Coppedge, Michael. 1994. *Strong Parties and Lame Ducks*. Stanford, CA: Stanford University Press.

Criddle, Byron. 1984. 'Candidates.' In: David E. Butler and Dennis Kavanagh (eds.), *The British General Election of 1983*. London: Macmillan.

—— 1988. 'Candidates.' In: David E. Butler and Dennis Kavanagh (eds.), *The British General Election of 1987*. London: Macmillan.

—— 1992. 'MPs and Candidates.' In: David E. Butler and Dennis Kavanagh (eds.), *The British General Election of 1992*. London: Macmillan.

—— 1997. 'MPs and Candidates.' In: David E. Butler and Dennis Kavanagh (eds.), *The British General Election of 1997*. London: Macmillan.

Crisp, Brian F., Maria Escobar-Lemmon, Bradford S. Jones, Mark P. Jones, and Michelle M. Taylor-Robinson. 2004. 'Vote-Seeking Incentives and Legislative Representation in Six Presidential Democracies.' *Journal of Politics*, 66 (3), pp. 823–46.

Crittenden, John A. 1982. *Parties and Elections in the United States*. Englewood Cliffs, NJ: Prentice Hall.

Cross, William. 2002. 'Grassroots Participation in Candidate Nominations.' In: Joanna Everitt and Brenda O'Neill (eds.), *Citizen Politics: Research and Theory in Canadian Political Behaviour*. Oxford: Oxford University Press.

—— 2004. *Political Parties*. Vancouver: University of British Columbia Press.

—— 2006. 'Candidate Nomination in Canada's Political Parties.' In: Jon Pammet and Christopher Dornan (eds.), *The Canadian General Election of 2006*. Toronto: Dundurn Press.

—— 2008. 'Democratic Norms and Party Candidate Selection: Taking Contextual Factors into Account.' *Party Politics*, 14 (5), pp. 596–619.

Crotty, William. 2006. 'Party Origins and Evolution in the United States.' In: Richard S. Katz and William J. Crotty (eds.), *Handbook of Party Politics*. London: Sage.

Cutts, David, Sarah Childs, and Edward Fieldhouse. 2008. ' "This Is What Happens When You Don't Listen": All-Women Shortlists at the 2005 General Election.' *Party Politics*, 14 (5), pp. 575–95.

Czudnowski, Moshe M. 1975. 'Political Recruitment.' In: Fred I. Greenstein and Nelson W. Polsby (eds.), *Handbook of Political Science, Volume 2*. Reading, MA: Addison-Wesley.

Dahl, Robert A. 1970. *After the Revolution?* New Haven, CT: Yale University Press.

Dahlerup, Drude (ed.). 2006. *Women, Quotas and Politics*. New York: Routledge.

Dalton, Russell. 2008. *Citizen Politics*, 5th edition. Washington, DC: Congressional Quarterly Press.

Davidson-Schmich, Louise K. 2006. 'Implementation of Political Party Gender Quotas: Evidence from the German Länder 1990–2000.' *Party Politics*, 12 (2), pp. 211–32.

De Luca, Miguel, Mark P. Jones, and Maria I. Tula. 2002. 'Back Rooms or Ballot Boxes? Candidate Nomination in Argentina.' *Comparative Political Studies*, 35 (4), pp. 413–36.

De Winter, Lieven. 1988. 'Belgium: Democracy or Oligarchy?' In: Michael Gallagher and Michael Marsh (eds.), *Candidate Selection in Comparative Perspective: The Secret Garden of Politics*. London: Sage.

—— 1997. 'Intra- and Extra-Parliamentary Role Attitudes and Behaviour of Belgian MPs.' *Journal of Legislative Studies*, 3 (1), pp. 128–54.

—— and Marleen Brans. 2003. 'Belgium: Political Professionals and the Crisis of the Party State.' In: Jens Borchert and Jürgen Zeiss (eds.), *The Political Class in Advanced Democracies: A Comparative Handbook*. Oxford: Oxford University Press.

Denver, David. 1988. 'Britain: Centralized Parties with Decentralized Selection.' In: Michael Gallagher and Michael Marsh (eds.), *Candidate Selection in Comparative Perspective: The Secret Garden of Politics*. London: Sage.

Depauw, Sam. 2003. 'Government Party Discipline in Parliamentary Democracies: The Cases of Belgium, France and the United Kingdom in the 1990s.' *Journal of Legislative Studies*, 9 (4), pp. 130–46.

—— and Steven Van Hecke. 2005. 'Preferential Voting and Personal Vote-Earning Attributes: The Benelux Countries and the 1999–2004 EP Elections.' Paper presented at the European Consortium for Political Research General Conference, Budapest.

Deschouwer, Kris. 1994. 'The Decline of Consociationalism and the Reluctant Modernization of Belgian Mass Parties.' In: Richard S. Katz and Peter Mair (eds.),

*How Parties Organize: Change and Adaptation in Party Organizations in Western Democracies*. London: Sage.

Dickson, A. D. R. 1975. 'MPs' Readoption Conflicts: Their Causes and Consequences.' *Political Studies*, 23 (1), pp. 62–70.

Dotan, Yoav and Menachem Hofnung. 2005. 'Why Do Elected Representatives Go to Court?' *Comparative Politics*, 38 (1), pp. 75–103.

Duverger, Maurice. 1954. *Political Parties: Their Organization and Activity in the Modern State*. London: Methuen.

Edwards, Julia and Laura McAllister. 2002. 'One Step Forward, Two Steps Back? Women in the Two Main Political Parties in Wales.' *Parliamentary Affairs*, 55 (1), pp. 154–66.

Engelmann, Frederick C. and Mildred A. Schwartz. 1975. *Canadian Political Parties: Origin, Character, Impact*. Scarborough: Prentice Hall of Canada.

Engstrom, Richard L. and Richard N. Engstrom. 2008. 'The Majority Vote Rule and Runoff Primaries in the United States.' *Electoral Studies*, 27 (3), pp. 407–16.

Enterline, Andrew J. and Kristian S. Gleditsch. 2000. 'Threats, Opportunity, and Force: Repression and Diversion of Domestic Pressures, 1948–1982.' *International Interactions*, 26 (1), pp. 21–53.

Epstein, Leon D. 1960. 'British MPs and Their Local Parties: The Suez Cases.' *American Political Science Review*, 54 (2), pp. 374–90.

—— 1964. 'A Comparative Study of Canadian Parties.' *American Political Science Review*, 58 (1), pp. 46–59.

—— 1967. *Political Parties in Western Democracies*. New York: Praeger.

—— 1977a. 'A Comparative Study of Australian Parties.' *British Journal of Political Science*, 7 (1), pp. 1–21.

—— 1977b. 'The Australian Political System.' In: Howard R. Penniman (ed.), *Australia at the Polls: The National Elections of 1975*. Washington, DC: American Enterprise Institute.

—— 1980. *Political Parties in Western Democracies*. New Brunswick, NJ: Transaction Publishers.

—— 1986. *Political Parties in the American Mold*. Madison, WI: University of Wisconsin Press.

Erickson, Lynda. 1997. 'Canada.' In: Pippa Norris (ed.), *Passages to Power: Legislative Recruitment in Advanced Democracies*. Cambridge: Cambridge University Press.

—— and R. K. Carty. 1991. 'Parties and Candidate Selection in the 1988 Canadian General Election.' *Canadian Journal of Political Science*, 24 (2), pp. 331–49.

Esteban, Jorge de and Luis López Guerra. 1985. 'Electoral Rules and Candidate Selection.' In: Howard R. Penniman and Eusebio M. Mujal-Leon (eds.), *Spain at the Polls 1977, 1979 and 1982*. Washington, DC: American Enterprise Institute.

Eulau, Heinz and Paul D. Karps. 1977. 'The Puzzle of Representation: Specifying Components of Responsiveness.' *Legislative Studies Quarterly*, 2 (3), pp. 233–54.

Ezra, Marni. 2001. 'A Reexamination of Congressional Primary Turnout.' *American Politics Research*, 29 (1), pp. 47–64.

Faas, Thorsten. 2003. 'To Defect or Not to Defect? National, Institutional and Party Group Pressures on MEPs and Their Consequences for Party Group Cohesion in the European Parliament.' *European Journal of Political Research*, 42 (6), pp. 841–66.

Farrell, David M. 1992. 'Ireland.' In: Richard S. Katz and Peter Mair (eds.), *Party Organizations: A Data Handbook on Party Organizations in Western Democracies, 1960–90*. London: Sage.

Farrell, David M. 1994. 'Ireland: Centralization, Professionalization and Competitive Pressures.' In: Richard S. Katz and Peter Mair (eds.), *How Parties Organize: Change and Adaptation in Party Organizations in Western Democracies*. London: Sage.

Fell, Dafydd. 2005. 'Democratization of Candidate Selection in Taiwanese Political Parties.' Paper presented at the Annual Meeting of the American Political Science Association, Washington, DC.

Fenno, Richard F. 1996. *Senators on the Campaign Trail: The Politics of Representation*. Norman: OK University of Oklahoma Press.

Field, Bonnie N. 2006. 'Transition to Democracy and Internal Party Rules: Spain in Comparative Perspective.' *Comparative Politics*, 39 (1), pp. 83–102.

Fiorina, Morris P. 1974. *Representatives, Roll Calls, and Constituencies*. Lexington, MA: D. C. Heath.

Fukui, Haruhiro. 1997. 'Japan.' In: Pippa Norris (ed.), *Passages to Power: Legislative Recruitment in Advanced Democracies*. Cambridge: Cambridge University Press.

Gabel, Matthew and Kenneth Scheve. 2007. 'Mixed Messages, Party Dissent and Mass Opinion on European Integration.' *European Union Politics*, 8 (1), pp. 37–59.

Galderisi, Peter F. and Marni Ezra. 2001. 'Congressional Primaries in Historical and Theoretical Context.' In: Peter F. Galderisi, Marni Ezra, and Michael Lyons (eds.), *Congressional Primaries and the Politics of Representation*. Lanham, MD: Rowman and Littlefield.

—— —— and Michael Lyons. 2001. 'Introduction: Nomination Politics and Congressional Representation.' In: Peter F. Galderisi, Marni Ezra, and Michael Lyons (eds.), *Congressional Primaries and the Politics of Representation*. Lanham, MD: Rowman and Littlefield.

Gallagher, Michael. 1980. 'Candidate Selection in Ireland: The Impact of Localism and the Electoral System.' *British Journal of Political Science*, 10 (4), pp. 489–503.

—— 1988*a*. 'Introduction.' In: Michael Gallagher and Michael Marsh (eds.), *Candidate Selection in Comparative Perspective: The Secret Garden of Politics*. London: Sage.

—— 1988*b*. 'Ireland: The Increasing Role of the Centre.' In: Michael Gallagher and Michael Marsh (eds.), *Candidate Selection in Comparative Perspective: The Secret Garden of Politics*. London: Sage.

—— 1988*c*. 'Conclusion.' In: Michael Gallagher and Michael Marsh (eds.), *Candidate Selection in Comparative Perspective: The Secret Garden of Politics*. London: Sage.

—— 1991. 'Proportionality, Disproportionality and Electoral Systems.' *Electoral Studies*, 10 (1), pp. 33–51.

—— 2003. 'Ireland: Party Loyalists with a Personal Base.' In: Jens Borchert and Jürgen Zeiss (eds.), *The Political Class in Advanced Democracies*. Oxford: Oxford University Press.

—— and Michael Marsh (eds.), 1988. *Candidate Selection in Comparative Perspective: The Secret Garden of Politics*. London: Sage.

—— Michael Laver, and Peter Mair. 2006. *Representative Government in Modern Europe: Institutions, Parties and Government*. Boston, MA: McGraw-Hill.

Galligan, Yvonne. 2003. 'Candidate Selection: More Democratic or More Centrally Controlled?' In: Michael Gallagher, Michael Marsh, and Paul Mitchell (eds.), *How Ireland Voted 2002*. Houndmills: Palgrave Macmillan.

Gauja, Anika. 2006. 'An Assessment of the Impact of Party Law on Intra-Party Democracy in Common Law Nations.' Paper presented at the International Political Science Association World Congress, Fukuoka.

Gerber, Elisabeth R. and Rebecca B. Morton. 1998. 'Primary Election Systems and Representation.' *Journal of Law, Economics, and Organization*, 14 (2), pp. 304–24.

Glaser, James M. 2006. 'The Primary Runoff as a Remnant of the Old South.' *Electoral Studies*, 25 (4), pp. 776–90.

Goldberg, Giora. 1992. *Political Parties in Israel: From Mass Parties to Electoral Parties.* Tel Aviv: Ramot [in Hebrew].

—— and Steven A. Hoffman. 1983. 'Nominations in Israel: The Politics of Institutionalization.' In: Asher Arian (ed.), *The Elections in Israel 1981*. Tel Aviv: Ramot.

Goodliffe, Jay and David B. Magleby. 2000. 'Campaign Spending in Primary Elections in the U.S. House.' Paper presented at the Midwest Political Science Association Annual Meeting, Chicago.

—— —— 2001. 'Campaign Finance in U.S. House Primary and General Elections.' In: Peter F. Galderisi, Marni Ezra, and Michael Lyons (eds.) *Congressional Primaries and the Politics of Representation*. Lanham, MD: Rowman and Littlefield.

Graham, B. D. 1986. 'The Candidate-Selection Policies of the Indian National Congress, 1952–1969.' *Journal of Commonwealth and Comparative Politics*, 24 (2), pp. 197–218.

Grofman, Bernard and Arend Lijphart (eds.). 1986. *Electoral Laws and Their Political Consequences*. New York: Agathon Press.

Gunlicks, Arthur B. 1970. 'Intraparty Democracy in Western Germany: A Look at the Local Level.' *Comparative Politics*, 2 (2), pp. 229–49.

Hardarson, Ólafur Th. 1995. *Parties and Voters in Iceland: A Study of the 1983 and 1987 Althingi Elections*. Reykjavik: University of Iceland.

Hazan, Reuven Y. 1997a. 'The 1996 Intra-Party Elections in Israel: Adopting Party Primaries.' *Electoral Studies*, 16 (1), pp. 95–103.

—— 1997b. 'Executive–Legislative Relations in an Era of Accelerated Reform: Reshaping Government in Israel.' *Legislative Studies Quarterly*, 22 (3), pp. 329–50.

—— 1999a. 'Constituency Interests without Constituencies: The Geographical Impact of Candidate Selection on Party Organization and Legislative Behavior in the 14th Israeli Knesset, 1996–99.' *Political Geography*, 18 (7), pp. 791–811.

—— 1999b. 'Yes, Institutions Matter: The Impact of Institutional Reform on Parliamentary Members and Leaders in Israel.' *Journal of Legislative Studies*, 5 (3–4), pp. 301–24.

—— 2002. 'Candidate Selection.' In: Lawrence LeDuc, Richard G. Niemi, and Pippa Norris (eds.), *Comparing Democracies 2: New Challenges in the Study of Elections and Voting*. London: Sage.

—— 2003. 'Does Cohesion Equal Discipline? Towards a Conceptual Delineation.' *Journal of Legislative Studies*, 9 (4), pp. 1–11.

—— 2007. 'Kadima and the Centre: Convergence in the Israeli Party System.' *Israel Affairs*, 13 (2), pp. 266–88.

—— and Paul Pennings (eds.), 2001. *Democratizing Candidate Selection: Causes and Consequences*. Special issue of *Party Politics*, 7 (3).

—— and Gideon Rahat. 2006. 'The Influence of Candidate Selection Methods on Legislatures and Legislators: Theoretical Propositions, Methodological Suggestions and Empirical Evidence.' *Journal of Legislative Studies*, 12 (3–4), pp. 366–85.

—— and Gerrit Voerman. 2006. 'Electoral Systems and Candidate Selection.' *Acta Politica*, 41 (3–4), pp. 146–62.

Heidar, Knut. 1994. 'The Polymorphic Nature of Party Membership.' *European Journal of Political Research*, 25 (1), pp. 61–86.

Helander, Voitto. 1997. 'Finland.' In: Pippa Norris (ed.), *Passages to Power: Legislative Recruitment in Advanced Democracies*. Cambridge: Cambridge University Press.

Herrnson, Paul S. 1997. 'United States.' In: Pippa Norris (ed.), *Passages to Power: Legislative Recruitment in Advanced Democracies*. Cambridge: Cambridge University Press.

Hinojosa, Magda. 2009. '"Whatever the Party Asks of Me": Women's Political Representation in Chile's Unión Demócrata Independiente.' *Politics and Gender*, 5 (3), pp. 377–407.

Hix, Simon. 2004. 'Electoral Institutions and Legislative Behavior: Explaining Voting Defection in the European Parliament.' *World Politics*, 56 (2), pp. 194–223.

Hofnung, Menachem. 1996*a*. 'The Public Purse and the Private Campaign: Political Finance in Israel.' *Journal of Law and Society*, 23 (1), pp. 132–48.

—— 1996*b*. 'Public Financing, Party Membership and Internal Party Competition.' *European Journal of Political Research*, 29 (1), pp. 73–86.

—— 2006. 'Financing Internal Party Races in Non-Majoritarian Political Systems: Lessons from the Israeli Experience.' *Election Law Journal*, 5 (4), pp. 372–83.

—— 2008. 'Unaccounted Competition: The Finance of Intra-Party Elections.' *Party Politics*, 14 (6), pp. 726–44.

Holland, Martin. 1981. 'The Selection of Parliamentary Candidates: Contemporary Developments and their Impact on the European Elections.' *Parliamentary Affairs*, 34 (1), pp. 28–46.

—— 1987. 'British Political Recruitment: Labour in the Euro-Elections of 1979.' *British Journal of Political Science*, 17 (1), pp. 53–70.

Hopkin, Jonathan. 2001. 'Bringing the Members Back In? Democratizing Candidate Selection in Britain and Spain.' *Party Politics*, 7 (3), pp. 343–61.

—— and Caterina Paolucci. 1999. 'The Business Firm Model of Party Organization: Cases from Spain and Italy.' *European Journal of Political Research*, 35 (3), pp. 307–39.

Htun, Mala. 2004. 'Is Gender Like Ethnicity? The Political Representation of Identity Groups.' *Perspectives on Politics*, 2 (3), pp. 439–58.

Inter-Parliamentary Union. 1986. *Parliaments of the World: A Comparative Reference Compendium*. Aldershot: Gower.

Jackson, John S. 1994. 'Incumbency in the United States.' In: Albert Somit, Rudolf Wildenmann, Bernhard Boll, and Andrea Römmele (eds.), *The Victorious Incumbent: A Threat to Democracy?* Aldershot: Dartmouth.

Jackson, Keith. 1980. 'Candidate Selection and the 1978 General Election.' In: Howard R. Penniman (ed.), *New Zealand at the Polls: The General Election of 1978*. Washington, DC: American Enterprise Institute.

Janda, Kenneth. 1980. *Political Parties: A Cross-National Survey*. New York: Free Press.

Jones, Mark P. 2002. 'Explaining the High Level of Party Discipline in the Argentine Congress.' In: Scott Morgenstern and Benito Nacif (eds.), *Legislative Politics in Latin America*. Cambridge: Cambridge University Press.

—— 2008. 'The Recruitment and Selection of Legislative Candidates in Argentina.' In: Peter M. Siavelis and Scott Morgenstern (eds.), *Pathways to Power: Political Recruitment and Candidate Selection in Latin America*. University Park: PA. Pennsylvania State University Press.

Kangur, Riho. 2005. 'Candidate Selection in Estonian Parliamentary Parties 1999–2003: Toward Institutionalization.' Paper presented at the European Consortium for Political Research General Conference, Budapest.

Kanthak, Kristin and Rebecca Morton. 2001. 'The Effects of Electoral Rules on Congressional Primaries.' In: Peter F. Galderisi, Marni Ezra, and Michael Lyons (eds.) *Congressional Primaries and the Politics of Representation*. Lanham, MD: Rowman and Littlefield.

Katz, Richard S. 1997. *Democracy and Elections*. New York: Oxford University Press.

——2001. 'The Problem of Candidate Selection and Models of Party Democracy.' *Party Politics*, 7 (3), pp. 277–96.

——and Robin Kolodny. 1994. 'Party Organization as an Empty Vessel: Parties in American Politics.' In: Richard S. Katz and Peter Mair (eds.), *How Parties Organize: Change and Adaptation in Party Organizations in Western Democracies*. London: Sage.

——and Peter Mair (eds.). 1992. *Party Organizations: A Data Handbook on Party Organizations in Western Democracies, 1960–90*. London: Sage.

—— —— 1995. 'Changing Models of Party Organization and Party Democracy: The Emergence of the Cartel Party.' *Party Politics*, 1 (1), pp. 5–28.

Kazee, Thomas A. and Mary C. Thornberry. 1990. 'Where's the Party? Congressional Candidate Recruitment and American Party Organizations.' *Western Political Quarterly*, 43 (1), pp. 61–80.

Kenig, Ofer. 2007. *Party Leaders' Selection Methods and their Political Consequences*. Ph.D. dissertation. Jerusalem: Hebrew University of Jerusalem.

——2009a, 'Democratizing Party Leadership Selection in Israel: A Balance Sheet.' *Israel Studies Forum*, 24 (1), pp. 62–81.

——2009b. 'Democratization of Party Leadership Selection: Do Wider Selectorates Produce More Competitive Contests?' *Electoral Studies*, 28 (2), pp. 240–7.

——and Shlomit Barnea. 2009. 'The Selection of Ministers in Israel: Is the Prime Minister "A Master of His Domain"?' *Israel Affairs*, 15 (3), pp. 261–78.

Key, V. O., Jr. 1949. *Southern Politics in State and Nation*. New York: Vintage Books.

——1954. 'The Direct Primary and Party Structure: A Study of State Legislative Nominations.' *American Political Science Review*, 48 (1), pp. 1–26.

——1967. *Politics, Parties, and Pressure Groups*, 5th ed. New York: Crowell Company.

Kirchheimer, Otto. 1966. 'The Transformation of the West European Party Systems.' In: Joseph LaPalombara and Myron Weiner (eds.), *Political Parties and Political Development*. Princeton, NJ: Princeton University Press.

Kitschelt, Herbert. 1988. 'Organization and Strategy of Belgian and West German Ecology Parties: A New Dynamic of Party Politics in Western Europe?' *Comparative Politics*, 20 (2), pp. 127–54.

Kittilson, Miki Caul. 2006. *Challenging Parties, Changing Parliaments: Women and Elected Office in Contemporary Western Europe*. Columbus: OH. Ohio State University Press.

——and Susan E. Scarrow. 2003. 'Political Parties and the Rhetoric and Realities of Democratization.' In: Bruce E. Cain, Russell J. Dalton, and Susan E. Scarrow (eds.), *Democracy Transformed? Explaining Political Opportunities in Advanced Industrial Democracies*. Oxford: Oxford University Press.

Kitzinger, Uwe W. 1960. *German Electoral Politics: A Study of the 1957 Campaign*. Oxford: Clarendon Press.

Knapp, Andrew. 2002. 'France: Never a Golden Age.' In: Paul Webb, David Farrell, and Ian Holliday (eds.), *Political Parties in Advanced Industrial Democracies*. Oxford: Oxford University Press.

Kochanek, Stanley A. 1967. 'Political Recruitment in the Indian National Congress: The Fourth General Election.' *Asian Survey*, 7 (5), pp. 292–304.

Kolodny, Robin and Richard S. Katz. 1992. 'The United States.' In: Richard S. Katz and Peter Mair (eds.), *Party Organizations: A Data Handbook on Party Organizations in Western Democracies, 1960–90*. London: Sage.

Koole, Ruud and Monique Leijenaar. 1988. 'The Netherlands: The Predominance of Regionalism.' In: Michael Gallagher and Michael Marsh (eds.), *Candidate Selection in Comparative Perspective: The Secret Garden of Politics*. London: Sage.

—— and Hella van de Velde. 1992. 'The Netherlands.' In: Richard S. Katz and Peter Mair (eds.), *Party Organizations: A Data Handbook on Party Organizations in Western Democracies, 1960–90*. London: Sage.

Kristjánsson, Svanur. 1998. 'Electoral Politics and Governance: Transformation of the Party System in Iceland, 1970–1996.' In: Paul Pennings and Jan-Erik Lane (eds.), *Comparing Party System Change*. London: Routledge.

—— 2002. 'Iceland: From Party Rule to Pluralist Political Society.' In: Hanne Marthe Narud, Mogens N. Pedersen, and Henry Valen (eds.), *Party Sovereignty and Citizen Control: Selecting Candidates for Parliamentary Elections in Denmark, Finland, Iceland and Norway*. Odense: University Press of Southern Denmark.

—— 2004. 'Iceland: Searching for Democracy along Three Dimensions of Citizen Control.' *Scandinavian Political Studies*, 27 (2), pp. 153–74.

Krook, Mona Lena. 2009. *Quotas for Women in Politics: Gender and Candidate Selection Reform Worldwide*. Oxford: Oxford University Press.

Krouwel, André. 1999. *The Catch-All Party in Western Europe 1945–1990: A Study in Arrested Development*. Ph.D. dissertation. Amsterdam: Vrije Universiteit Amsterdam.

Kuitunen, Soile. 2002. 'Finland: Formalized Procedures with Member Predominance.' In: Hanne Marthe Narud, Mogens N. Pedersen, and Henry Valen (eds.), *Party Sovereignty and Citizen Control: Selecting Candidates for Parliamentary Elections in Denmark, Finland, Iceland and Norway*. Odense: University Press of Southern Denmark.

Kunovich, Sheri and Pamela Paxton. 2005. 'Pathways to Power: The Role of Political Parties in Women's National Political Representation.' *American Journal of Sociology*, 111 (2), pp. 505–52.

Laffin, Martin, Eric Shaw, and Gerald Taylor. 2007. 'The New Sub-National Politics of the British Labour Party.' *Party Politics*, 13 (1), pp. 88–108.

Langston, Joy. 2001. 'Why Rules Matter: Changes in Candidate Selection in Mexico's PRI, 1988–2000.' *Journal of Latin American Studies*, 33 (3), pp. 485–511.

—— 2006. 'The Changing Party of the Institutional Revolution: Electoral Competition and Decentralized Candidate Selection.' *Party Politics*, 12 (3), pp. 395–413.

—— 2008. 'Legislative Recruitment in Mexico.' In: Peter M. Siavelis and Scott Morgenstern (eds.), *Pathways to Power: Political Recruitment and Candidate Selection in Latin America*. University Park: Pennsylvania State University Press.

Lawless, Jennifer L. and Kathryn Pearson. 2008. 'The Primary Reason for Women's Underrepresentation? Reevaluating the Conventional Wisdom.' *Journal of Politics*, 70 (1), pp. 67–82.

Lijphart, Arend. 1969. 'Consociational Democracy.' *World Politics*, 21 (2), pp. 207–25.

—— 1977. *Democracy in Plural Societies: A Comparative Exploration*. New Haven, CT: Yale University Press.

—— 1984. *Democracies: Patterns of Majoritarian and Consensus Government in Twenty-one Countries*. New Haven, CT: Yale University Press.

—— 1985. 'The Field of Electoral Systems Research: A Critical Survey.' *Electoral Studies*, 4 (1), pp. 3–14.

—— 1994. *Electoral Systems and Party Systems: A Study of Twenty-Seven Democracies, 1945–1990*. Oxford: Oxford University Press.

—— 1999. *Patterns of Democracy: Government Forms and Performance in Thirty-six Countries*. New Haven, CT: Yale University Press.

—— and Bernard Grofman (eds.). 1984. *Choosing an Electoral System: Issues and Alternatives*. New York: Praeger.

Linek, Lukás and Jan Outly. 2006. 'Selection of Candidates to the European Parliament in the Main Czech Political Parties.' Paper presented at the International Political Science Association World Congress, Fukuoka.

Loewenberg, Gerhard. 1966. *Parliament in the German Political System*. Ithaca, NY: Cornell University Press.

Loosemore, John and Victor J. Hanby. 1971. 'The Theoretical Limits of Maximum Distortion: Some Analytical Expressions for Electoral Systems.' *British Journal of Political Science*, 1 (4), pp. 467–77.

Lovenduski, Joni and Pippa Norris. 1994. 'The Recruitment of Parliamentary Candidates.' In: Lynton Robins, Hilary Blackmore, and Robert Pyper (eds.), *Britain's Changing Party System*. London: Leicester University Press.

Lundell, Krister. 2004. 'Determinants of Candidate Selection: The Degree of Centralization in Comparative Perspective.' *Party Politics*, 10 (1), pp. 25–47.

Mair, Peter. 1987. 'Party Organization, Vote Management, and Candidate Selection: Toward the Nationalization of Electoral Strategy in Ireland.' In: Howard R. Penniman and Brian Farrell (eds.), *Ireland at the Polls 1981, 1982 and 1987: The Study of Four General Elections*. Durham, NC: Duke University Press.

—— 1994. 'Party Organizations: From Civil Society to the State.' In: Richard S. Katz and Peter Mair (eds.), *How Parties Organize: Change and Adaptation in Party Organizations in Western Democracies*. London: Sage.

—— 1997. *Party System Change: Approaches and Interpretations*. Oxford: Oxford University Press.

—— and Ingrid van Biezen. 2001. 'Party Membership in Twenty European Democracies, 1980–2000.' *Party Politics*, 7 (1), pp. 5–21.

Maisel, Louis Sandy and Mark D. Brewer. 2007. *Parties and Elections in America*, 5th ed. Lanham, MD: Rowman and Littlefield.

—— and Walter J. Stone. 2001. 'Primary Elections as a Deterrence to Candidacy for the U.S. House of Representatives.' In: Peter F. Galderisi, Marni Ezra, and Michael Lyons (eds.), *Congressional Primaries and the Politics of Representation*. Lanham, MD: Rowman and Littlefield.

Malloy, Jonathan. 2003. 'High Discipline, Low Cohesion? The Uncertain Patterns of Canadian Parliamentary Party Groups.' *Journal of Legislative Studies*, 9 (4), pp. 116–29.

Manin, Bernard. 1997. *The Principles of Representative Government*. Cambridge: Cambridge University Press.

Mansbridge, Jane. 2003. 'Rethinking Representation.' *American Political Science Review*, 97 (4), pp. 515–28.

Marsh, Michael. 2000. 'Candidates: Selection.' In: Richard Rose (ed.), *International Encyclopedia of Elections*. Washington, DC: Congressional Quarterly Press.

—— 2005. 'Parties and Society.' In: John Coakley and Michael Gallagher (eds.), *Politics in the Republic of Ireland*. London: Routledge.

Marshall. Thomas R. 1978. 'Turnout and Representation: Caucuses versus Primaries.' *American Journal of Political Science*, 22 (1), pp. 169–82.

Masahiko, Asano. 2004. *Electoral Reform and Candidate Selection: Japan's Liberal Democratic Party (1960–2003)*. Ph.D. dissertation. Los Angeles: University of California – Los Angeles.

Massicotte, Louis, André Blais, and Antoine Yoshinaka. 2004. *Establishing the Rules of the Game: Election Laws in Democracies*. Toronto: University of Toronto Press.

Mateo-Diaz, Mercedes. 2005. *Representing Women? Female Legislators in West European Parliaments*. Colchester: European Consortium for Political Research Press.

Matland, Richard E. 1993. 'Institutional Variables Affecting Female Representation in National Legislatures: The Case of Norway.' *Journal of Politics*, 55 (3), pp. 737–55.

—— 2004. 'The Norwegian Experience of Gender Quotas.' Paper presented at the International IDEA/CEE Network for Gender Issues Conference, Budapest.

—— 2005. 'Enhancing Women's Political Participation: Legislative Recruitment and Electoral Systems.' In: Julie Ballington and Azza Karam (eds.), *Women in Parliament: Beyond Numbers*. Stockholm: International IDEA Handbook Series. www.idea.int/publications/wip2/upload/WiP_inlay.pdf [accessed February 24, 2010].

—— and Donley T. Studlar. 1996. 'The Contagion of Women Candidates in Single-Member District and Proportional Representation Electoral Systems: Canada and Norway.' *Journal of Politics*, 58 (3), pp. 707–33.

—— —— 2004. 'Determinants of Legislative Turnover: A Cross-National Analysis.' *British Journal of Political Science*, 34 (1), pp. 87–108.

Matthews, Donald R. 1985. 'Legislative Recruitment and Legislative Careers.' In: Gerhard Loewenberg, Samuel C. Patterson, and Malcolm E. Jewell (eds.), *Handbook of Legislative Research*. Cambridge, MA: Harvard University Press.

—— and Henry Valen. 1999. *Parliamentary Representation*. Columbus: OH. Ohio State University Press.

McHarg, Aileen. 2006. 'Quotas for Women! The Sex Discrimination (Election Candidates) Act 2002.' *Journal of Law and Society*, 33(1), pp. 141–59.

Meier, Petra. 2004. 'The Mutual Contagion Effect of Legal and Party Quotas.' *Party Politics*, 10 (5), pp. 583–600.

Merriam, Charles E. and Louise Overacker. 1928. *Primary Elections*. Chicago: University of Chicago Press.

Michels, Robert. 1915. *Political Parties: A Sociological Study of the Oligarchical Tendencies of Modern Democracy*. Glencoe, IL: Free Press.

Mikulska, Anna and Susan Scarrow. 2008. 'Assessing the Political Impact of Candidate Selection Rules: Britain in the 1990s.' Paper presented at the Annual Meeting of the American Political Science Association, Boston.

Miller, Raymond. 1999. 'New Zealand and Scotland: Candidate Selection and the Impact of Electoral System Change.' Paper presented at the European Consortium for Political Research Joint Sessions of Workshops, Mannheim.

Milne, S. R. 1966. *Political Parties in New Zealand*. Oxford: Clarendon Press.

Mitchell, James and Jonathan Bradbury. 2004. 'Political Recruitment and the 2003 Scottish and Welsh Elections: Candidate Selection, Positive Discrimination and Party Adaptation.' *Representation*, 40 (4), pp. 289–302.

Mitchell, Paul. 2000. 'Voters and Their Representatives: Electoral Institutions and Delegation in Parliamentary Democracies.' *European Journal of Political Research*, 37 (3), pp. 335–51.

Montabes, Juan and Carmen Ortega. 2005. 'Candidate Selection in Two Rigid List Systems: Spain and Portugal.' Paper presented at the European Consortium for Political Research Joint Sessions of Workshops, Mannheim.

Moraes, Juan Andrés. 2008. 'Why Factions? Candidate Selection and Legislative Politics in Uruguay.' In: Peter M. Siavelis and Scott Morgenstern (eds.) *Pathways to Power: Political Recruitment and Candidate Selection in Latin America*. University Park: Pennsylvania State University Press.

Mulgan, Richard. 2004. *Politics in New Zealand*, 3rd ed. Auckland: Auckland University Press.

Müller, Wolfgang C. 1992. 'Austria.' In: Richard S. Katz and Peter Mair (eds.), *Party Organizations: A Data Handbook on Party Organizations in Western Democracies, 1960–90*. London: Sage.

Murphy, R. J. and David Farrell. 2002. 'Party Politics in Ireland: Regularizing a Volatile System.' In: Paul Webb, David Farrell, and Ian Holliday (eds.), *Political Parties in Advanced Industrial Democracies*. Oxford: Oxford University Press.

Murray, Rainbow. 2007. 'How Parties Evaluate Compulsory Quotas: A Study of the Implementation of the "Parity" Law in France.' *Parliamentary Affairs*, 60 (4), pp. 568–84.

Narud, Hanne Marthe. 2003. 'Norway: Professionalization – Party-Oriented and Constituency-Based.' In: Jens Borchert and Jürgen Zeiss (eds.), *The Political Class in Advanced Democracies: A Comparative Handbook*. Oxford: Oxford University Press.

—— and Henry Valen. 2008. 'The Norwegian Storting: The "People's Parliament" or Coop for "Political Broilers".' *World Political Science Review*, 4 (2), pp. 1–34.

—— Mogens N. Pedersen, and Henry Valen. 2002*a*. 'Parliamentary Nominations in Western Democracies.' In: Hanne Marthe Narud, Mogens N. Pedersen, and Henry Valen (eds.), *Party Sovereignty and Citizen Control: Selecting Candidates for Parliamentary Elections in Denmark, Finland, Iceland and Norway*. Odense: University Press of Southern Denmark.

—— —— —— 2002*b*. 'Conclusions.' In: Hanne Marthe Narud, Mogens N. Pedersen, and Henry Valen (eds.), *Party Sovereignty and Citizen Control: Selecting Candidates for Parliamentary Elections in Denmark, Finland, Iceland and Norway*. Odense: University Press of Southern Denmark.

—— —— —— (eds.). 2002*c*. *Party Sovereignty and Citizen Control: Selecting Candidates for Parliamentary Elections in Denmark, Finland, Iceland and Norway*. Odense: University Press of Southern Denmark.

Navia, Patricio. 2008. 'Legislative Candidate Selection in Chile.' In: Peter M. Siavelis and Scott Morgenstern (eds.), *Pathways to Power: Political Recruitment and Candidate Selection in Latin America*. University Park: PA. Pennsylvania State University Press.

Newman, Roland and Shelley Cranshaw. 1973. 'Towards a Closed Primary Election in Britain.' *Political Quarterly*, 44 (4), pp. 447–52.

Norrander, Barbara. 1986. 'Measuring Primary Turnout in Aggregate Analysis.' *Political Behavior*, 8 (4), pp. 356–73.

Norris, Pippa. 1997a. 'Introduction: Theories of Recruitment.' In: Pippa Norris (ed.), *Passages to Power: Legislative Recruitment in Advanced Democracies*. Cambridge: Cambridge University Press.

—— (ed.). 1997b. *Passages to Power: Legislative Recruitment in Advanced Democracies*. Cambridge: Cambridge University Press.

—— 2004. *Building Political Parties: Reforming Legal Regulations and Internal Rules*. Report commissioned by the International IDEA. www.idea.int/parties/upload/pippa%20norris%20ready%20for%20wev%20_3_.pdf [accessed February 24, 2010].

—— 2006. 'Recruitment.' In: Richard S. Katz and William Crotty (eds.), *Handbook of Party Politics*. London: Sage.

—— and Joni Lovenduski. 1993. '"If Only More Candidates Came Forward": Supply-Side Explanations of Candidate Selection in Britain.' *British Journal of Political Science*, 23 (3), pp. 373–408.

—— —— 1995. *Political Recruitment: Gender, Race and Class in the British Parliament*. Cambridge: Cambridge University Press.

—— —— 1997. 'United Kingdom.' In: Pippa Norris (ed.), *Passages to Power: Legislative Recruitment in Advanced Democracies*. Cambridge: Cambridge University Press.

—— R. K. Carty, Lynda Erickson, Joni Lovenduski, and Marian Simms. 1990. 'Party Selectorates in Australia, Britain and Canada: Prolegomena for Research in the 1990s.' *Journal of Commonwealth and Comparative Politics*, 28 (2), pp. 219–45.

O'Brien, Michael S. 1993. *A Comparative and Historical Analysis of Candidate Selection Practices in the Liberal Party of Canada*. M.A. thesis. Halifax: Dalhousie University.

Obler, Jeffrey L. 1970. *Candidate Selection in Belgium*. Ph.D. dissertation. Madison: University of Wisconsin.

—— 1973. 'The Role of National Party Leaders in the Selection of Parliamentary Candidates: The Belgian Case.' *Comparative Politics*, 5 (2), pp. 157–84.

—— 1974. 'Intraparty Democracy and the Selection of Parliamentary Candidates: The Belgian Case.' *British Journal of Political Science*, 4 (2), pp. 163–85.

Ohman, Magnus. 2002. 'Determining the Contestants: Candidate Selection in Ghana's 2000 Elections.' *Critical Perspectives*, 8. Ghana: Ghana Center for Democratic Development.

—— 2004. *The Heart and Soul of the Party: Candidate Selection in Ghana and Africa*. Uppsala: Uppsala University Press.

Olson, Mancur. 1965. *The Logic of Collective Action: Public Goods and the Theory of Groups*. Cambridge, MA: Harvard University Press.

Ornstein, Norman J., Thomas E. Mann, and Michael J. Malbin. 2000. *Vital Statistics on Congress 1999–2000*. Washington, DC: American Enterprise Institute Press.

Ostrogorski, M. 1964 [1902]. *Democracy and the Organization of Political Parties, Volume 1: England*. Garden City, NY: Anchor Books.

Paterson, Peter. 1967. *The Selectorate: The Case for Primary Elections in Britain*. London: Macgibbon and Kee.

Patzelt, Werner J. 1999. 'Recruitment and Retention in Western European Parliaments.' *Legislative Studies Quarterly*, 24 (2), pp. 239–79.

Pedersen, Karina. 2001. 'Ballots and Technology in the Danish Parties: Enhanced Participation?' Paper presented at the European Consortium for Political Research Joint Sessions of Workshops, Grenoble.

Pedersen, Mogens N. 2002. 'Denmark: The Interplay of Nominations and Elections in Danish Politics.' In: Hanne Marthe Narud, Mogens N. Pedersen, and Henry Valen (eds.), *Party Sovereignty and Citizen Control: Selecting Candidates for Parliamentary Elections in Denmark, Finland, Iceland and Norway*. Odense: University Press of Southern Denmark.

Pennock, J. Roland. 1968. 'Political Representation: An Overview.' In: J. Roland Pennock and John W. Chapman (eds.), *Representation*. New York: Atherton.

Persily, Nathaniel. 2001. 'Toward a Functional Defense of Political Party Autonomy.' *New York University Law Review*, 76 (3), pp. 750–824.

Phillips, Anne. 1995. *The Politics of Presence*. Oxford: Clarendon.

Pierre, Jon and Anders Widfeldt. 1992. 'Sweden.' In: Richard S. Katz and Peter Mair (eds.), *Party Organizations: A Data Handbook on Party Organizations in Western Democracies, 1960–90*. London: Sage.

Pitkin, Hanna F. 1976. *The Concept of Representation*. Berkeley: CA. University of California Press.

Poguntke, Thomas. 1992. 'Unconventional Participation in Party Politics: The Experience of the German Greens.' *Political Studies*, 40 (2), pp. 239–54.

—— 1993. *Alternative Politics: The German Green Party*. Edinburgh: Edinburgh University Press.

—— and Bernhard Boll. 1992. 'Germany.' In: Richard S. Katz and Peter Mair (eds.), *Party Organizations: A Data Handbook on Party Organizations in Western Democracies, 1960–90*. London: Sage.

—— and Paul Webb (eds.). 2005. *The Presidentialization of Politics: A Comparative Study of Modern Democracies*. Oxford: Oxford University Press.

Porter, Stephen R. 1995. *Political Representation in Germany: The Effects of the Candidate Selection Committee*. Ph.D. dissertation. Rochester, NY: University of Rochester.

Putnam, Robert. 1976. *The Comparative Study of Political Elites*. Englewood Cliffs, NJ: Prentice Hall.

Putnam, Robert D. 2000. *Bowling Alone: The Collapse and Revival of American Community*. New York: Simon and Schuster.

Quinn, Thomas. 2004. *Modernizing the Labour Party*. Houndmills: Palgrave Macmillan.

Rae, Douglas W. 1967. *The Political Consequences of Electoral Laws*. New Haven, CT: Yale University Press.

Rahat, Gideon. 2008*a*. 'Candidate Selection in Israel: Between the One, the Few and the Many.' In: Asher Arian and Michal Shamir (eds.), *The Elections in Israel 2006*. New Brunswick, NJ: Transaction Publishers.

Rahat, Gideon. 2008*b*. 'Entering Through the Back Door: Non-party Actors in Intra-party (S)electoral Politics.' In: David M. Farrell and Rüdiger Schmitt-Beck (eds.), *Non-Party Actors in Electoral Politics: The Role of Interest Groups and Independent Citizens in Contemporary Election Campaigns*. Baden-Baden: Nomos.

—— 2009. 'Which Candidate Selection Method Is the Most Democratic?' *Government and Opposition*, 44 (1), pp. 68–90.

—— Forthcoming. 'The Political Consequences of Candidate Selection to the 18<sup>th</sup> Knesset.' In: Asher Arian and Michal Shamir (eds.) *The Elections in Israel 2009*. New Brunswick, NJ: Transaction Publishers.

—— and Reuven Y. Hazan. 2001. 'Candidate Selection Methods: An Analytical Framework.' *Party Politics*, 7 (3), pp. 297–322.

———— 2007. 'Political Participation in Party Primaries: Increase in Quantity, Decrease in Quality.' In: Thomas Zittel and Dieter Fuchs (eds.), *Participatory Democracy and Political Participation: Can Participatory Engineering Bring Citizens Back In?* London: Routledge.

—— and Tamir Sheafer. 2007. 'The Personalization(s) of Politics: Israel 1949–2003.' *Political Communications*, 24 (1), pp. 65–80.

—— and Neta Sher-Hadar. 1999a. *Intra-party Selection of Candidates for the Knesset List and for Prime-Ministerial Candidacy 1995–1997*. Jerusalem: Israel Democracy Institute [in Hebrew].

———— 1999b. 'The 1996 Party Primaries and Their Political Consequences.' In: Asher Arian and Michal Shamir (eds.), *Elections in Israel 1996*. Albany: State University of New York Press.

—— Reuven Y. Hazan, and Richard S. Katz. 2008. 'Democracy and Political Parties: On the Uneasy Relationship Between Participation, Competition and Representation.' *Party Politics*, 16 (6), pp. 663–83.

Ranney, Austin. 1965. *Pathways to Parliament: Candidate Selection in Britain*. London: Macmillan.

—— 1968. 'Candidate Selection and Party Cohesion in Britain and the United States.' In: William J. Crotty (ed.), *Approaches to the Study of Party Organization*. Boston: MA. Allyn and Bacon.

—— 1981. 'Candidate Selection.' In: David Butler, Howard R. Penniman, and Austin Ranney (eds.), *Democracy at the Polls*. Washington, DC: American Enterprise Institute.

—— 1987. 'Candidate Selection.' In: Vernon Bogdanor (ed.), *The Blackwell Encyclopaedia of Political Institutions*. Oxford: Blackwell Reference.

Rice, Stuart A. 1925. 'The Behavior of Legislative Groups: A Method of Measurement.' *Political Science Quarterly*, 40 (1), pp. 60–72.

Riedwyl, Hans and Jürg Steiner. 1995. 'What Is Proportionality Anyhow?' *Comparative Politics*, 27 (3), pp. 357–69.

Riker, William H. 1984. 'Electoral Systems and Constitutional Restraints.' In: Arend Lijphart and Bernard Grofman (eds.), *Choosing an Electoral System: Issues and Alternatives*. New York: Praeger.

Roberts, Geoffrey. 1988. 'The German Federal Republic: The Two-Lane Route to Bonn.' In: Michael Gallagher and Michael Marsh (eds.), *Candidate Selection in Comparative Perspective: The Secret Garden of Politics*. London: Sage.

Rush, Michael. 1969. *The Selection of Parliamentary Candidates*. London: Nelson.

—— 1988. 'The "Selectorate" Revisited: Selecting Parliamentary Candidates in the 1980s.' In: Lynton Robins (ed.), *Political Institutions in Britain*. London: Longman.

Samuels, David. 2008. 'Political Ambition, Candidate Recruitment, and Legislative Politics in Brazil.' In: Peter M. Siavelis and Scott Morgenstern (eds.), *Pathways to Power: Political Recruitment and Candidate Selection in Latin America*. University Park: PA. Pennsylvania State University Press.

Sartori, Giovanni. 1965. *Democratic Theory*. New York: Praeger.

—— 1973. 'What Is "Politics"?' *Political Theory*, 1(1), pp. 5–26.

—— 1976. *Parties and Party Systems: A Framework for Analysis*. Cambridge: Cambridge University Press.

Scarrow, Howard A. 1964. 'Nomination and Local Party Organization in Canada: A Case Study.' *Western Political Quarterly*, 17 (1), pp. 55–62.

Scarrow, Susan E. 1994. 'The "Paradox of Enrollment": Assessing the Costs and Benefits of Party Membership.' *European Journal of Political Research*, 25 (1), pp. 41–60.

—— 1999*a*. 'Democracy Within – and Without – Parties: Introduction.' *Party Politics*, 5 (3), pp. 275–82.

—— 1999*b*. 'Parties and the Expansion of Direct Democracy, Who Benefits?' *Party Politics*, 5 (3), pp. 341–62.

—— 2000. 'Parties Without Members? Party Organization in a Changing Electoral Environment.' In: Russell J. Dalton and Martin P. Wattenberg (eds.), *Parties Without Partisans: Political Change in Advanced Industrial Democracies*. Oxford: Oxford University Press.

—— 2002. 'Party Decline in the Parties State? The Changing Environment of German Politics.' In: Paul Webb, David Farrell, and Ian Holliday (eds.), *Political Parties in Advanced Industrial Democracies*. Oxford: Oxford University Press.

—— 2005. *Political Parties and Democracy in Theoretical and Practical Perspectives: Implementing Intra-Party Democracy*. Washington, DC: National Democratic Institute for International Affairs. www.ndi.org/files/1951_polpart_scarrow_110105.pdf [accessed October 7, 2009].

—— Paul Webb, and David M. Farrell. 2000. 'From Social Integration to Electoral Contestation: The Changing Distribution of Power within Political Parties.' In: Russell J. Dalton and Martin P. Wattenberg (eds.), *Parties Without Partisans: Political Change in Advanced Industrial Democracies*. Oxford: Oxford University Press.

Schattschneider, E. E. 1942. *Party Government*. New York: Holt, Rinehart and Winston.

Scherlis, Gerardo. 2008. 'Machine Politics and Democracy: The Deinstitutionalization of the Argentine Party System.' *Government and Opposition*, 43 (4), pp. 579–98.

Schumpeter, Joseph A. 1943. *Capitalism, Socialism and Democracy*. London: George Allen and Unwin.

Schüttermeyer, Suzanne S. and Roland Strum. 2005. 'Der Kandidat – das (fast) unbekannte Wesen: Befunde und Überlegungen zur Aufstellung der Bewerber zum Deutschen Bundestag.' *Zeitschrift für Parlamentsfragen*, 36 (3), pp. 539–53 [in German].

Selle, Per and Lars Sväsand. 1991. 'Membership in Party Organizations and the Problem of Decline of Parties.' *Comparative Political Studies*, 23 (4), pp. 459–77.

Seyd, Patrick and Paul F. Whiteley. 1995. 'Labour and Conservative Party Members: Change Over Time.' *Parliamentary Affairs*, 48 (3), pp. 456–72

Shaw, Eric. 2001. 'New Labour: New Pathways to Parliament,' *Parliamentary Affairs*, 54 (1), pp. 35–53.

Sheafer, Tamir and Shaul Tzionit. 2006. 'Media-Political Skills, Candidate Selection Methods and Electoral Success.' *Journal of Legislative Studies*, 12 (2), pp. 179–97.

Shepherd-Robinson, Laura and Joni Lovenduski. 2002. *Women and Candidate Selection in British Political Parties*. London: Fawcett Society.

Sheppard, Simon. 1998. 'The Struggle for the Agenda: New Zealand Labour Party Candidate Selections 1987–93.' *Political Science*, 49 (2), pp. 198–228.

Shiratori, Rei. 1988. 'Japan: Localism, Factionalism and Personalism.' In: Michael Gallagher and Michael Marsh (eds.), *Candidate Selection in Comparative Perspective: The Secret Garden of Politics*. London: Sage.

Shomer, Yael. 2009. 'Candidate Selection, Procedures, Seniority, and Vote-Seeking Behavior.' *Comparative Political Studies*, 42 (7), pp. 945–70.

Siavelis, Peter M. 2002. 'The Hidden Logic of Candidate Selection for Chilean Parliamentary Elections.' *Comparative Politics*, 34 (4), pp. 419–38.

—— 2005. 'The Hidden Logic of Candidate Selection for Chilean Parliamentary Elections.' *Estudios Públicos*, [online] 98 (1), pp. 1–32. Available at: www.cepchile.cl/dms/lang_2/doc_3540.html [accessed February 24, 2010].

—— and Scott Morgenstern (eds.). 2008. *Pathways to Power: Political Recruitment and Candidate Selection in Latin America*. University Park: PA. Pennsylvania State University Press.

Sieberer, Ulrich. 2006. 'Party Unity in Parliamentary Democracies: A Comparative Analysis.' *Journal of Legislative Studies*, 12 (2), pp. 150–78.

Somit, Albert, Rudolf Wildenmann, Bernhard Boll, and Andrea Römmele (eds.). 1994. *The Victorious Incumbent: A Threat to Democracy?* Aldershot: Dartmouth.

Squires, Judith. 2005. *The Implementation of Gender Quotas in Britain*. Paper written for the International IDEA project on Electoral Quotas for Women. www.quotaproject.org/CS/CS_Britain_Squires.pdf [accessed February 24, 2010].

Standing, William H. and James A. Robinson. 1958. 'Inter-Party Competition and Primary Contesting: The Case of Indiana.' *American Political Science Review*, 52 (4), pp. 1066–77.

Stephens, Gregory R. 2008. *Electoral Reform and the Centralization of the New Zealand National Party*. M.A. thesis. Wellington: Victoria University.

Stirnemann, Alfred. 1989. 'Recruitment and Recruitment Strategies.' In: Anton Pelinka and Fritz Plasser (eds.), *The Austrian Party System*. Boulder, CO: Westview Press.

Sundberg, Jan. 1997. 'Compulsory Party Democracy: Finland as a Deviant Case in Scandinavia.' *Party Politics*, 3 (1), pp. 97–117.

—— 2002. 'The Scandinavian Party Model at the Crossroads.' In: Paul Webb, David Farrell, and Ian Holliday (eds.), *Political Parties in Advanced Industrial Democracies*. Oxford: Oxford University Press.

Suri, K. C. 2007. *Political Parties in South Asia: The Challenge of Change*. Stockholm: International Institute for Democracy and Electoral Assistance.

Szabo, Stephen F. 1977. *Party Recruitment in the Federal Republic of Germany: Candidate Selection in a West German State*. Ph.D. dissertation. Washington, DC: Georgetown University.

Taagepera, Rein and Matthew S. Shugart. 1989. *Seats and Votes: The Effects and Determinants of Electoral Systems*. New Haven, CT: Yale University Press.

Tan, Alexander C. 1998. 'The Impact of Party Membership Size: A Cross-National Analysis.' *Journal of Politics*, 60 (1), pp. 188–98.

Taylor-Robinson, Michelle M. 2001. 'Candidate Selection in Costa Rica.' Paper presented at the International Congress of the Latin American Studies Association, Washington, DC.

Teorell, Jan. 1999. 'A Deliberative Defense of Intra-Party Democracy.' *Party Politics*, 5 (3), pp. 363–82.

Thiébault, Jean-Louis. 1988. 'France: The Impact of Electoral System Change.' In: Michael Gallagher and Michael Marsh (eds.), *Candidate Selection in Comparative Perspective: The Secret Garden of Politics*. London: Sage.

Tremblay, Manon (ed.). 2008. *Women and Legislative Representation: Electoral Systems, Political Parties, and Sex Quotas*. New York: Palgrave Macmillan.

Turner, Julius. 1953. 'Primary Elections as the Alternative to Party Competition in "Safe" Districts.' *Journal of Politics*, 15 (2), pp. 197–210.

Valen, Henry. 1988. 'Norway: Decentralization and Group Representation.' In: Michael Gallagher and Michael Marsh (eds.), *Candidate Selection in Comparative Perspective: The Secret Garden of Politics*. London: Sage.

—— Hanne Marthe Narud, and Audun Skare. 2002. 'Norway: Party Dominance and Decentralized Decision-Making.' In: Hanne Marthe Narud, Mogens N. Pedersen, and Henry Valen (eds.), *Party Sovereignty and Citizen Control: Selecting Candidates for Parliamentary Elections in Denmark, Finland, Iceland and Norway*. Odense: University Press of Southern Denmark.

Vanhanen, Tatu. 1990. *The Process of Democratization: A Comparative Study of 147 States 1980–1988*. New York: Crane Russak.

Von Beyme, Klaus. 1996. 'Party Leadership and Change in Party Systems: Towards a Postmodern Party State?' *Government and Opposition*, 31 (2), pp. 135–59.

Vowels, Jack. 2002. 'Parties and Society in New Zealand.' In: Paul Webb, David Farrell, and Ian Holliday (eds.), *Political Parties in Advanced Industrial Democracies*. Oxford: Oxford University Press.

Ware, Alan. 1987. *Citizens, Parties, and the State: A Reappraisal*. Cambridge: Polity Press.

—— 1996. *Political Parties and Party Systems*. Oxford: Oxford University Press.

—— 2002. *The American Direct Primary: Party Institutionalization and Transformation in the North*. Cambridge: Cambridge University Press.

Wattenberg, Martin P. 1991. *The Rise of Candidate-Centered Politics*. Cambridge, MA: Harvard University Press.

Webb, Paul. 2002. 'Political Parties in Britain: Secular Decline or Adaptive Resilience?' In: Paul Webb, David Farrell, and Ian Holliday (eds.), *Political Parties in Advanced Industrial Democracies*. Oxford: Oxford University Press.

Weeks, Liam. 2007. 'Candidate Selection: Democratic Centralism or Managed Democracy?' In: Michael Gallagher and Michael Marsh (eds.), *How Ireland Voted 2007*. London: Palgrave.

Weldon, Steven. 2006. 'Downsize My Polity? The Impact of Size on Party Membership and Member Activism.' *Party Politics*, 12 (4), pp. 467–81.

Wertman, Douglas. 1977. 'The Italian Electoral Process: The Election of June 1976.' In: Howard R. Penniman (ed.), *Italy at the Polls: The Parliamentary Elections of 1976*. Washington, DC: American Enterprise Institute.

Wertman, Douglas. 1981. 'The Christian Democrats: Masters of Survival.' In: Howard R. Penniman (ed.), *Italy at the Polls, 1979: A Study of the Parliamentary Elections.* Washington, DC: American Enterprise Institute.

—— 1988. 'Italy: Local Involvement, Central Control.' In: Michael Gallagher and Michael Marsh (eds.), *Candidate Selection in Comparative Perspective: The Secret Garden of Politics.* London: Sage.

Wessels, Bernhard. 1997. 'Germany.' In: Pippa Norris (ed.), *Passages to Power: Legislative Recruitment in Advanced Democracies.* Cambridge: Cambridge University Press.

Whiteley, Paul F. and Patrick Seyd. 1999. 'Discipline in the British Conservative Party: The Attitudes of Party Activists Toward the Role of their Members of Parliament.' In: Shaun Bowler, David M. Farrell, and Richard S. Katz (eds.), *Party Discipline and Parliamentary Government.* Columbus, OH: Ohio State University Press.

Williams, R. J. 1981. 'Candidate Selection.' In: Howard R. Penniman (ed.), *Canada at the Polls 1979 and 1980.* Washington, DC: American Enterprise Institute.

Wright, William E. 1971. 'Recruitment.' In: William E. Wright (ed.), *A Comparative Study of Party Organization.* Columbus, OH: Charles E. Merrill.

Wu, Chung-Li. 2001. 'The Transformation of the Kuomintang's Candidate Selection System.' *Party Politics*, 7 (1), pp. 103–18.

—— and Dafydd Fell. 2001. 'Taiwan's Party Primaries in Comparative Perspective.' *Japanese Journal of Political Science*, 2 (1), pp. 23–45.

Wuhs, Steven T. 2006. 'Democratization and the Dynamics of Candidate Selection Rule Change in Mexico, 1991–2003.' *Mexican Studies*, 22 (1), pp. 33–55.

Youn, Jung-Suk. 1977. *Recruitment of Political Leadership in Postwar Japan, 1958–1972.* Ph.D. dissertation. Ann Arbor: University of Michigan.

Young, Alison. 1983. *The Reselection of MPs.* London: Heinemann Educational.

Young, Lisa and William Cross. 2002. 'The Rise of Plebiscitary Democracy in Canadian Political Parties.' *Party Politics*, 8 (6), pp. 673–99.

## Internet Sources

Arizona Constitution. Article 7, Chapter 10. Direct Primary election law. www.azleg.gov/const/7/10.htm [accessed February 24, 2010].

California Secretary of State. Election and Voter Information. www.sos.ca.gov/elections/elections_decline.htm [accessed February 24, 2010].

Conservative Party of Canada. 2009. Candidate Nomination Rules and Procedures. www.conservative.ca/media/NominationRules2009.pdf [accessed February 24, 2010].

Constitution of the Swedish Social Democratic Party. 2001. www.socialdemokraterna.se/upload/Internationellt/Other%20Languages/SAPconstitution_eng.pdf [accessed February 24, 2010].

Finland, Ministry of Justice, Election Act. 1998. www.finlex.fi/en/laki/kaannokset/1998/en19980714.pdf [accessed February 24, 2010].

Florida Department of State, Division of Elections. 2008. A Compilation of the Election Laws of the State of Florida. http://election.dos.state.fl.us/publications/pdf/2008–2009/08–09ElectionLaw.pdf [accessed February 24, 2010].

Global Database of Quotas for Women. 2009. International Institute for Democracy and Electoral Assistance. www.quotaproject.org/index.cfm [accessed February 24, 2010].

Idaho Secretary of State. Idaho Blue Book. Chapter 1: Profile. http://www.sos.idaho.gov/elect/BLUEBOOK.HTM [accessed February 24, 2010].

Israel Parties Law. 1992. [in Hebrew]. www.knesset.gov.il/laws/special/heb/knesset_laws.pdf [accessed February 24, 2010].

Liberal Party of Canada. 2009. National Rules for the Selection of Candidates for the Liberal Party of Canada. www.liberal.ca/pdf/docs/national-nomination-rules.pdf [accessed February 24, 2010].

Netherlands Institute for Multiparty Democracy (NIMD). 2007. *Report Expert Meeting Intra-party Democracy.* www.nimd.org/documents/R/report20nimd20expert20meeting 20intra-party20democracy201220april202007.pdf [accessed February 24, 2010].

State of Hawaii, Office of Elections. Hawaii Election Laws. The Constitution of the State of Hawaii. http://hawaii.gov/elections/info/laws [accessed February 24, 2010].

Worldwide Political Science Abstracts. http://csaweb105v.csa.com/factsheets/polsci-set-c.php [accessed February 24, 2010].

# Author Index

# Subject Index